MW00896846

POWERFUL POLITICAL WOMEN

Stirring Biographies of Some of History's Most Powerful Women

BY

JOAN MCMAHON FLATT

iUniverse, Inc.
Bloomington

Powerful Political Women
Stirring Biographies of Some of History's Most Powerful Women

iUniverse books may be ordered through booksellers or by contacting:

iUniverse
1663 Liberty Drive
Bloomington, IN 47403
www.iuniverse.com
1-800-Authors (1-800-288-4677)

ISBN: 978-1-4620-6812-8 (sc)
ISBN: 978-1-4620-6818-0 (hc)
ISBN: 978-1-4620-6819-7 (e)

Library of Congress Control Number: 2011960851

Printed in the United States of America

iUniverse rev. date: 08/28/2012

CONTENTS

POWERFUL POLITICAL WOMEN

BY
JOAN MCMAHON FLATT

For Wayne and My Precious Lamb Children, Richard, David, Dianne, Doug, Daniel and Darlene

INTRODUCTION

My father Daniel Francis McMahon (named after his uncle, one of the leaders of Tammany Hall) first introduced me to politics. As a young girl growing up near New York City, I remember conversations around the dinner table involving local and national matters. Moreover, my father was a strong Irish nationalist. The name *Mahon*, according to historical records, dates back to the 10th century. Mahon had become King of Munster in A.D. 951 upon the death of his father and together with his brother, Brian Boru of Kincora, fought against the invading Norsemen.

The Battle of Bealach Leachta in A.D. 978 marked the first major defeat of the Danish Vikings in Ireland and helped establish Brian Boru as the first and last High King. Unfortunately, Mahon was captured and killed in the battle at Aghabullogue. Seeking revenge, Brian Boru attacked his brother's assassins and killed their leader, Maolmuidh, at Leacha Dubh. Fulfilling a curse put on Maolmuidh for the killing of Mahon, he was buried on the north side of the hill "where the sun never shines and the harsh wind never stops." Three grave stones were erected on the battle site and two remain to this day. One is known as Leacht Mahon. In Celtic culture *Mc* indicates son of, and with the royal name McMahon handed down through the ages my father strongly felt his Celtic origins. Indeed, I was raised with a great sense of pride in my heritage.

As the grandson of Irish immigrants who arrived in New York City in coffin ships during the potato famine of the 1840s, my father certainly was sympathetic to the Irish Republican Army. I even remember talk of weapons being stored in upstate New York and then shipped to Ireland. I grew up hearing all this conversation, and I guess the feeling that things could change through political action was nurtured in me. My father bequeathed to me a strong sense of activism.

But mine was a different issue that demanded my attention. When I was born, women in the United States had only had the right to vote in most states since 1920. In colonial America, most women could not sign contracts or own property. Radcliffe was the female connection to Harvard, where women were not admitted. In England, Cambridge did not award degrees to women until 1947.

Amazing, almost unbelievable, I thought. And so I decided to explore women's history and write a book about the evolution of the development of women's political history from Esther to Hillary. As Emile Zola once said, "Do not forget those who fought the battles for you." With these short profiles of political women, it is my intent to educate and inform my readers of the long journey of women for political power.

Throughout history, certain women have stood out in the cultural moment of their generation. All over the world the circumstances of the age brought out passion, heroism, determination, dedication, and talent in a few confident women who would stand on the stage of history and fight for the political rights of women. They were like torches burning in the night, inspiring those that followed to fight against injustice and for ultimate equality.

Indeed, leadership is a public engagement with history. Whether the leadership is noble or evil, leaders impart their personal stamp on history. Individuals can and do make a difference. To this day, the women in this book embolden the rest of us to live according to our best selves. These women ignited the fuse between the individual and the group and thus altered history. Events shape leaders but leaders also shape events.

I decided to start with Esther. She was not a political woman in the true sense of the word as we understand it today, but she made a great contribution to the world by saving the Hebrew nation. The women I have selected seem to me to have special relevance for our own times. Many others could have been included, but because of a lack of time and space, were left out. However, it is not my intention to diminish their importance.

The issue of women's political rights has stirred nations around the world and is an ongoing struggle even in 2012. The matter has been taken up by queens, parliamentarians, businessmen, journalists, clergymen, caricaturists, novelists, and playwrights. In the nineteenth and twentieth centuries, advocates flocked to meetings and demonstrated in the streets, risking jail time, the loss of family and position in the community, and sometimes physical punishment. The women's revolution included all classes and races and took place in many different countries.

These are women who over the generations broke down barriers, sometimes risking their lives, believing they could make a change. The women of past generations offer many lessons in political leadership to women of the twenty-first century. It is important to understand women's history and the evolution of the sociological and psychological factors that brought women to the position they now hold in society. Culture and tradition (religious, economic, and political) have dictated the norms by which men and women live. We are the off-spring of the Greco-Judeo-Christian tradition. In ancient Greek culture, Demosthenes separated women into three categories: wives to have children, courtesans to be companions, and prostitutes for sexual needs. The one constant, however, in all these cultures was the importance of the family for raising children. This view still holds today. In Greek culture, all women's political and economic rights were to be exercised by male members of the family because women were considered mentally and politically incompetent.

In Roman society, women attended social functions and intermingled on a daily basis with men. They were also afforded some economic and political rights. Greek writers cast aspersions on the Romans for this stand; Greek men often divorced their wives. In contrast, the Romans highly valued family life, often considering it a vital link to political power. Some of the Roman attitudes toward women prevailed until the Middle Ages in parts of Europe. However, with the fall of the Roman Empire and the rise of Christianity, women were subjected to strict rules that regulated their rights within the family, church, and society.

Yet women throughout history kept forging their path away from patriarchal norms, pressing for private and public rights. Many great female leaders of the past and present had to balance career with family. These women were assertive, competitive, and ready to fight for the same rights and privileges held by men. Often these personality traits were viewed as unfeminine and were much vilified.

Gone is the age when women were mere trophies and subjects of their husbands and when they were expected to leave the realm of politics to men. Like corks bobbing in the stream, many women floated quietly along through their lives. Now there are women who direct the currents of history. Eleanor Roosevelt once wrote: "The future belongs to those who believe in the beauty of their dreams." (Nancy Pelosi. *Know Your Power.* [New York: Doubleday, 2008]. 173).

In 1984, Geraldine Ferraro was the first woman to be nominated by a major political party as a vice-presidential candidate in the United States. However, she and her running mate Walter Mondale were defeated in the election. In 2008, a woman, Sarah Palin, governor of Alaska, for the first time won the Republican nomination as a vice-presidential candidate. At the same time, Hillary Clinton made a very strong showing in her bid for the presidency in the Democrat primary with more than eighteen million votes cast for her.

I end my book with Nancy Pelosi and women of the twenty-first century. Nancy achieved the highest pinnacle of political power of any woman in American history when she was elected Speaker of the House of Representatives, third highest political office in the United States. We women of the twentieth-first century owe much to the women who came before us, from Esther in the Bible to Nancy Pelosi and others of the twenty-first century. They motivated and activated us and our memories of them will endure. Women politicians are nothing new; they have been around for a long time.

We must be guided into the future by the foresight and wisdom of women such as those who met in Seneca Falls, New York, in 1848. At that time a woman, if she were employed, worked for low wages. Her pay, her children, and even the clothes on her back belonged to her husband. Imagine the joy and expectations of the women who traveled in horse drawn carriages to the first Women's Rights Convention in America led by Elizabeth Cady Stanton.

Women in the twentieth-first century have come a long way especially in western societies. Today there are many female heads of state. Women, more than ever before, have a sense of engagement and empowerment. Plato wrote about the imprint of man's soul about the state; today we write about the mark of woman's soul upon the nation. Surely the early pioneers would be pleased with the progress of women's rights and freedoms. However, they are not universally shared. Women the world over must stand firm and fight for human rights across the globe.

For the sake of easy readability, I have not used footnotes or endnotes. I have provided a general bibliography, if readers are interested in further investigation of the themes and subject matter of this book. The list should provide a "first base" for reader exploration.

"The future is nothing, but the past is myself, my own history, the seed of my present thoughts, the mold of my present disposition." *Essays of the Road* R.L. Stevenson

Persian Queen Esther Accusing Hamon by Gustave Dore She saved the Jewish nation. (Wikipedia Commons) Dore Bible Illustrations

CHAPTER ONE

Esther, Savior of the Jewish Nation

"...will I go in unto the king, which is not according to the law: and if I perish, I perish."

Esther is a Babylonian name: Esther's Hebrew name was Hadassah. She lived in the fifth century B.C. during the time when the Persians controlled the Middle East from India to Palestine. At that time, many Jews had been deported to other lands by the Babylonians. Nevertheless, they clung to their national identity and religion while at the same time adapting to the cultural mores of their new masters. In some cases, Jews acquired new names to conceal their true identities. In the Book of Esther in the Bible, Esther, an orphan, was raised by her cousin, Mordecai, who encouraged her to hide her Jewish identity.

Xerxes, who reigned from 519 to 465 B.C., was the great Persian king who ravaged the lands of Greeks, Babylonians, and Egyptians and any other nations in his way. According to the Bible story, Xerxes decided to throw a spectacular banquet to show off his wealth in his new palace at Susa. He invited his beautiful wife, Queen Vashti, to the feast, so that she could show off her feminine charms to the invited guests. No doubt, Xerxes wanted to show her off like a prize cow; he regarded her as one of his personal possessions. However, Vashti declined his invitation.

She may have had good reasons for refusing. It is probable that the men at the party would have become drunk and behaved cruelly and lewdly. She may have preferred to have her own party with her female friends and without the watchful eyes of their husbands. In any case, Vashti did not use much common sense in disobeying her royal husband. The consequences were severe.

The other men complained to the king that he must do something about his wife; otherwise, all the women would soon be mocking their husbands and doing as they pleased. How would he punish her? As a result of her misconduct, she would never again be allowed in the presence of the king, and all her worldly possessions would go to her replacement. Soon Vashti was found dead on the street. Then Xerxes decided to arrange a competition, like a beauty contest, where the fairest damsel in the land would compete for Vashti's vacant spot.

During the reign of Xerxes, Mordecai was a member of the Susa City Council, and he decided to promote his cousin Esther in this competition. Women came in from all over the empire and were placed in the care of the eunuch Hegai who was in charge of the royal harem. For one year, the contestants received beauty treatments and charm lessons before they individually went before the king. Hegai gave preferential treatment to the beautiful Esther, for he was impressed with her intelligence as well as her charm and beauty. He sincerely cared about the welfare of the king and believed Esther was the prime candidate to win the contest. He instructed her on how to captivate the king in speech and manner. Thus, as soon as Esther appeared before Xerxes, the king was totally mesmerized. Immediately, he wished to make her his bride. He, too, found her intelligent as well as beautiful, someone who could speak on his level about important and serious matters.

Mordecai happened to hear two guards plotting to kill the king. This he reported to Esther who in turn reported it to her husband Xerxes. Of course, Mordecai became a great hero for saving the life of the king.

Meanwhile, Hamon, the king's right-hand man, secretly was seeking the downfall of the king. Hamon was an arrogant, haughty man who demanded submission from everyone because of his powerful position. On one occasion, Mordecai refused to pay homage to Hamon because he claimed he would only pay homage to God. His conduct was immediately reported to the king.

Hamon maintained that Jewish immigrants were trying to undermine the king's authority and should be exterminated, when in reality it was Hamon who was the traitor. Furthermore, Hamon agreed to put up a vast amount of silver as bounty money for the murder of these supposed Jewish insurgents. The king agreed, and a decree was sent out for all Persians to rise up against their Jewish enemies on the thirteenth day of the last month of the year. This date was chosen by a roll of Hamon's dice (Purim). All Jews were to be killed everywhere in the kingdom.

All was not lost, however, for Mordecai sent a message to Esther, informing her of the edict and requesting that she beg the king to retract his order. Now Esther had a problem; no one, including the king's wife, was allowed in the king's private apartment without a proper invitation. A person could be executed for this incursion, depending on the king's mood. Moreover, the king did not know Esther was Jewish; she had not revealed it. Thus her life, too, was in danger.

At this point, Esther sent a note back to Mordecai, advising him to spread the word that all Jews in the city should fast for three days. She and her maids would do the same. After that time, Esther would go to the king in spite of his decree not to disturb him under penalty of death. Esther's famous words will live forever: *"And if I perish, I perish."*

Fortunately, the king was in a good frame of mind. When he beheld Esther, he was so overcome by her beauty and charm, he promised her anything. She decided to play a little game of strategy, inviting him and the evil Hamon to a party in her apartments. When they arrived, the king again asked Esther what she would like as a gift. She invited them to return the next day at which time she would present her request.

Meanwhile, Hamon's anger against Mordecai increased every time they passed each other. Hamon perceived he was being insulted by this lowly man who would not bow down to him. Yet, Hamon's ego was inflated from having been invited to the queen's party. He shared his feelings with his wife who advised him to have a seventy-five-foot-high gallows built from which to hang Mordecai. Of course, Hamon would have to get the king's permission first.

Xerxes requested that his servant bring him his favorite book, *The Adventures of Ahasuerus, King of Persia,* so that he might read some stories to help him sleep. (Ahasuerus was Xerxes' Hebrew name.) In fact, he was reading stories about his own reign, no doubt written like a journal. The book fell open to the account where Mordecai saved the king's life. This reminded the king that he had not rewarded Mordecai properly for his great service.

Shortly after, Hamon came back to the palace to seek permission to hang Mordecai. But the king asked Hamon first how he would reward someone for a great service. Hamon misinterpreted, thinking he was going to be the one honored. So he naturally held lofty expectations: a grand parade, a royal horse for the honoree, magnificent robes and royal heralds proclaiming his great deeds, a great feast marking him as one of the king's favorites. Then the king added that Mordecai would be the honoree. Realizing he had made a huge blunder, Hamon retreated home.

The next day in the queen's apartments, Xerxes, in the presence of Hamon and attendants, again told the queen that he would give her whatever she requested. This time she decided to be forthcoming. She told him that she and her people had been condemned to be slaughtered by Hamon. Not just exiled but killed! Of course, the king was flabbergasted. The Jews for the most part were living in peace. He had been tricked by honey-mouthed Hamon into signing the edict to kill the Jews. Hamon at the same time begged forgiveness from Queen Esther. The king, however, had had enough and ordered that Hamon be hanged on the gallows constructed for Mordecai. Immediately, Mordecai became the king's right hand man; honorable, honest, humble Mordecai was elevated to one of the highest positions of royalty in the land.

The order passed by the king to kill Jews still was in effect. Once the king signed a decree, according to Persian law, it could not be revoked. Xerxes could not even countermand his own law. Consequently, the lives of all Jews in the kingdom were in jeopardy. So Esther appealed even more strongly to the king to save the lives of her people. The king decided the way around the problem was to issue a proclamation allowing the Jews the right to raise a militia to defend themselves. They could even seek revenge against their enemies. As a result, many of the Jews' enemies were killed, including the ten sons of Hamon.

Esther was a devout Jew who practiced her religion, often in secret, with great diligence, dedication, and devotion. As a consequence of this near extermination experience, she left a mark in Jewish history that would be remembered for all time. Thus, she and Mordecai established the Feast of Purim throughout the Persian Empire as a reminder of her people's deliverance. This reminder is still with us. Purim is an annual celebration usually celebrated in March or April. Purim is so-called because the villain of the story, Haman, cast the "pur" (lot) against the Jews to destroy them. It is one of the most fun holidays on the Jewish calendar when people dress up in all manner of costumes to celebrate the time the Jewish people were saved from extermination. A horrible genocide was averted because of the strength of one woman who risked her life for her people. She is an example of an historic woman who used her beauty, wits, and intelligence to reach a position of power in which she was able to change the course of history.

Sculpture of Egyptian Queen Hatshepsut Eighteenth dynasty of Egypt circa 1473-1458 B.C. depicted with a faux beard in male attire She ruled as Pharaoh and was known as the King of Upper and Lower Egypt. (public domain)

CHAPTER TWO

Hatshepsut, King-Queen of Egypt

"My command stands firm like mountains, and the sun's disk shines and spreads rays over the titulary of my august person, and my falcon rises high above the kingly banner unto all eternity."

How aptly Hatshepsut's mother named her, for her name in Egyptian means "foremost of women." Her exact date of birth is unknown. However, we do know she belonged to the eighteenth dynasty of pharaohs in an age called the New Kingdom. Historians believe that she died between the ages of thirty-five and fifty-five, probably around 1458 B.C., after having ruled for about twenty-two years. She reigned from about 1479 to 1458 B.C.

Hatshepsut was the daughter of Pharaoh Thuthmosis I, who was a successful military general not of royal blood. He served Amenhotep I well and because Amenhotep had no sons, he named Thuthmosis his successor. Thuthmosis had many wives but only one could be named queen, and Ahmose was the chosen one. Hatshepsut was born of this union, which gave her special prestige. However, other wives bore sons. When Thuthmosis I died, one of his sons became pharaoh. Hatshepsut married Thuthmosis II, her half-brother, probably at age twelve. Thus, the power, money, and royal blood line were kept in one family through incestuous relationships.

Giving birth to a son was the most important role for the queen. Hatshepsut bore only one child the female, Neferure. One of the minor wives produced a son who would become pharaoh after Thuthmosis II. Hatshepsut, no doubt, was not thrilled about this but accepted the fact.

Hatshepsut's next most important role was to serve as "God's Wife." The king was regarded as a god, and she was responsible for carrying out many religious duties. The pharaoh gave unity to the Egyptian religion that was sacred, solemn, splendid, and sensuous. Archeologists maintain Hatshepsut assisted the king in serving sacrificial feasts to the gods at the temple in Karnak. Because she was queen, she was allowed in the inner sanctuary of the temple to make offerings to the god Amun. In addition, she performed rites to defend the kingdom against its enemies in time of war. It was believed that by burning the names of her enemies, her enemies would be destroyed. Moreover, her duties also required her to accompany her husband on ceremonial processions through the holy city of Thebes. It must have been a beautiful sight seeing the entire royal family in their royal regalia parading through the streets.

When Hatshepsut was about thirty years old, her husband, Thuthmosis II, died after reigning fifteen years. The son of Isis, one of the lesser wives, inherited the kingship. Since Isis was not royal, neither was her child, but he would grow up to be pharaoh if he married his half-sister. History suggests that he married Neferure, Hatshepsut's daughter.

Until Thuthmosis III was old enough to reign, Egypt needed a regent during the interregnum. So Hatshepsut, aunt and step-mother of Thuthmosis III, stepped boldly into that position. She had had many years of experience in palace life. She knew the protocol and how to handle her advisers. She was experienced in handling foreign diplomats, military leaders, and priests of the various gods. Women had acted as regents before in Egyptian history, so Hatshepsut was not the first Egyptian woman to own and inherit property. She already had considerable power and influence. In many ways, Egyptian women had more rights in ancient Egypt than they do today. Thuthmosis III was probably less than two years of age when Hatshepsut took the reins of office.

At first, Hatshepsut appeared to rule in the name of her stepson, but at some point, she made a bold move. She took on the very identity of a king, and she began to take on the religious duties that formerly belonged to the king. Next, she had herself crowned king with the double crown of two Egypts, north and south. Her coronation name was Maatkare, which signifies cosmic order. A woman serving as king would certainly need some cosmic order!

In the Egyptian language, there is no word for queen; the spouse of the king was simply referred to as wife of the king. Hence, Hatshepsut had to call herself pharaoh. Moreover, she decided to dress like a man: she donned a short kilt, put on a king's broad collar around her neck, and attached a faux beard to her chin. Often, she referred to herself as a male. Her daughter, Neferure, acted as God's wife at various public, state, and social functions. This was good training for the roles she was expected to fulfill as the wife of Thuthmosis III in a future time.

Apparently, however, Hatshepsut maintained her femininity, for one inscription describes her as "more beautiful than anything." No doubt she applied creams, lotions, and cosmetics, and adorned herself with gold jewelry and precious gems that befitted her position. She must have been an impressive sight decked out in her royal garb either as king or queen.

As Hatshepsut started her reign, she immediately launched an attack on her Nubian enemies who were quickly subdued. Then she focused on trade. Egypt needed wood from Lebanon and copper and turquoise from Sinai.

Hatshepsut's reign was peaceful except for the war against Nubia. Under her leadership, Egypt's power lay not in military conquests but in great architectural monuments, some of which have lasted almost two thousand years. Her greatest architectural achievement was the Deir el-Bahri Temple near Thebes dedicated to Amun, the divine father of all pharaohs. She called the Deir el-Bahri Temple "Holy of Holies." She possessed a great artistic sensibility. The temple was constructed in three tiers supported by columns and set into the side of a mountain. A tree lined avenue of sphinxes led up to the temple, and ramps led from terrace to terrace. Reliefs still visible today on the lowest terrace depicted the transport of obelisks by barge to Karnack. This temple was to be Hatshepsut's tomb. When she became king, she was eligible to be buried in the Valley of the Kings. However, she chose a site surrounded by the Valley of the Kings and the Valley of the Queens. But as was discovered in 2007, this was not her final resting place. Many archeologists claim Hatshepsut's mummy is enshrined in one of two Royal Mummy Rooms in the Cairo Museum.

Hatshepsut had artists carve and paint reliefs on the temple walls, telling her life story. According to her, she was conceived by the god Amun and Queen Ahmose, a divine conception. Carvings of her coronation and performance of sacred rites and rituals were engraved on the sacred walls of the temple. These depictions suggested that she was chosen by the gods to rule as pharaoh; apparently, the gods did not care about her gender. The architect Senenmut designed the temple and many other monuments during this age of architectural grandeur. Whether they were closer than friends is hotly debated in academic circles. Thus, Senenmut left for history the story of Hatshepsut's life, which would never have been known without him. Egyptologists in the nineteenth century began interpreting the carvings on the walls and, in a sense, brought Hatshepsut back to life.

Senenmut was one of Hatshepsut's major advisers. Evidently, his parents were above ordinary workers on the social scale, for he did receive some education. He chose to serve in the military and later became a scribe. His professional and personal attributes were soon recognized, and he moved into the halls of power. Even before Hatshepsut was king, Senenmut was hired as a tutor for Neferure her daughter. It is believed that at this point, Hatshepsut and the tutor became close. He had many responsibilities and various roles to play. He is credited with being the genius behind the many monuments built during her twenty-two year reign.

The king-queen's building projects were carried out in all the major cities of Egypt. Most of the monuments have been lost along with the cities. Evidence exists that her building programs were carried out in Nubia, Kom Ombo, Hierakonpolis, Elkab, Armant, and the island of Elephantine. She renewed and restored monuments that had been damaged in wars before her reign and greatly improved the infrastructures of important urban areas.

Hatshepsut added two obelisks to the Karnak temple: they were covered in gold foil and commemorated her twenty-two year reign. She added a new pier-shrine where Amun's processional boat could land. She also added a new walkway, new palace, and great improvements to the connecting processional walkways to the various chapels and shrines.

The king-queen wanted most to be remembered for the expedition she sent to Punt. Here one notes the difference between man's and woman's nature. Most kings and male leaders want to be most remembered for their military conquests and exploits. Hatshepsut gloried in her story of a peaceful but exciting expedition into the "land of wonders."

Several expeditions were sent by her, but this is the only one of which we have an account. Chancellor Neshi, one of the senior officials of the king-queen, was placed in charge. Journeying to Punt was a brave endeavor, for Punt was located far down the east coast of Africa, the area that is now the Eritrean/Ethiopian coast. There could be found the finest frankincense and myrrh, which were used in religious rituals, cosmetics, and mummification.

On the walls of Deir el-Bahri, one can see to this day a boat traveling to Punt with sailors rowing standing up. This gives us a good idea of what the vessels in the expedition looked like as they ventured down the Nile. Each boat had about thirty rowers. Then the boats had to be portaged across the desert to the Red Sea. In the temple, there is a carving of the king of Punt hospitably receiving the expedition from Egypt. Neshi, Hatshepsut's envoy, carried many gifts of weapons and jewelry from the king-queen. In return, the Egyptians received trees of incense and myrrh and exotic animals and birds for the pharaoh's zoo.

This world of Punt was so different from the world that the adventurers from Egypt came. Here the domed houses were built on stilts and wildlife was everywhere. Among the treasures carried back were thirty frankincense and myrrh trees, giraffes, baboons, ebony, spices, gold, elephant tusks, and panther skins. The expedition was aimed primarily at developing trade as well as for exploration. In addition, the explorers brought back incredible tales of wonder to stir the imagination of anyone exposed to the chronicles of Neshi. Fortunately for us, some of the story is carved into the walls of Deir el-Bahri Temple so we, too, can still wonder.

By having the story of her life carved into her monuments at Karnak and elsewhere, Hatshepsut believed she would be immortalized forever. However, this was not to be. Attempts to remove all traces of her life occurred twenty years after her death. Statues of her were smashed and buried (some recently found); her face was gouged out of many of the carvings. The religious belief of Egyptians was that if all traces of a person's human existence on the temple walls were destroyed, the deceased could not enter eternal life but would be doomed to darkness forever. No one knows for certain why the attacks occurred.

Perhaps her stepson-nephew, Thuthmosis III, wanted to be rid of her once and for all. It took a long while for him to assume the throne, so perhaps he wanted revenge. No one really knows what happened to her; she just disappeared in history. Did she die from natural causes or was she murdered? Maybe Egyptians believed at the time that there was no room for a woman king. Maybe she had too much power and wealth. Perhaps, the Egyptian leadership at some point felt compelled to erase all evidence of her existence, so that future generations would never know that a queen once ruled Egypt. Whatever the reason, Hatshepsut is back with us. She is a stronger presence than ever with what many archaeologists believe is the positive identification of her mummy in 2007.

Thuthmosis III, her stepson and successor, became one of the greatest pharaohs in Egyptian history. He was a great builder and warrior-king. During his nineteen year reign, this brilliant leader fought seventeen military campaigns in the Levant. Another military victory that is still studied today was won against the Canaanites at Megiddo (present day Israel). His son Amenhotep succeeded him.

Although Hatshepsut reigned for only twenty-two years three thousand years ago, she left a great legacy. She was the leader of the greatest civilization on earth at the time. She conquered her enemies, maintained the peace, developed trade, and focused on great architectural monuments, some of which survive to this day. She was a woman of great strength, intelligence, perseverance, ambition, pride, and diplomatic prowess. On one of her obelisks in Karnak there is inscribed her words: "Now my heart turns this way and that, as I think what the people will say. Those who see my monuments in years to come, and who shall speak of what I have done." How fortunate are we in the twenty-first century to know about this woman of ancient history! How do our women leaders of today compare to the "foremost of women?"

1st Century B.C. Statue of Cleopatra VII of Egypt She sought to maintain the power of Egypt.(public domain)

CHAPTER THREE

Cleopatra, Seductress or Politician?

"I will not be triumphed over."

After the death of Alexander the Great in 323 B.C., his empire was divided among his three generals. One of the generals established the Ptolemy dynasty in Egypt that lasted more than three hundred years. The Greek conquerors merged their culture and sensibilities with the ancient religions and cultures of Egypt. Cleopatra, who ruled from 51-30 B.C., was a descendent of these Macedonians, not of pharaohs, and she grew up in this world of mixed cultures.

During the Third Intermediate Period of Egyptian history, women in the elite class had great power. Besides being mothers and wives, they were also priestesses, musicians, and choir members. They could own real and personal property. Moreover, they held the highest political and religious ranks. The queen held the title of "God's Wife of Amun;" she was, in a sense, a divinely sanctioned first lady. However, women of all classes traditionally were restricted to the home. Only men moved freely in the public spheres.

History tells us nothing of Cleopatra's mother. Thus, we can only recognize Cleopatra through her father. We do know that her father was acknowledged to have had many sexual liaisons. She grew up in the palace as a royal princess surrounded by servants and tutors. She no doubt visited the great library in Alexandria where she became enthralled with learning. She spoke seven languages, and she was the first Ptolemy ruler who spoke Egyptian. Her father Ptolemy Auteles was interested in the arts including music, theater, and dance. He was captivated with stagecraft and used theatrical devices as propaganda to further his aims and ambitions, much like politicians use the media today.

Her father's example influenced Cleopatra, and she used similar tactics in her later life in some of her most extravagant public exhibitions. Auteles was not liked at home or abroad, yet he ruled for twenty-nine years. Corruption and the excesses of the Ptolemies had reduced the nation to a client-kingdom (subordinate to a more powerful state in international affairs, satellite or puppet state) under the Romans. So when Cleopatra took control, the land of Egypt was in great turmoil.

Cleopatra began her rule by using the cult of the mother goddess, Isis, as a means of reinforcing her own image as goddess. Royalty had generally been considered divine among the Egyptians. The Romans, however, knew otherwise. Cleopatra used her supposed divine nature as a practical device to control her people and to further her ambitions. Isis was considered the queen of heaven, while Cleopatra was content to be the queen of earth.

In Rome Caesar, Pompey, and Crassus joined together in the First Triumvirate, which amounted to a shared dictatorship. The Romans grabbed Egyptian territories wherever and whenever possible. Auteles and Egypt were in debt due to his excesses and bribes to the point that the populace in Alexandria wanted him deposed. With his treasury almost depleted, the client-king fled to Rome to see whether he could procure more loans. Apparently, the triumvirate was divided on what to do about restoring Auteles to his throne. They knew about his unpopularity and ineptitude as ruler. Finally, it was agreed that the king should be restored with the stipulation that a huge amount of money be paid to Caesar and Pompey as well as to the Roman treasury.

During Auteles' absence, the people of Alexandria placed Archelaus on the throne. He had married Auteles' eldest daughter Berenice to establish his claims to become ruler. However, the Romans were infuriated over Archelaus' action and denied him permission to rule. Soon the Romans marched into Egypt and reinstated Auteles. Berenice and Archelaus were executed, the common practice when someone was deposed. Auteles was left with four children of whom the eldest was Cleopatra, followed by Arisone and two brothers.

Cleopatra realized that the riches of Egypt had fallen to Rome. She saw her country in civil war and the economy in turmoil. Garrisoned Roman troops in the capitol separated the king and his people. She also realized the monstrous financial debt the Egyptians owed the Romans. Even among the Romans corruption was rampant. For example, two Romans who were delegated to collect monies from the Egyptians were charged with embezzlement and defrauding the Roman people. In an ironic twist,

Caesar let them off with a light sentence, for he had been beneficiary of a large part of the money.

The people of Alexandria, accustomed to the hard rule of their Greek rulers, now realized that they were better off under the yoke of the Romans. Egypt had no will to fight the Romans or to aid her neighbors. When the Egyptians took notice of what had happened to the Carthaginians, they did not want their own lands laid waste. They, therefore, chose to be accommodating and adaptable. Of course, the Romans walked over them in short order. Soon a new Roman province was formed in the west side of Egypt and placed under a Roman administrator.

Thus, when Cleopatra ascended the throne, the Romans were already encroaching on her kingdom. Corinth, Macedonia, Carthage, Syria, and Armenia were lands that were already under the control of the Romans, much like the satellite countries of Russia. The Romans controlled both the east and west. Surely, Egypt in the south would be next.

When Auteles died in 51 B.C., he left his kingdom under the auspices of Rome to his ten-year-old son Ptolemy XIII and his eighteen-year-old daughter Cleopatra VII. So it was into this chaotic whirlwind Cleopatra was thrown.

If the land of the Ptolemies was in upheaval, the Romans were also in a state of internal conflict. The politics of Rome was often complicated by the ambitions, rivalries, and treachery of the ruling class. One belief most Romans held was that Rome existed to rule the world. In their conquest of the world, troops, weapons, and money were needed. Roman troops were recruited and maintained abroad, and great levies of taxes sustained the Roman war machine. Egypt had to pay tribute to Rome. Cleopatra knew that only the Romans could help her save Egypt. She needed Rome on her side to maintain and increase her authority and power.

From the start, there was trouble between the co-rulers. The boy-king had a royal Egyptian council backing him with its motivations, ambitions, and desires. Furthermore, the Roman Senate had placed Ptolemy XIII under the protection of Pompey. In other words, Cleopatra was being forced out of power. She withdrew to Syria and prepared to recover her crown by her own wiles and force of arms if need be. In her world she had to kill or be killed to retain her position.

Meanwhile, Crassus, a third member of the Roman triumvirate was killed, leaving two great rivals, Caesar and Pompey. At first Cleopatra leaned towards Pompey since he already had strong influence in Egypt. In 49 B.C., the Egyptians drove Cleopatra out of Alexandria. But within the year, she was ready to dethrone her brother-husband. One of the king's council members led an army against Cleopatra. But by then she had Julius Caesar on her side, and he was willing to fight a war for her against Ptolemy XIII and Pompey.

After Pompey's defeat at Epirus in Greece, he decided to flee to Egypt. As Pompey was pulling ashore, the king's forces were already lined up to fight Cleopatra. A Roman soldier stabbed Pompey to death, probably with Caesar's blessing. Subsequently at Cleopatra's urging the Egyptian navy attacked Pompey's ships, and they were either sunk or scattered. Now Julius Caesar was sole leader of Rome and its vast empire.

Caesar came with his fleet and legions into the harbor of Alexandria. Badly needing money after his many campaigns, he was now guardian of the Egyptian crown and its wealth. Caesar demanded that the co-rulers end their hostility and meet before him. At this meeting he backed Cleopatra. Caesar, as sole ruler of Rome, viewed the riches of Egypt as endless.

Plutarch told an amazing story about the first encounter between Cleopatra and Caesar in Alexandria. The boy-king's army blocked the way for Cleopatra to enter the city. Not to be dissuaded, she took a small boat and arrived at the palace in darkness. Her friend Apollodorus wrapped her in a rug that he tied and carried her into the palace without notice. Caesar, when he beheld this ruse, was most enchanted by the wiles of this clever woman. According to Plutarch, Cleopatra was not a beautiful woman, and a few recently discovered coins with her likeness confirm this. However, she had a magnetic personality and great intellect. Caesar viewed her as a way to control Egypt; she saw him as a way to achieve her political survival. He soon had her installed as queen of Egypt.

Caesar had quite a reputation with women. He was fifty-two and Cleopatra was eighteen when he first encountered her rolling out of a rug. Her charm, spirit, and intelligence captivated all who came into her presence. She was multi-lingual and well educated. No doubt she and Caesar conversed in Greek about literature and philosophy. Indeed, Rome had adopted much of Greek culture, including their gods, drama, political system, literature, and philosophy. Caesar even desired to become the new ruler of the world like his Greek hero, Alexander the Great. Caesar's power and intelligence attracted Cleopatra while he saw in her the Hellenistic qualities that he greatly valued. She embodied the synthesis of the pharaohs and the Ptolemies. Caesar brought Cleopatra to Rome, and she lived openly with him as his mistress. Caesar's wife resented this, and many Romans were angered at the public display of immorality.

When the boy-king saw his sister cohabiting with Caesar, his ire was raised. The Egyptian army and inhabitants supported Ptolemy XIII and turned against Cleopatra and the Roman occupiers. For two years, the warring factions fought. In the end, Ptolemy XIII and his Egyptian supporters lost the battle. Ptolemy XIII was drowned, and for the first time in three centuries, a foreign power took over Alexandria. During this fighting the world famous library in Alexandria was destroyed by fire. Meanwhile, Caesar had an enraptured interlude in the arms of Cleopatra. To satisfy Egyptian customs, Ptolemy XIV, another younger brother, was designated a nominal co-ruler.

Caesar returned to Rome. After the birth of Caesarian, Caesar's son, Cleopatra and her son soon followed him, and they lived on Caesar's estate for more than a year. Her aim was to solidify the political relationship between Egypt and Rome. Through his power over the Senate, Caesar was able to achieve success for a time. The birth of Caesarian not only bound him and Cleopatra together as parents, but it also bound their two countries. They hoped that Caesarian would someday inherit the thrones of both Rome and Egypt.

Because Caesar was married to Calpurnia, he could not marry Cleopatra. Roman law did not allow polygamous marriages or marriage between a patrician and a foreigner. Although Caesar and Cleopatra were no longer lovers, Caesar provided Cleopatra the highest honors possible. He placed a gilded statue of her in the Roman Forum next to the statue of Venus Genetrix, a goddess claimed as founder of the Julian clan. Egypt and Rome were politically bound together at least in the eyes of Caesar and Cleopatra. Egypt would remain an independent nation under Rome's protection. This situation was of political advantage to both sides.

However, the republicans in Rome believed that introducing the statue of queen-goddess Cleopatra into the shrine of Caesar's clan was outrageous. Caesar would not consider himself merely a dictator, but a god like Cleopatra. His vaulting ambition and dreams of deification were blamed on his queen-goddess. Cleopatra was the great seductress with a brilliant mind. She was seen to have cast her "magic spell" on Caesar, and the tide of public opinion was turning against him. Already forces were at work to bring down Caesar.

Alexandria was the cultural and scientific center of the east, and Caesar longed for Rome to be such a center. Like her father, Cleopatra knew the art of spectacle and held great feasts and dramatic productions with music and dance for propaganda purposes. According to the Greek historian and biographer, Plutarch, Cleopatra dressed herself like Isis and wished to be addressed as the "new Isis," the greatest of all the Egyptian goddesses. The cult of Isis and her husband Osiris dated back two thousand years and presupposed the equality of the sexes since they were equally worshipped by all Egyptians. This was part of Cleopatra's public relations, for she portrayed herself as a mother and a war-goddess queen. Some of the greatest scholars and political leaders in Rome attended her dinners where politics, philosophy, and literature were discussed. To be invited to one of her banquets was a high social distinction.

By establishing a romantic and political relationship with Julius Caesar, Cleopatra had managed to retain her own power and the relative independence of her nation. However, when Caesar was assassinated in Rome on the Ides of March, 44 B.C., the situation suddenly changed. The Egyptian queen wanted to maintain cordial relations with Rome. The two countries had extensive trade, and both derived financial benefit from the exchange. Egypt was regarded as the "bread basket" of Rome.

But first, Cleopatra had to get her own kingdom in order. During her residence in Rome, Cleopatra had neglected her own land and people. When she returned to Alexandria, the nation was suffering from a drought. The diminished seasonal flooding of the Nile had caused the grain harvest to be drastically reduced. In addition as a direct result of the famine, disease was rampant. Sick and starving people might easily rise in revolt.

Cleopatra had to collect the grain that was still available in the countryside, gather it together in strategic locations, and redistribute the food where it was most needed. Farmers were required to give more of their produce as a tax to the government than in normal years. While Cleopatra's administrators were able to provide grain to the populous cities, foreign residents and the Jews were cruelly denied provisions of food and grain. Through her use of religious rituals and public ceremonies and her effective redistribution of food, the people had been held in check through the worst of famine and plague. Eventually agricultural production increased. To commeratate the end of the famine and Cleopatra's judicious handling of the crisis, new coins were minted showing a double cornucopia horn of plenty and her royal crown.

Next, Cleopatra turned to the task of preserving and strengthening her own rule. Cleopatra shed no tears when her first brother-husband Ptolemy XIII was drowned. She also ordered the execution of her younger sister Arizone. Then her second brother-husband Ptolemy XIV conveniently disappeared. Cleopatra's intention was to have her son by Julius Caesar,

Caesarian, placed on the throne beside her as co-ruler. The marriage of the queen to her own son was not a serious scandal to the Egyptians; incest was a common method of preserving the royal blood. Besides, Egyptian custom and law prohibited a female from ruling alone; a male had to rule with her.

Since Caesarian was half Roman, Egypt's queen expected that Caesarian would be acceptable as co-sovereign of their client-state. She thought that eventually Rome and Egypt would meld into one new empire with her son in command. To further enhance Caesarian's authority, he too was officially declared a descendent of the gods.

The Romans were shocked and disgusted by Cleopatra's cruel behavior in the pursuit of greater power. However, conditions in Rome were in turmoil.

Upon Caesar's assassination, the republic erupted into civil war. Two of Caesar's assassins, Brutus and Cassius, tried to seize control, but they were defeated by Mark Antony at the battle of Philippi in 42 B.C. The mantle of Caesar's power was divided among the Second Triumvirate, consisting of Mark Anthony, Lepidus, and Octavian, the adopted son and nephew of Julius Caesar. Mark Anthony was given control over the Eastern Roman territories, which included the client-kingdom of Egypt.

In vying against one another for more power, Lepidus resigned, leaving the Roman republic at the mercy of Octavian and Mark Antony. Instead of dividing the land between them peacefully, Mark Antony declared himself supreme ruler of the Eastern half of the republic. Octavian, however, refused to allow the separation of Rome.

Civil war was inevitable.

Cleopatra viewed Octavian as a possible threat to the birthright of her son, Caesarian. As Caesar's only natural son, he should have inherited the wealth and privileges of his father Julius. So Cleopatra decided to lend her support and that of her army and navy to the rebellious Mark Antony. Commanding her own fleet in a great display of pomp and splendor, Cleopatra set sail for Philippi to join forces with Antony. However, her fleet was nearly destroyed by a storm. Immediately, she began building new ships and raising another army.

Antony invited Cleopatra to meet with him in Tarus, a city in Asia Minor. Apparently they fell madly in love. In 41 B.C., Antony went to stay with Cleopatra in Alexandria and continued their love affair in earnest. They both seemed sincere in their love for each other, but politics remained as a strong motive for their conduct. Plutarch described their relationship as a "dreadful calamity."

Cleopatra wanted to secure her own throne and assure the prosperity and security of her nation. For many years she had ruled Egypt effectively without help from Rome. She was able to maintain her independence from Rome as an absolute monarch. Now she wanted to rule side by side with Antony. She even had coins minted which displayed his head on one side and hers on the other. Such an action could only be viewed as a taunt and challenge to Octavian.

After spending a passionate year in luxury and wantonness, Antony returned in 40 B.C. to the Roman capitol to confront Octavian. The two had many issues to argue about: money, possession of lands, control of armies, and ultimate control of the Roman government throughout the Roman world. Octavian and Antony agreed to a simple power-sharing plan: Octavian was in control of the west while Antony ruled the east. But the two halves still constituted a single Rome. Octavian wanted to prevent the breakup of the nation, and he also wanted to retain Antony as a friend and ally. Accordingly, Octavian offered his sister Octavia in marriage. Octavia had recently become a widow and was already pregnant. Away from Cleopatra's romantic influence, Antony impulsively married Octavia. It would be advantageous to him personally and politically to be linked with the family of Caesar. Antony apparently forgot that he had a royal paramour in Egypt who was pregnant with his twins.

For a while, Antony settled down to married life and resumed his administrative duties in Rome. Octavian must have been pleased, but Antony was not. Eventually he decided to abandon his new wife. He sailed to Syria where he begged Cleopatra to join him. According to Plutarch, when the Egyptian queen arrived in Syria, Antony offered her new lands to govern: Phoenicia, part of Syria, all of the isle of Cyprus, a great part of Cilicia, part of Judea, and a coastal part of Arabia.

Yet, the Queen wanted even more. Egypt's eastern frontier was constantly being invaded, so she requested satellite areas in Arabia, Syria, and Palestine where her armies could defend Egypt's borders. In spite of his passion, Antony denied her request for the whole of Judea.

It is not clear whether Antony and Cleopatra were ever formally joined in marital union. Many historians think they were, and if so their marriage would signify the union of Egypt and Rome. Antony recognized the twins as his heirs, along with Julius' son Caesarian. The twins were named Alexander Helios and Cleopatra Selene, after the Greek god of the sun and the goddess of the moon. Conservative Rome allowed for only one wife at a time while in Egyptian culture, a man could have multiple wives.

Impressed by Antony's reputation as a great military leader, Cleopatra viewed him not only as her consort, but as the protector and savior of her nation as well. Theirs was not just a passionate love affair; it was also a political and diplomatic affair. With Cleopatra's assistance, Antony might become another Alexander, and with his help and protection, she might become empress of a vast Roman-Egyptian empire.

Unfortunately for them, their ambitions were doomed to failure. Antony, for good reason, had a reputation as a libertine and drunkard who often lost sight of his duties and goals. In addition, Octavian had been insulted and pushed too far, and he was determined to have his revenge by crushing the combined forces of Antony and Cleopatra. For a time, the old Antony was revitalized by the prospect of a new war against Parthia. Cleopatra rode with Antony and his troops as far as the Euphrates River, from where she went on to visit some of her new territories.

But the military campaign against Parthia did not go well. Antony's army lost thirty thousand men, which further tarnished his image as a military leader. Some historians allege that Antony was so much under Cleopatra's spell, or so crazed with drugs and alcohol, that his judgment became wild and rash. When Cleopatra heard of the disaster, she rushed to aid him with fresh troops, ships, supplies, and money. She arrived too late.

After achieving a minor military success in Armenia, Antony returned to Alexandria in 34 B.C. Using his authority as co-consul of Rome, Antony reaffirmed Cleopatra's title of Queen of Egypt, Cyprus, Libya, and Syria. He also appointed Caesarian as co-ruler of Egypt, thus making legitimate Cleopatra's claim to queenship according to Egyptian custom.

Octavian regarded Antony as a threat to Roman interests as well as to his own. Antony's failing military leadership gave Octavian confidence that he could defeat Antony's and Cleopatra's forces in battle. Octavian wanted no merger of Egyptian and Roman cultures. All the client-kingdoms of Rome were to remain under Roman domination. Octavian and Antony prepared to do battle. In 32 B.C., with Cleopatra and her fleet, Antony sailed for Samos, an island off the coast of Italy.

The previous year, Octavian had been elected consul for the third time, and Antony was elected co-consul. Antony could not conduct another war without the help of Cleopatra, for she provided the money and resources needed to oppose Octavian and his forces. She competently began managing payment of troops. She even ordered the building of war ships and provided transport for Antony's army. She acted like a quartermaster overseeing the storage and shipment of food and grains.

Yet Antony could not attack the Roman capitol with the Egyptian queen at his side. This would have been contrary to the masculine and paternalistic values Rome stood for; in fact, Antony could never attain political ruling status in Rome unless he got rid of his paramour-queen. However, at this point in their relationship, they were forever linked. So Antony delayed a confrontation until Octavian attacked.

Although Antony had proven himself a competent general on land at Philippi, Cleopatra prevailed upon him instead to fight a naval battle. She firmly believed there was no way Octavian could defeat her flotilla. Once again, Antony conceded to her wishes.

As the battle of Actium commenced, it appeared that Antony would have an easy victory, but soon he was out-maneuvered by Octavian. The battle surged one way and then another. Suddenly after many hours of fighting, Cleopatra and sixty of her ships fled through the lines toward Greece. Antony in a small craft followed to her ship and boarded. The rest of Antony's fleet fled to Actium where they ultimately surrendered.

Cleopatra returned to Alexandria where she put on another one of her theatrical productions, as if all were well. Meanwhile, Antony in deep depression went to Paraetonium. Octavian waited a year before he decided to attack Egypt. With a decimated army and navy, Antony and Cleopatra would be easy prey for Octavian.

Antony joined Cleopatra at the Brucheion Palace in Alexandria. Here they feasted and partied and handed out lavish gifts to their guests and to the populace. Cleopatra, Antony, and all their guests swore to end their lives together if defeat came. Things were looking bleak. However, Cleopatra, ever the politician, sent an emissary carrying money to Octavian in Rome, hoping to placate him for a time and to determine his plans. Octavian kept the money but sent the diplomat back with no concessions.

Next, Cleopatra sent emissaries to Syria offering to give up her regal status if her children could inherit the crown. For his part, Antony agreed to give up his rank and authority and wanted only to exist as a private citizen. Octavian's reply was that Cleopatra must execute Antony. She realized that Antony's fate was sealed, but she did not trust Octavian. She worried that Octavian would steal all the wealth of Egypt.

Antony was in a great state of anxiety and would not be able to help her in her contest with Octavian. Yet her fate was linked to Antony. She set about moving the Ptolemy treasure into her mausoleum. This treasure could be a bargaining chip, for the treasures and wealth of Egypt were Octavian's main goal. The treasure in the lower part of the mausoleum was surrounded by combustible material that could destroy it in a short time.

Soon Octavian moved his army into Egypt. Antony's depleted army and navy were soon dispatched, and Antony retreated to Alexandria. He accused Cleopatra of betrayal. In fear of her life, she went to her mausoleum amid great stores of gold, silver, gems, and other treasures that she swore she would destroy lest they fall into Roman hands. She issued word that she was dead. Antony in great agony attempted suicide by self-inflicted sword wounds. Upon hearing the news, Cleopatra requested that the dying Antony be brought to her. He was laid in her bed and covered with a dress she ripped from her body. Moreover, she covered herself with his blood. As he lay dying, in great anguish she expressed her undying love. Indeed, Antony was the great love of her life.

Octavian, at about the same time, entered Alexandria. He wanted only to capture Cleopatra and her treasure, so he could parade her through the streets of Rome like a slave. When the Roman representative reached her, she begged only that her children be allowed to succeed her. Soon, however, she was captured.

Then, Octavian ordered an audience with his captured queen. He now had everything he wanted: her person, her treasure, and control of the Ptolemy dynasty and of Egypt. It is hard to imagine the depth of despair Cleopatra must have felt as she saw everything in her life torn from her. After three hundred years, the Ptolemy dynasty was at an end. She had fought hard to keep it alive and independent. Now all was lost, and there was no way out except by death. Suicide was viewed as a noble death in Roman culture. Her mind was made up; she would not allow herself to be made a spectacle in Rome. No further indignities would befall her. In the end, she deprived Octavian of some of his glory: he would never have her as a trophy of his victory.

The victor made plans to send Cleopatra and her children to Rome. In the meantime, he allowed Cleopatra to bury Antony in an honorable way; she too wished to be buried honorably near Antony. She requested that he allow her one more chance to pour a libation to the gods, and he granted her that wish.

Her physician Olympus wrote a report that was handed down through the family of Plutarch and recorded by historians. As the story goes, Cleopatra was in her mausoleum resting from her bath and dinner. One of her servants brought her a basket which appeared to be full of figs. That is how the basket passed through the guards. Cleopatra at some point requested a tablet on which she wrote a message, and she asked that it be sent to Octavian. When Octavian read it, he knew that she was dead. She had expressed the desire to be buried next to Antony. An asp in the fig basket had killed Cleopatra. By dying from the venom of an asp bite, Cleopatra hoped to transform herself into the Egyptian deity Isis. The asp was sacred to Amun-Ra, and the pharaohs wore its figure on their headdresses and their insignias. Cleopatra believed the sun-god welcomed her into the family of Egyptian gods.

When she died, she was wearing her magnificent ceremonial robes that she wore in public. Even in death, she appeared to be the Macedonian-Egyptian queen-goddess. Her manner of death was a fitting theatrical finish to her dramatic life. Most of us think of Cleopatra, the love goddess, the femme fatal, as a woman who used her manipulative and conniving skills to get what she wanted. Behind those skills, there lurked a shrewd mind with brilliant plans. Her ultimate design was to keep the throne and insure the continuance of the Ptolemy dynasty. She cleverly mingled the blood lines of Julius Caesar and Mark Antony with that of her own royal family. Yet in the end she failed.

Cleopatra, queen-goddess of Egypt, has been immortalized in books, plays, poems, movies, and legends. Some of the greatest ancient writers have written, albeit subjectively, about her life. She may have been the world's first celebrity: five ballets, forty-five operas, seventy-seven plays, and at least seven movies are about her. Her affairs with Caesar and Antony have titillated our senses and imagination for all these many years and continue to do so. With her tragic demise after a twenty year reign, Egypt was absorbed into the Roman Empire. The "magic spell" of one woman in her efforts to save her nation brought about the downfall of two of the world's greatest leaders. She was a ruler first and last.

Livia Drusilla II marble sculpture with wheat sheaf and cornucopia 1st century B.C. She was the wife of Augustus Caesar, mother of Tiberius, and grandmother of Claudius. Musee du Louvre, Paris (Wikipedia Commons credit line Borghese Collection purchase 1807, Source/Photographer, original upload 4 June, 2004 by ChristO, Accession number Ma1242 MR 259)

CHAPTER FOUR

Livia, Rome's Ideal Woman

"To a chaste woman naked men are no different than statues."

Livia Drusilla was one of the most impressive women in Roman history. Her power and influence were almost unlimited. She was the wife of Augustus Caesar, mother of Tiberius, grandmother of Claudius, and great-grandmother of Nero. Her roles as wife of Augustus and several times as regent stand out in history. Two thousand years later, her life still impresses us.

She was born in 58 B.C., the daughter of Marcus Livius Claudianus and his wife Aufidia. In 42 B.C., her father married her off to her patrician cousin, Tiberius Claudius Nero. Both men were fighting against Octavian on the side of Julius Caesar's assassins. Marcus Claudianus committed suicide at the battle of Philippi along with Gaius Cassius and Marcus Brutus. However, Livia's husband kept on fighting against Octavian but this time on the side of Mark Antony. To escape prosecution from Octavian's forces, the family fled to Sicily and then to Greece.

Amnesty was later granted to all who fought against the victorious Octavian, and Livia returned to Rome with her family. By this time she had a son Tiberius who would succeed Octavian and later become emperor. She was pregnant with another son when she met Octavian who instantly fell in love with her. He was already married to Scribonia who also was pregnant. Octavian demanded a divorce, and on the day the divorce became official, Scribonia gave birth to a daughter, Julia. Livia's husband, Tiberius Nero, also agreed to a divorce.

Such marital entanglements were not uncommon in patrician society. Marital alliances and exchanges often enhanced the political upward climb of male politicians. Women were used as a means to influence and manipulate those who could promote their husband's or son's careers.

Moreover, Roman women were allowed to attend public functions and had more private freedoms than their Greek counterparts at this time. They could sue for divorce, make contracts, and hold title to real property.

Cassius Dio, the Roman writer, wrote that Tiberius Nero gave Livia to Octavian just as a father would give a daughter in marriage. He was even present at the wedding banquet celebrating Livia's and Octavian's marriage. Again, it appears there was also a political motivation for the marriage. Through the marriage of Octavian and Livia, Nerones families were joined together with Octavian, which consolidated his power even more. In all of his marriages, Octavian sought out political advantage. Yet it appears they were genuinely devoted to each other. Octavian and Livia were married for fifty-one years but had no children. Therefore, the factor of heredity became a major issue.

When Mark Antony committed suicide, Octavian's major opposition was eliminated; Octavian became Roman Emperor and adopted the name of Augustus Caesar. As Emperor, Augustus was one of the most outstanding leaders the world has ever known. He completely reformed the Roman Empire, making it so strong it lasted for hundreds of years. Livia was always at his side at all state functions. She appeared to be the model mother and wife being unpretentious and forgiving of her husband's infidelities. She ignored his notorious womanizing, pretending neither to hear nor notice any of the objects of his interest. Augustus, in turn, rewarded Livia with great honors. For example, she was allowed to control her own finances, and with a circle of her own friends she promoted her own candidates for public office.

Behind the scenes, Livia was promoting Tiberius, her own son, to be Augustus' successor. Her other son Drusus became a trusted general. He married Augustus' favorite niece Antonia Minor. Augustus had only one daughter Julia by his wife Scribonia. Tiberius married her, thus entwining the families more closely. In A.D. 4, Augustus formally named Tiberius his successor and heir to the empire. Even though Livia worked in unofficial ways, she was a brilliant political analyst who succeeded in furthering her own ends.

Historians disagree on the integrity of Livia. The suspicions start with the mysterious death of Augustus' nephew, Marcellus. Cassius Dio maintained that Livia was responsible for the deaths of Julia's sons whom Augustus had adopted as his own sons, and they were his true heirs.

Indeed, they were of his blood line, whereas Tiberius was not. It does seem suspicious that three possible heirs died rather young—Lucious-Gaius-Agrippa Postumus. The Roman writers Cassius Dio and Tacitus allude to the possible involvement of Livia in their deaths. With all three contenders eliminated, Tiberius was in first place to inherit. According to Tacitus, Livia exerted profound influence on the aging Augustus. Cassius Dio also raises the possibility that Livia had a hand in the death of Augustus by poisoning. On the other hand, many modern historians refute these accounts.

In A.D. 14, Augustus died and soon was deified. He left one third of his estate to Livia and two thirds to Tiberius. She was also granted inclusion in the Julian family, which gained her patrician status. Henceforth, she was referred to as Julia Augusta. She held such power in A.D. 20 that the Senate passed a law making it an act of treason to speak against her. She was so esteemed that she sat with the Vestal Virgins at theater events.

Her power and prestige eventually annoyed Tiberius who was probably jealous of her popularity. Evidently she constantly harped on the notion that she was responsible for his becoming emperor. Cassius Dio tells us that Tiberius loathed his mother and retired to Capri because he could not bear to be near her. Tiberius may have been adversely affected by his mother's divorce from his father making him a step-child in the house of Augustus. Another source of resentment for Tiberius was that he was compelled to leave the wife he loved and was forced to marry Augustus' daughter, Julia.

At one point, he refused the Senate's offer to bestow upon Liva the unprecedented title of Mater Patriae (Mother of the Fatherland). Cassius Dio and Tacitus portrayed Livia as a meddling, domineering woman who frequently interfered with her son's political decisions. For example, Urgulania, a friend of Livia's, was implicated in the death of the great Roman General Germanicus. She was exonerated solely on the basis of her friendship with Livia. On one occasion, Livia placed a statue of Augustus in the center of Rome with her own name prominently displayed before that of Tiberius. When women invoked oaths, moreover, they had to use Livia's name. As early as 16 B.C., Livia's portrait was stamped on Roman coins, depicting her famous hairstyles, representing the ideal woman. She was a smart, shrewd, and scheming woman.

When Livia died in A.D. 29 at the age of eighty-six, Tiberius did not attend her funeral. He excused himself on the basis of business involvements and sent Caligula to deliver the funeral oration. Tiberius denied his mother all the honors bestowed upon her by the Senate as well as the supreme honor of deification for which she longed. Livia had lived over fifty years as a strong power player and empress. Therefore, she assumed she should have the same political influence and tried to interfere in her son's political decisions, which generally speaking were more republican than were those of Augustus. With the past history between the two, strong bitterness only intensified.

The story of Claudius, Caligula's nephew and Livia's grandson, is a fascinating one. He was ugly and deformed and he stuttered. Because of his unattractiveness, he was generally ostracized from the political limelight. This served to his advantage: through his solitary studies he became a political and historical scholar. Under the direction of Livia, he studied under Livy, the great historian, who had received much acclaim under Augustus. Subsequently, Claudius wrote chronicles of Rome and the Etruscans as well as several biographies. Fortunately for Claudius, he was never close to Caligula. Therefore, when it was time for a new emperor to be chosen, the army and public supported Claudius.

As emperor, Claudius restored many of the honors his grandmother had been denied by her son, and he had her deified in A.D. 42. Some of the honors conferred upon her were extravagant: an elephant-drawn chariot transported her image to all public games; races were held in her name; and a statue of her was placed in the temple of Augustus. Officially, she became known as the Diva Augusta (Divine Augusta).

Livia was born at a time in Roman history when women were valued for little more than their family connections, their property, or the public image they were able to display. Yet Livia, behind-the-scenes, shaped the rule of two Roman emperors. In her official role as Empress, she represented the ideal Roman wife and mother. All the Julio-Claudian emperors were her direct descendents. Tacitus' obituary referred to her as: "An imperious mother and an amiable wife....She was a match for the diplomacy of her husband and the dissimulation of her son." She has emerged as one of the most significant women in Roman history.

Bronze statue of Boudica with her daughters in her war chariot near Westminster Pier, London
The statue was commissioned by Prince Albert, executed by Thomas Thornycroft and completed in 1905. Born circa A.D. 25, she united the British native tribes in a last stand against the Romans. She died in battle circa A.D. 60. (Wikimedia Commons)

CHAPTER FIVE

Boudica, Legendary Warrior Queen of the Britons

"But now, it is not as a noble descended from noble ancestry, but as one of the people that I am avenging, lost freedom, my scourged body, and the outraged chastity of my daughters." Tacitus

Little historical evidence exists regarding Boudica. The word *Boudica* is Celtic, meaning victory, and perhaps her name is a variant of the Celtic goddess of victory. Much of what we know about her comes from the *Annals* of the Roman writer Tacitus and the Greek writer Cassius Dio. Fifty years after the events occurred, Tacitus wrote his history based on the eye-witness testimony of General Agricola, his father-in-law, who served on the Roman General Suetonius' staff. Cassius Dio wrote his version one hundred years after the death of Boudica. But their accounts of her life were forgotten until Boudica's name was resurrected from some manuscripts found in a monastery by Giovanni Boccaccio, the author of the *Decameron*, during the fourteenth century.

Boudica was married to the wealthy Celtic Iceni king, Prasutagus, who ruled as a subordinate of the Romans. He had made an agreement with the Romans in exchange for retaining power over his tribe and was a client-king. When he died in A.D. 60, his will stipulated that half his kingdom should go to the Roman Emperor Nero and the other half to his two daughters. Thus he thought his kingdom would be left in peace. However, under Roman law wives and daughters of client-kings could not inherit. On the other hand, Britons regarded Boudica as their new rightful leader and her daughters as legal heirs. The Icenian kingdom soon fell into the hands of the conquerors. The Britons were unsophisticated in financial matters and were constantly being exploited. Nero's tutor and adviser

Seneca demanded that Boudica pay all of her husband's and her tribe's debts, plus interest immediately. Boudica was unable to do so.

In Celtic society, females could reach upper echelons of power and prestige. They were involved in the arts, politics, and the religion of the society. In addition, they could own land, choose their own husbands, and initiate divorce. The Britons seemed to be comfortable with the idea of powerful women who could serve as independent rulers, not just as consorts. They also served as warrior instructors, as warriors, and even as military leaders.

Boudica possessed a great deal of military knowledge albeit below the more experienced standard of the Roman generals. Often depicted as a barbarian queen, Boudica, on the contrary, was of noble birth. She was relatively sophisticated and bi-lingual. The Roman historian Cassius Dio in *Roman History*, Book 62 described her in this way:

> In build she was very tall, in her demeanor most terrifying, in the glint of her eye most fierce, and her voice was harsh; a great mound of the tawniest hair fell to her hips; around her neck was a large golden torc; and she wore a tunic of many colors upon which a thick cloak was fastened with a brooch. This was her general attire. (Vanessa Collingridge. *Boudica*. [New York: Overlook Press, 2005].180).

Romans and Celts both esteemed warrior queens. Cartimandua, the female ruler of vast Brigantian lands, had strong Roman support. The lives of Roman women were not as free or pleasant, generally speaking, as those of Celtic women. Iceni women had more privileges and often were given positions of leadership. Under the Romans most women were relegated to domestic careers: their proper place was deemed to be in the home.

Under Roman rule, the Celts were divided into different kingdoms. The lands of the Celtic Iceni covered most of East Anglia, Norfolk, north Suffolk, and northeast Cambridgeshire. Some of the natives had lived there since the Bronze Age. Later, other Celtic tribes during the Iron Age emigrated from Europe. The various tribes were often at war with each other and were never a united force. Celts shared a common language, history, and culture but never a shared identity. If they had come together, they might have beaten the Romans when they first invaded.

However, many of the tribes enjoyed their ties to Rome. Trade between the Gauls and other continental groups had been going on long before the Roman invasion. From Britain, the Romans imported tin, iron, silver, and grain.

The Romans and Celtic tribes had enjoyed peaceful relationships before the death of Prasutagus in A.D. 60. However, without a strong king to lead them, the Celts, especially the Iceni, were extremely vulnerable.

The Romans plundered Boudica's lands and possessions and considered them legal bounty. The natives faced unbearable religious and cultural oppression. Queen Boudica was ignominiously lashed and her two daughters were savagely raped, making them unmarriageable. It is believed the daughters were around twelve to fourteen years of age when they were violated. By their actions, the Romans expected to assure the utter oppression of the Celtic tribes in Britain and to instill mortal fear. Meanwhile, the high ranking Icenians and the king's relatives were reduced to slavery.

But their cruelty had the opposite effect. The Icenians were enraged. Boudica, queen, mother, and warrior would have her revenge. She was witnessing the overthrow of her culture and traditions. There were other long-standing resentments as well. Like modern freedom fighters, Boudica and her followers were fighting for self-preservation, dignity, and freedom. They decided to revolt, and the Trinobantians joined the uprising. Other tribes also came forth to support them in arms, and they effectively formed a pan-tribal alliance. Guerrilla-type warfare was an effective tool against the Romans all over the island. Many Roman veterans had been given lands at Camulodunum (Colchester) that had formerly belonged to the native Britons. In addition, Celtic collaborators living and working in Camulodunum embittered other natives. They were treated as slaves, held in bondage, disarmed, and their lands taken from them. The last straw was the erection of a statue of Claudius, which to the natives stood as a symbol of their enslavement.

Druids had great power and influence over the Celtic tribes. Druidism was stirring up trouble with its elements of superstition and fear. Druids were not only priests, but scientists, scholars, and teachers. They often made the laws and served as judges. The priests exploited the problems of Boudica and used her as a martyr to unite the different factions. She was made a priestess and even raised to the status of goddess.

The Britons were now at war against their oppressors. It is believed Boudica, with the help of the Druids, raised an army of one hundred thousand strong. The Romans were determined to eradicate Druidism, the ancient Celtic religion of the Britons, which was the cement that bound the tribes together. The Romans believed that the Druids on the Isle of Mona were stirring up the insurrection. The Roman warriors destroyed the great forests where they thought the gods of the Druids resided.

Since Boudica, the Druids, and the Britons were in complete rebellion, the Roman Emperor appointed Quintus Petillus Cerealis as governor of Britain. He arrived in Britain with fresh new troops. They garrisoned in Lincoln and built forts in York and Carisle. Cerealis began to search out and destroy the Druids, but when word arrived that Comulodunum (Colchester) was under attack, he rushed to its defense. The Romans had built no defense around Comulodunum. Besides retired Roman soldiers, only a few officers and active soldiers were garrisoned there. Although the city was the capitol of Roman power, the Celts realized that it would be easy prey. The Britons took the town by surprise and slaughtered the population within two days. Then they burned the city to the ground. There was total annihilation of people and buildings. Slain and tortured bodies were everywhere. The victorious Celts offered the heads of captives to Boudica, "goddess of victory."

When the Roman governor Petilius Cerealis arrived too late to rescue the town and its people, his own legion was cut to pieces in short order. Fortunately, he was able to escape. After seeing the carnage, Catus Decianus, the cowardly procurator of the province quickly fled to Gaul.

Next, Londinium (London) was marked for destruction and plunder. Actually, London was not an official colony and the population was small. However, it was a center for trade and commerce. Since Decianus had vacated his role and Ceraelis' military forces had been decimated, Suetonius, the governor in charge of London, decided his fate would be sealed if he stayed in the city. His forces were too small to take on Boudica's army, and he had to take a stand elsewhere.

He left London with all who wished to leave under his protection. Of course, many merchants did not want to abandon their businesses and chose to stay behind, as did many elderly, mothers, and children. Others remained because they did not have transportation or did not believe in the seriousness of the situation. Those who did not leave were butchered, raped, and tortured in the most barbaric way.

The town of Verulamium (St. Albans) was the Britons' next target. Approximately, seventy thousand Roman citizens or allies of Rome perished in the three towns. The Britons did not take prisoners to keep as slaves, nor did they exchange prisoners. For two years, the Britons pillaged the settlements. Meanwhile, Suetonius rounded up approximately ten thousand men and went on the offensive. A master strategist, he chose well the battlefield on which to fight. The general selected a field circled by wood with a narrow entrance and a forest at the rear. Suetonius exhorted his men to fight bravely for the glory of Rome. The Britons had to attack from the front on a slightly upward slope. When the Britons attacked, they were caught in a trap. Their troops in total disarray were no match for the well-trained Romans. Moreover, old internecine problems flared again, causing military strife.

Intoxicated with victory and overconfident, the Celts charged against the Roman troops, who were well armed, highly disciplined, and well-organized. The Britons were so confident of victory that they even left their families in wagons on the outskirts of the plain to watch the battle. They vastly outnumbered the Romans; some estimates put the figure at four to one.

Boudica addressed her army before the last battle against the Romans where she faced off with Suetonius. The exact location of the battle is unknown, but most historians believe it took place in A.D. 60 or 61 along the old Roman Road known as Watling Street between London and Wroxeter in Shropshire. Imagine the scene which has been immortalized by many artists, poets, dramatists, and film makers. Boudica is standing in her horse drawn chariot, her raven hair flying in the wind. Her two daughters stand in front of her while she exhorts her army to battle. Tacitus in his *Annals,* XIV. 35 captured the emotion of the moment in his purely fictitious speech from the mouth of Boudica:

> But now it is not as a woman descended from illustrious ancestry, but as one of the people that I am avenging my lost freedom, my lashed body, and the outraged honor of my daughters. Roman greed has developed to such an extent that not even our persons, nor even our age or our virginity are left unpolluted. But heaven is on the side of just vengeance: one legion which dared to fight has been destroyed; the rest are cowering in their camps or anxiously seeking a means of escape. They will not stand even din and shout of so many thousands, let alone our attack and our weapons. If you balance the strength of our armies and the reason for this war, then you must conquer or die. This is a woman's decision: as for men, they can live or become slaves. (Vanessa Collingridge. *Boudica.* [New York: Overlook Press, 2005]. 234).

Queen Elizabeth I and Queen Victoria, (Boudica, Celtic name for victory) her namesake, drew great inspiration from this speech as have many other powerful women in history down to the feminists of the 20th century.

The naked Celtic warriors often fought with their bodies tattooed and painted. They entered the battle yelling and bellowing like a pack of wild animals. Their purpose was to instill terror in the hearts of their enemies. The women fought with their hair streaming and struck with their swords and spears. At first, some of the Roman troops were dumbfounded. But urged on by their officers, the Romans in wedge formation, charged through the middle of the Britons' lines, thus splitting the Britons' troops. On the flanks, the Romans placed other legions, which essentially encircled the Celts. As the Britons tried to retreat, the wagons holding women and children who had come to view the victory of their warriors, hampered their way, and they were trapped. The Romans, with their superior strategy and skills, slaughtered every man, woman, and child they could reach. When the battle was over, Seutonius annihilated every native man, woman, and child he and his troops could find. The Romans sought out any sympathizers on the rest of the island and their villages, crops, and homes were destroyed. Many were killed or just starved to death. Seutonius' revenge and punishment was so harsh that Nero called him back to Rome after a year of his barbaric tactics.

According to some historians, Boudica, rather than being taken alive, committed suicide like Cleopatra. In fact, Boudica almost defeated the Romans and drove them from her lands. As de facto leader, she ruled less than two years, thus ending the last native uprising against the Romans. The Roman legions occupied Britain for almost four hundred years until they left in A.D. 410 never to return. The Roman legions were needed at home.

Throughout British history, the image of this woman of strong determination has been molded to fit the times. Elizabeth I, Winston Churchill, and Margaret Thatcher all invoked her name in time of war. Boudica still lives in our historical imagination. The memory of this "Iron Queen" who reigns in the pantheon of British heroes will never die.

Empress Theodora A.D. 500-548 and her attendants in 6th century mosaic at the Basilica of St. Vitale of Ravenna, Italy Theodora, wife of Justinian, was perhaps the most powerful and influential woman in Byzantine history. (Wikimedia Commons)

CHAPTER SIX

Theodora, Empress of Byzantium

"The throne is a glorious sepulcher."

When Constantine became Roman emperor, he moved the capitol, from the city of Rome in the west to a town called Byzantium in present-day Turkey. He changed the name to Constantinople, and he chose a co-emperor to administer the lands of the West Roman Empire. Constantinople was the mercantile center of the world, lying across trade routes between east and west and north and south. Today, the city is called Istanbul. When the great Roman Empire fell in A.D. 476, the eastern sector of what remained became the Byzantine Empire. Constantinople was designated the capitol. Religious and political factions vied with each other for power; savage tribes from the east and west attacked its vast lands. The stability of the Empire was in dire peril. The Emperor Justinian, who was crowned in A.D. 527, was able to preserve his empire.

To stem the corrupt abuses in the bureaucracy, Justinian changed the legal code. This revised body of laws is still known as the Justinian Code and remains the basis of legal systems in many eastern nations. Great achievements in art and architecture also marked his reign. Eight hundred years after Justinian's death, Dante Alighieri expressed his views on the egocentric consul: "Caesar I was and am." Justinian tried to recover the lost territories of western Rome and succeeded in regaining the Italian peninsula and even vast regions of Spain.

The bubonic plague devastated the empire in A.D. 543 and abruptly ended an age of splendor. This was the time when the period of antiquity was coming to an end and the Middle Ages were beginning. Fear of God's wrath and justice put people in a religious frame of mind. The Christian church gained new power and influence over the common people and even the nobility. There was less focus on the building of secular buildings and more on churches and monasteries. It was a time when emperors would bend their knees to popes.

Justinian provided support for the church, which in turn, provided needed services to the people with alms houses for the poor and free hospitals for the needy, elderly, widows, and orphans. Free bread was offered to the hungry.

However, the accomplishments of Justinian's rule were not his alone, for Justinian ruled with his wife, Theodora, a name which in Greek meant "gift of God." She was known for her passion, intelligence, and bravery. Theodora served the king as his trusted adviser and is credited with helping to save the empire as well as enhancing its power and influence.

Theodora lived from about A.D. 500-548. Many historians believe she was born on the island of Crete, while others maintain she was born in Syria. Much of the information on her early life comes from the *Secret History* by Procopius who gave us a great view of her early life, albeit prejudicial. His work was not published in his lifetime and became common knowledge approximately three hundred years ago. According to the Byzantine historian Procopius, her father was a bear trainer at the Hippodrome in Constantinople; her mother was an actress and dancer. Thus, she came from the lowest level of Byzantine society since all actresses were considered prostitutes. After her father's death, her mother remarried.

The stepfather sought the job of bear-keeper that his predecessor held, but he was denied the job. The bureaucracy often demanded bribes and showed favoritism in awarding government positions. Corruption was common. The stepfather requested the help of a strong multi-faceted faction known as the Greens but again was turned down.

Faced with the threat of poverty, Theodora's mother formed a plan to save herself and her family. It was common for people to come to the arena where they could raise their voices for justice, fairness, and special favors. So she trained her three girls as little actresses. Dressed in white, with garlands in their hair and bouquets in their hands, the girls and their mother entered the Kynegion Arena. They implored Asterius, the Green leader, for relief. He in turn cast a look of scorn upon the poor widow and her girls. With the supplicants on their knees and Asterius displaying an arrogant and cruel manner, the audience was not looking at this leader as a kind ruler but rather as a cruel tyrant. In ancient culture, kindness was supposed to be shown from the leaders to the oppressed and less fortunate.

But Theodora's mother did not give up. She instructed her girls to go to the other side of the arena where another faction, the Blues, had congregated. Again they knelt and pleaded. Their leader, who happened to need a bear-trainer, immediately declared the widow's new husband employed. From this act of charity, the leader of the Blues received much approval.

Yet, Theodora never forgot the insults of the Greens on that day, and forevermore identified herself with the Blues. She was determined to overcome poverty and to rise to the status of the wealthy and powerful. She used the talents available to her to achieve her goal.

First, Theodora became a mime and later a notorious actress after appearing in the nude. Female actors of that time were regarded as prostitutes, and with her legendary parties, she lived the part. She developed toughness, shrewdness, courage, and survival techniques that she used effectively throughout her life. Her career, unfortunately, was one of the few ways a woman could earn a living. Men that went near her were considered perverts, and respectable men avoided her.

At the age of sixteen, Theodora became the mistress of the governor of Pentapolis, Hecebolus, by whom she had a son. She traveled with him to northern Africa where he eventually abandoned her. She decided to return to Constantinople, but she took time on the way to stop in Alexandria, Egypt. There she met the Patriarch Timothy who treated her with great kindness. Timothy made such an impression on her that ever after she referred to him as her spiritual father. She was still only twenty-one, but her life was changed forever. She converted to Monophysitism, a sect of Christianity that held that Jesus Christ's nature was divine, and he merely had a human appearance. This view was outside the mainstream teaching of the Christian Church. Monophysites were considered heretics by most Christians.

Another person who greatly influenced Theodora's development was the highly intellectual Patriarch of Antioch, Serverus. He began his life as a pagan, studied as a lawyer, then became a monk in Alexandria. He was expelled from the monastery because his arguments in defense of his theological views on Monophysitism caused a riot. The Emperor Anastasius, however, was impressed and made him archbishop of Antioch in A.D. 513. From Serverus, Theodora learned the art of rhetoric and argument, and she developed a taste for intelligent conversation. Bright and very articulate, she could argue her points in a logical convincing manner.

Back in Constantinople in A.D. 522, Theodora took up the reputable career of a weaver, working in a house near the palace. Shortly after, she attracted the attention of Justinian. He was forty years old, about twice her age, when he fell in love with her. Justinian no doubt had many sexual liaisons before Theodora, but he was totally smitten by her beauty. The Greek male often preferred the company of other men and courtesans to his own family. Young men and women were often trained for these roles intellectually and socially.

Justinian wanted to wed Theodora but was prohibited by Roman law from marrying an actress; this law applied to all government officials and patricians. However, Justinian arranged to have the current emperor Justin I, his uncle, nullify the old law. Therefore, in A.D. 525 Justinian married Theodora. The same right was given to other patricians and officials. It was presupposed of course that the actress would reform her life. Besides her physical charms, Theodora's intelligence and strong character also attracted Justinian. In Theodora, Justinian saw many great qualities that would distinguish her as queen.

Although Theodora held the honorific title of Empress, Byzantine law prevented her from officially reigning as co-monarch. However, she came to be co-monarch de facto since the new Emperor frequently sought her advice on many affairs of state. She was staunchly loyal to her husband, and her biographer Procupious confirmed her fidelity. She confided in no one but Justinian and was constantly on the alert for any adviser, official, or general who might thwart her husband's aims. She soon understood that the life in the palace was not that different from her former life in the Hippodrome.

Through her marriage, she instantly gained great wealth and power. Justinian was the heir of his Uncle Justin I. When Justin I abdicated the throne in A.D. 527, Justinian and Theodora were crowned Emperor and Empress of the Byzantine Empire.

Justinian had been on the throne for five years when great civil unrest erupted. A high tax required by Justinian's fiscal policies was one of the major problems, and unfair judicial practices angered the people as well. Justinian's ambitious goals required a great deal of money: military campaigns to reconquer the Italian peninsula, North Africa, and Spain; monumental building projects, such as palaces, churches, fortresses, and aqueducts; and payments to barbarian nations for their diplomatic and military support. In addition, both Theodora and Justinian had generous natures, and each gave much-needed aid to the city of Antioch when it was struck by earthquakes in two consecutive years. The only way to pay for all these ventures was by excessive taxation, which was often administered by corrupt agents. The populace was ready for an uprising to protest their exploitation. The people demanded solutions for their present problems. Once again, Justinian relied on Theodora for her help and guidance.

Chariot racing had been the passion of the Roman people since the days of the republic. The chariots were two-wheeled and were drawn by four horses. Wherever Romans lived, there was chariot racing. At times, the races seemed more important than God, family, or the Empire. The Hippodrome, which could hold one hundred thousand spectators, was one place where voices could be raised openly against the government.

The fans were divided into factions of Greens and Blues. Besides being sporting clubs, each faction had religious interests. The Blues tended to be more conservative politically and religiously, and they were mostly of the upper class. On the other hand, the Greens were mostly of the working class and generally less orthodox in their religious views. Both groups had a nucleus of gang-like members that engaged in all kinds of criminal activity.

In A.D. 532, a major dispute erupted between the Blues and Greens. Justinian was perceived as supporting the Blues making the Greens feel alienated and bitter. Seeing themselves as the chosen ones, the Blues became arrogant and antagonistic against the Greens. The underlying economic and judicial injustices were the real cause of unrest.

Matters were about to explode.

Meanwhile, Justinian was taking a firm hand trying to establish law and order. He ordered the execution of seven convicted murderers. While strung up, the scaffold broke and one Green and one Blue survived. Monks immediately took the lucky ones to St. Lawrence Church for asylum. At this point, the Blues and Greens united, begging for mercy for the intended victims. Justinian refused to show leniency. Subsequently, at the end of twenty-two chariot races when there were to be twenty-four, the Blues and Greens in a show of unity shouted, "Long live the benevolent Blues and Greens."

Justinian remained firm. In protest, the Nika Riot began. It lasted ten days and left the city of Constantinople virtually in ruins. The riot almost toppled the emperor and empress. The rioters set fire to many buildings, threw open the jails and attacked the palace. Churches, including the Hagia Sophia, as well as civic buildings were set on fire; the rioters demanded a new emperor. The Demanche, spokespersons for the Blues and Greens, called for the dismissal of Justinian and his three top advisers, the Prefect of Constantinople, and the heads of the treasury and judiciary.

At this point, Theodora showed her leadership and courage by helping to quell the Nika Riot. Justinian was advised to leave the city, but Theodora refused to show any sign of weakness. Under no circumstance would Justinian and Theodora abandon the city. Their course of action was exactly what the opposition did not want, and it would lead to their defeat. She maintained that it would be better to die for the throne than to flee in shame and dishonor, and she is reported to have said, "*For a king death is better than dethronement and exile.*"

Theodora was an actress, and she used her theatrical skills to the utmost. Justinian's generals were so moved by her words that they attacked the Hippodrome and won a battle against the insurgents. Overall, about thirty thousand people were killed. As a result, the crown was saved, and Theodora's fiery speech like Boudica's, had been a rallying call to victory.

Within ten years, Theodora and Justinian rebuilt Constantinople into one of the most magnificent cities in the world. Bridges, aqueducts, roads, and more than twenty-five churches adorned the city. The lavishly-decorated Hagia Sophia, Church of the Holy Wisdom, stands even today as one of the great ecclesiastical architectural wonders of the world. Its dome measures 108 feet in diameter, and its crown stands 180 feet above the ground. Splendid mosaics and marbles decorate the walls. During the fifteenth century, it became a mosque, and today it stands as a museum.

Theodora and Justinian were equals before the revolt, and they held power jointly. Now she simply took command, pursued her enemies and flaunted her wealth. She had her own palace. The Empress often showed a violent nature in defending her position. The ever practical Theodora was constantly alert to problems and threats against the empire, while the intellectual Justinian was more concerned with the theoretical issues of law and justice and designing plans for an ideal Christian society.

On pragmatic social and political issues that were of special interest to her, Theodora prevailed upon Justinian to pass specific legal reforms. Forced prostitution was prohibited, and shelters were established for women who wanted to abandon prostitution as a way of life. Young girls would no longer be sold into prostitution, nor would they be forced to sign contracts that would virtually reduce them to sex slaves. Under her new law, prostitutes were released from binding contracts which impeded their personal freedom. Two hundred and twenty-seven women took advantage of the law immediately after its passage. Perhaps Theodora felt empathy for these pitiful creatures because she remembered her own days at the Hippodrome and her own abandonment.

In any event, she advocated more rights for women in divorce cases. Theodora also strove to have laws passed that would stop the killing of women adulteresses. She changed the status of females born to slaves so that they did not automatically become slaves. The Roman writer Procopius maintained that Theodora was a proponent of legal abortion as well as a practitioner. A champion of women, Theodora sought equal political and economic rights for all. She was certainly the most influential person in Byzantine society to advocate the rights of women under the law.

Other reforms advanced by Theodora included: the right of women to own and inherit private property, to share guardianship of their children in divorce cases, to reclaim their dowries upon the death of their husbands. She sought the death penalty for men convicted of rape, and she often had men beaten when they abused their wives or refused to obey her rules. Staunchly loyal to her friends, the Empress treated her adversaries severely and would often send them to one of her dungeons. Men often would put up with anything from their wives rather than suffer Theodora's wrath. Many men accused her of sexism by favoring women over men.

Religion was an important part of Theodora's life; Monophysitism was her life-long passion even though Justinian remained Orthodox in his views. Theodora persuaded Justinian to stop his persecution of the Monophysites and to treat them with tolerance. Several of Theodora's friends were in positions of the highest power: Severus, Patriarch of Antioch; Athimus, Patriarch of Constantinople; and Theodosius, Patriarch of Alexandria.

In A.D. 536, Pope Agapetus visited Justinian and Theodora in Constantinople. Since Agapetus was considered weak-willed, she hoped he could be induced to reverse his religious Orthodox position. Justinian was in an awkward position. Most of the Italian peninsula that Justinian wanted to recapture was as strongly Orthodox as the Pope, so he could not offend the Pope or the people. The old Roman lands of the west would be lost if the Pope encouraged the people to resist Belisarious, Justinian's general, and his army.

Theodora made Justinian understand that papal demands could only be met with much shedding of blood. Her main role as adviser to the king was to insure the continuity of their own power. She realized correctly that disunity of the Church could split the empire apart. She encouraged Justinian to maintain a unified Christianity. Although the emperor did not depose or excommunicate the leading Monophysites, their maltreatment soon began. Theodora decided the only solution was to get one of her own friends appointed Pope, so that peace could unite the heretical Monophysites and the Orthodox. When Pope Agapetus died, Theodora sprang into action.

Under her influence, Justinian entertained the idea of finding a Pope who would bring the two hostile camps together and prevent a split in the Christian church. Theodora prevailed upon Justinian to support Vigilius, the Papal Nuncio to Constantinople, believing him to be a Monophysite sympathizer. With the full support of the Emperor and Empress, Vigilius was dispatched to Rome. But he was too late; Silverius had already been installed as the new Pope by the Gothic King Theodahad. Justinian and Theodora, who thought they held the power of the papacy, were infuriated. However, shortly after Silverius' ascension to the throne of St. Peter, his patron died, leaving the new Pope without a power base. He had not yet established himself with the western Church, nor did he have the approval of the Byzantines. Realizing his precarious situation, Silverius invited Belisarius' and Justinian's troops into the city of Rome in a conciliatory gesture. This was a wrong move.

At first Theodora tried to convince Silverius to reinstate Anthimus to the Patriarchal throne in Constantinople. Silverius refused. He was now her enemy since she could not control him. She ordered Belisarius to depose the Pope and have Vigilius installed as the new Pope in his place. Belisarius, who thought he could convince Silverius to compromise, met with him. The Pope would not change his deeply felt religious beliefs.

Plots were hatched for his immediate removal. Silverius was charged with plotting to let the Gothic forces into Rome in order to rid Rome of the Byzantines. What Theodora did to Silverius showed what a treacherous woman she could be. Silverius trusted Belisarius and was betrayed by him, but Theodora planned and ordered the treacherous treatment of the Pope.

Silverius was invited to the quarters of Belisarius, and according to an eye-witness, he was immediately taken prisoner, stripped of his papacy, and banished to a monastery. The next day, A.D. March 29, 537, while surrounded by Justinian's army, Vigilius was named pope.

When Justinian heard of Belisarius' treatment of Silverius, the Emperor ordered his general to Constantinople. Justinian deduced that Theodora was behind the plot to overthrow the Pope, so that her own candidate could ascend the throne of St. Peter. Orders for a trial were never carried out. What would have become of Vigilius if Silverius could prove that the charges against him were trumped up? At any rate, a trial never took place, and Silverius died less than a year later. Procopius hinted at Theodora's involvement in his murder and suggested that she was also aware of the terrible tortures inflicted on him.

With Vigilius her favorite on the throne, Theodora now had control of the church or so she thought. The years rolled by and Vigilius still did not subscribe to Theodora's wishes. Most historians believe his behavior was more influenced by the Catholic clergy and Orthodox people of old Rome than by Theodora. Pope Vigilius could not subscribe to her wishes. After the highly suspect election of Vigilius, wars raged for many years between the Goths and the Byzantines. The Italian peninsula was devastated. What appears to have sustained the Roman people was their Christian faith, although a number of differing theological views were held.

Meanwhile, Theodora was giving her blessing in the East to the Monophysite heresy while the Goths favored Gnosticism (doctrine of salvation by knowledge), another popular heresy of the time. Even though Vigilius had made promises to her, he could not waver from the faith of his predecessors. Theodora was far away, and he was in Rome surrounded by his Catholic clergy and devout followers in the Orthodox tradition. Finally, Theodora realized that her trust in Vigilius was misguided; he never would recognize the Monophysites as anything but heretics.

At about this time, a terrible plague hit the east and even Justinian fell victim. A third to one half of the population died. So Theodora put her religious problems aside, at least for the time being. She had to deal with more pressing problems, as she took over the rule of the empire and decided how the wars in old Rome and Syria would be conducted. She took over the governance of the entire empire.

In governing, she had to deal with serious economic problems as a result of the epidemic and the overextension of the army abroad. When Justinian recovered, he believed that he could bring unity between the Monophysites and the Orthodox because of one issue, the Nestorian heresy. The Nestorians were a heretical sect that declared that Mary was not to be referred to as the mother of God, but rather as the mother of the man Jesus. Justinian's condemnation was the Edict of the Three Chapters. For a time, the two groups worked together to stamp out this new heresy, but in the end this strategy did not work because leaders on both sides opposed it. Theodora decided now she must get rid of Vigilius. Justinian had his own reasons for removing the Pope from Rome since the city was under siege from the Goths, and Justinian did not want the Pope taken hostage. At any rate, Vigilius was taken by force, and eventually ended up in Constantinople, which was considered safer.

When Vigilius reached the capitol, he had an audience with Theodora. She prevailed upon him to appease the Monophysites, and he signed an official judgment in A.D. 548, backing away from the Orthodox position that he had held for years. He was consequently known as a vacillator. Theodora believed she had been victorious but did not live to see the end of the drama with Vigilius. She died shortly after. In A.D. 548, the clergy of the west forced Vigilius to sign a retraction of his judgment. Almost immediately, the Orthodox faction began to harass the Monophysites again.

The Roman Church eventually prevailed over all its heretical rivals. As Theodora had wished him to do in her lifetime, Justinian tried to keep the peace between the factions. This was a great tribute to Theodora and also benefited the empire.

Theodora was a benefactor not only to her friends but to the needy and downtrodden. She founded many monasteries. She provided a safe haven for Monophysite leaders in her palace and in the monastery at Sycae. She even sheltered one deposed patriarch for twelve years. These are but a few examples of her compassion.

After her death from cancer in A.D. 548, Theodora's body was buried in the Church of the Holy Apostles in Constantinople. She and Justinian had built this magnificent church many years before.

Beautiful mosaics of Theodora and Justinian exist to this day in the church of San Vitale at Ravenna in northern Italy, which were completed a year before her death. A print of one of the murals with her image appears at the beginning of this chapter.

History affords us an opportunity to look through a window into the past. How do we translate Theodora into today's woman? Although we cannot apply sixth century standards to our own time, we can see that, in many parts of the world, women are still dealing with some of the same issues. This notorious woman in Byzantine history used her position to improve living standards for other women. She will be judged in history for her accomplishments in social and political reforms.

Theodora's legacy not only includes her position in advancing women's rights, but also the pivotal role she played in keeping the peace between the two major Christian sects, Orthodox and Monophysites. She restored stability to the Roman Empire. The bear-trainer's daughter, who knelt in supplication in the Kynegion so many years before, now in the end of her life and rule had all the population of the Roman Empire kneeling before her. She who once stood naked before the vulgar crowd was laid to rest dressed in ceremonial robes and laden with jewels. She had transformed herself from the infamous to the illustrious and was the true Empress of Byzantium!

Mural of Eleanor of Acquitaine 1122-1204 at the Chapel of St. Radegunde, Chinon in a royal procession with her son, John I of England She is the only woman to have served as queen of both England and France. (Wikimedia Commons copyright expired)

CHAPTER SEVEN

Eleanor of Aquitaine, Queen of France and England

"Trees are not known by their leaves, nor even by their blossoms, but by their fruit."

The governing force in the lives of Christian women in the Middle Ages was the Catholic Church. Women were dominated by men. Often reared in convents, the girls of the elite class were generally married off at age fourteen or even younger, either for political purposes or to enhance their parents' financial or social standing. A girl's property and rights were transferred to her husband upon marriage. A girl or even a mature woman was treated like a slave.

Women and girls were generally the subjects of men: their fathers, and in case of the father's death, a friend or relative, and later, a husband. Eleanor, however, was unusual. Endowed with intelligence and creative energy and favored by changing political circumstances, she became a major force, both politically and culturally.

Eleanor of Aquitaine was born in 1122. Her grandmother was considered an adulteress: she had married the powerful Duke of Aquitaine, William IX, after leaving her husband who was much lower on the social scale. Eleanor's mother Aenor was one of the children by her mother's first husband. In order to insure the daughter's high status, a marriage was arranged between Aenor and William's son, William X. Eleanor was the first born of this union.

Eleanor's mother and younger brother William both died when Eleanor was eight, leaving her heiress-presumptive. Like his father, William X was a patron of storytellers and troubadours. Consequently, the intelligent Eleanor nurtured a lifelong love of literature and music. At the court of

Poitiers, Eleanor gave much of her wealth and prestige to rising artists, troubadours, and writers who sang and wrote of courtly love and romance; she became one of the foremost patrons of the twelfth century.

Eleanor developed a close relationship with her father who prepared her for her future role of duchess. When her father died on a pilgrimage to Santiago de Compostela in 1137, she became at age fifteen the richest woman in France—even richer than the king. On his deathbed, William asked his advisers to commend Eleanor's care to Louis the Fat, King of France.

Subsequently, Louis married his son and heir, the future King Louis VII, to the beautiful, intelligent, ambitious, and wealthy Eleanor. This union brought Aquitaine under the French crown, thereby increasing Louis' holdings and power. However, Eleanor's lands would remain independent of France until the next generation when it was assumed her son would be King of France and Duke of Aquitaine.

Eleanor was a free spirit and not popular with her mother-in-law. Her dress and language were constantly criticized by her elders, but her husband adored her and granted her every wish. Nevertheless, the couple had little in common. She was stubborn and high-spirited, and he was quiet, scholarly, and religious. Shortly after the marriage, Louis the Fat died and his son became king making Eleanor Queen of France. Eleanor was not the type to become engrossed in domestic issues, but she relished the role of Queen. Her husband, who respected her intelligence, often consulted her on matters of state. The marriage itself, however, proved boring to Eleanor.

In the twelfth century, the kingdom of France was small and mostly centered around Paris. The territories Eleanor inherited comprised vast lands between the River Loire in the north and the Pyrenees in the south, the Atlantic Ocean on the west and the Rhone Valley on the east. There were rich monasteries, small walled towns, fertile farms, and moated castles. In Aquitaine, Eleanor's subjects held her in high regard.

Aquitaine had been founded by the Romans in the first century B.C. The laws of Aquitaine were more favorable to women than in most places in Europe, simply because they were laid down before Christian Church law prevailed. Women could inherit property in their own right and even rule autonomously over the land they inherited. Women of all classes dressed and acted in any fashion they chose. Even a wife's adultery was not punished by death or imprisonment, although, in the conservative north, these acts were considered scandalous.

Generally, the education of women was not considered important; they were taught domestic skills at home or in a convent. Women were valued mainly as workers, as occasional sex partners, and as possessions. Rarely did they learn to read and write. Eleanor was the exception who learned to read in her native language as well as in Latin. Like her grandfather, she enjoyed romantic literature, music and poetry, and became a great patron of the troubadours. Furthermore, she was an avid sportswoman: she learned to ride at an early age, and she also enjoyed the sport of hawking. No doubt she was also taught household management and needlepoint. She was charming, energetic, intelligent, and beautiful with a mind of her own.

The concept of courtly love and romantic literature and poetry flourished in the twelfth century. This was the age of troubadours, who sang of the military exploits of Charlemagne, Roland, and King Arthur. When the Christian Church prevailed with its practice of subordinating women, one of the few places for the scholarly woman to flee was the convent. Here she could maintain control of her intellect as well as her body, without the domination of males, except for priests and monarchs. Some women developed into great writers, scholars, and creative thinkers.

Pope Eugenius requested Louis to lead a Crusade to the Middle East to rescue the Frankish kingdoms from disaster. The Muslims were waging wars of expansion and had captured the city of Edessa, which had been under Christian control for fifty years. The German Emperor joined with Louis, and their dual endeavor is known as the Second Crusade.

Not wanting to sit quietly at home while Louis was off on an adventure, Eleanor joined him and his army with a company of three hundred women. Nicetas Choniates compared her to Penthesilkea, the mystical queen of the Amazons, and according to some stories, she and her ladies dressed as Amazons at the initiation of the campaign. She also offered the services of one thousand of her knights and vassals to the Second Crusade, and she and many of the women contributed their services as nurses. When the Crusaders reached Antioch, they were met by Eleanor's uncle, Raymond of Poitiers. There was much gossip circulated concerning an affair between the crusader and his niece.

When Raymond pleaded for help from King Louis, he was refused, but Eleanor took the side of her uncle. Unable to change Louis' mind, Eleanor demanded an annulment. The crusade was doomed to failure from the start, largely because Louis was a weak and ineffectual leader.

While traveling around the Mediterranean, Eleanor was exposed to emerging maritime codes. Later she would establish new admiralty laws in her own lands and in England. She also developed trade agreements with Constantinople and ports of trade with nations of the Holy Lands.

Even before the Crusade, Eleanor and Louis VII were becoming estranged. It appears she and King Henry of England schemed to have her marriage to Louis dissolved. In contrast to Louis, her intellectual and reserved husband, Henry was a man of great ambition and energy. In 1152 with the approval of Pope Eugenius, the marriage of Eleanor and Louis was annulled on the basis of consanguinity; their two daughters, however, were declared legitimate. Furthermore, Eleanor's lands were returned to her. She hoped that one of her sons would inherit them and become king.

Several attempts were made by various nobles to kidnap Eleanor in order to marry her and claim her lands. Instead, Eleanor sent envoys to Henry, Count of Anjou and Duke of Normandy, to come and marry her. Actually, she was more closely related to Henry than to Louis, but nevertheless they married although she was eleven years older. Thus, she became Queen of England. This marriage changed the course of European history for the next four hundred years, since it was a causal factor in disputes between France and England over her lands. She transferred her rich territories of Aquitaine and Poitiers from France to her husband, Henry, the Plantagenet king.

There were rumors of Eleanor's sexual involvement with Henry's father Geoffrey of Anjou, who had advised his son against any involvement with her. During the next thirteen years of their marriage, Eleanor bore Henry five sons and three daughters. Henry had a reputation for philandering and sired many illegitimate children. His notorious affair with Rosamund Clifford signaled the end.

In 1167, Eleanor left court at Christmas time for her own city of Poitiers. The separation, no doubt, was sparked by Henry's flagrant affair. Eleanor now wanted more power than Henry was willing to grant her, so she started plotting against him.

Although Henry ruled over an increasingly large kingdom of his own, he tried to control Eleanor's patrimony of Aquitaine and her court at Poitiers. Back in England, Eleanor continued to scheme.

Archbishop Thomas Becket, the Papal legate to England and Henry's Chancellor, was murdered in his church by Henry's soldiers, arousing horror and contempt in Eleanor and the whole of Europe. The argument prevailed for seven years over the diverting of church funds to the crown.

Becket was a church lawyer who took the moral ground that church revenues should go to the poor and not the king. Becket had found a deeper meaning in life, and he honored God above the king. Trumped-up charges of embezzlement were levied against him, and he demanded a trial in an ecclesiastical court rather than a civil one. In the end, his former friend Henry, fearing for his power, had Becket murdered.

Henry II's eldest son, also named Henry, was encouraged by his father's enemies to launch a revolt in 1173-1174. His brothers Richard and Geoffrey, along with their mother, joined the plot against Henry II. Richard was her favorite son, and she strongly wanted to wrest control from her husband, so as to bestow it upon her son. She sent the two sons to Paris to join the younger Henry. In addition, she encouraged the lords of the south to participate in the plot. Disguised as a man, Eleanor was arrested on her way to Paris to join her sons. For a year her whereabouts were unknown. Later, Henry took Eleanor aboard a ship to England, and she was confined sometimes in Winchester Castle, Sarum Castle, and Nottingham Castle. Eleanor was imprisoned from 1173 to 1189. Near Shrewsbury, England, and close to Haughmond Abbey is "Queen Eleanor's Bower," thought to be one of her prisons.

While Eleanor was away, Henry started a liaison with the younger, beautiful Rosamond. After a seven-year relationship, Rosamond mysteriously died. At the time, it was rumored that Eleanor had her poisoned. Henry may have tried to provoke Eleanor into seeking an annulment while he was engaging in his affair with Rosamond. He wanted to make Eleanor the Abbess of Fontevrault, which would require her to take a vow of poverty. Thus, she would give up her titles and half of her lands to him. Eleanor refused.

In 1183, Henry the Young, along with his brothers Geoffrey and Richard, tried to ambush Henry at Limoges. Henry II's troops sacked the town, forcing Henry the Young to retreat. Shortly thereafter, the young Henry caught dysentery and died. On his deathbed, he begged for forgiveness and mercy for his mother and companions.

Philip II of France claimed that certain lands in Normandy belonged to his Queen. Henry II maintained they belonged to Eleanor and would revert to her upon his death.

Eleanor returned to Normandy and remained there for six months. In 1184, she went back to England. There she enjoyed much freedom, although supervised, and traveled with her husband throughout the realm. She even helped him in governing their lands.

When King Henry II died in 1189 on the eve of the Third Crusade, Richard was the undisputed heir. One of his first acts as king was to send an emissary to England for the release of Eleanor, who had been imprisoned for fifteen years. Eleanor rode to Westminster and received oaths of allegiance from prelates and lords on behalf of the young king. Ruling England as regent while Richard the Lionheart went off to the Third Crusade, she protected her son's domains. She signed herself as "Eleanor, by the grace of God, Queen of England." She founded many churches and schools. When Richard was captured, Eleanor personally negotiated his release by going to Germany.

Moreover, while Richard was away, Eleanor defended him against his brother, John, who was trying to seize the throne. She dealt with the Capetians and other continental threats. When Richard returned to England, Eleanor arranged reconciliation between the two brothers. After Richard's death while engaged in defending his lands in France, Eleanor became even more involved due to the incompetence of her son, John, who inherited the throne. Like Richard, John respected and heeded the advice of his mother. He is best remembered for the Magna Carta, which he was forced to sign by nobles in 1215. This document is the basis of British law today. Furthermore, John lost territories to the French and was forced to make peace, leading to his nickname John "Lackland."

An independent woman of power and wealth, Eleanor has come down in history as one of the most commanding women of all time. She traveled much of her life and died in her eighties at a monastery dear to her heart in 1204. She had been Queen of France and England. In addition, she had two sons who became kings of England (Richard and John); a grandson who became Holy Roman Emperor (Otto Brunswick, duke of Poitou); and a granddaughter who became queen of France (Blanche who married the son of the king of France). Eleanor was tirelessly involved with the family's dynastic struggles and in feudal politics in general. Her life and the lives of her sons and grandchildren influenced the destiny of Europe and the Holy Land.

In an age when women had little control over of their lives, Eleanor rose far above the norms of the time. She ruled France for fifteen years and England for fifty more. She began the Plantagenet reign that lasted three hundred years; she can certainly be called the "grandmother" of Europe.

This queen of two nations is entombed in Fontevraud next to her husband, Henry, and near her son, Richard. The play and movie *Lion in Winter* is based on the life of Eleanor. In 1968, Katharine Hepburn won an Academy Award for her portrayal of the queen.

Detail of the painting "Our Lady of the Fly" attributed to Gerard David 1520 and or someone of the circle of Jan Mabuse
Exuding charm and power along with religious devotion, Isabella was regarded as an almost mystical figure. (Public domain)

CHAPTER EIGHT

Isabella I of Spain, "Mother of the Americas"

"The distance is great from the firm belief to the realization from concrete experience."

Isabella I was born in 1451 in the town of Madrigal de las Altas Torres. Her father was John II, King of Castile; her mother was his second wife Isabella of Portugal. In 1454, when she was three, her father died and the throne passed to her brother, Henry IV. The young girl was taken to Areval by her mother where her education was conducted in relative isolation. Much emphasis was placed on her Catholic religious education, and she remained a devout Catholic for the rest of her life. When her mother showed increasing signs of insanity, young Isabella and a younger brother, Alfonso, were taken to live with her half-brother King Henry in his palace in Segovia. The king and his wife carefully supervised the education and activities of the children who were heirs to the throne. Isabella had to learn much more when she ascended the throne about diplomacy and statecraft. This blonde, blue-eyed princess grew up to be one of the most important women in world history.

King Henry IV was not popular with the nobility. He was deemed not very smart and an ineffectual leader. The nobles preferred Henry's half-brother Alfonso. The opposition's attempt to have Alfonso proclaimed king ended in defeat when Alfonso was poisoned in 1468. Some nobles approached Isabella age seventeen and pleaded with her, as Alfonso's chosen heir, to take the crown. She refused: she wanted to settle the insurrection peacefully. King Henry IV later agreed to name Isabella as his own heir to the throne.

Although Henry had a daughter, Joan, by his first wife, he willingly declared Isabella as his successor in order to maintain peace and keep his throne. Later he retracted and named Joan as his successor. Although he had agreed not to force Isabella to marry against her will, he, like his father before him, tried to arrange a number of suitable alliances. Instead, Isabella chose Ferdinand, the heir to the throne of Aragon. They arranged to meet and were secretly married. King Henry ruled for only five more years after Isabella married Ferdinand.

On Henry's deathbed, he vacillated once more by refusing to name an heir. Nevertheless, rumors circulated that he had named Joan his heir. Henry had already agreed to a marriage for Joan with King Alfonso V of Portugal. By marrying Joan, King Alfonso could also claim the crown of Castile. But when King Henry died, Isabella's counselor, Archbishop Carrillo, arranged for her immediate coronation as Queen of Castile and Leon.

Ferdinand heard the news in Zaragoza and was quite unhappy, realizing that he was merely king-consort with his wife who was really in charge. Isabella showed her tact and wisdom and declared herself and Ferdinand co-rulers of the two kingdoms. Her motto was: *Tanto monta, monta tanto.* (As much as the one is worth, so much is the other.) She and Ferdinand signed a prenuptial agreement to lay out the terms of the union of their kingdoms. From the beginning, the two were often heralded as "kings." Even though Ferdinand was still only a prince, Isabella insisted that when they appeared publicly together, they should be heralded jointly as kings.

Castile and Portugal fought a five year war over who was the legitimate heir to the throne of Castile and Leon. A peace treaty between the Kingdoms was signed in 1479 when Joan gave up her claim to the throne and was remanded to a convent. Until the day she died, she signed her letters, "I, the Queen." Thus, Isabella became undisputed Queen of Castile and Leon after ten years of fighting. About the same time Ferdinand became King of Aragon upon the death of his father.

Ferdinand's kingdom included not only Aragon in the north but Valencia and Catalonia in the southwest. In combination with the vast lands ruled by Isabella, a new great kingdom of Spain would emerge. At first, however, Castile and Leon were the dominant members of the new emerging nation, and at the end of the fifteenth century the population of Leon and Castile was six million compared to one million in Aragon, Valencia, and Catalonia.

To fuse these disparate lands together, a strong bureaucracy would be needed to assure a common system of governance. Order needed to be restored and the power and authority of the monarchy strengthened. In addition, corruption among the nobility and government officials had to be stamped out.

By her own moral integrity, religious convictions, and sincere piety, Isabella exercised a beneficial influence over the court. She discouraged inordinate luxury and frivolous diversions. Ferdinand, like Charlemagne his predecessor, would not wear any clothes that were not sewn or spun by his wife or daughters.

The two monarchs recognized the threats of ambitious, powerful nobility, and the violent disputes of dukes and princes among themselves and with the developing towns. Ferdinand and Isabella issued new laws affirming the rights and obligations of the people and condemned certain excesses of the nobility. To protect the townspeople, a permanent military or police force called La Santa Hermandad (The Holy Brotherhood) was established. The new organization was financed by the local communities in exchange for protection and law enforcement.

The justice system was reorganized. The Holy Brotherhood had its troops enforce the laws and keep the peace; they could make arrests and try law breakers in their own courts. To facilitate trade and business, coinage was standardized. Nobles who had formerly victimized and oppressed the towns were attacked, their lands confiscated and their castles destroyed.

In 1480, the monarchs oversaw five royal councils that worked with civilian representatives to institute a series of laws that would help unify Spain, combining their respective provinces under one central government. Isabella and Ferdinand also believed that a common religion was a necessary factor to unify the nation. This would lead to the Spanish Inquisition.

Another means of weakening the nobility was the employment of men of lower status in higher positions of responsibility. The Royal Council of Castile, which formerly had been composed of high-ranking nobles, was now comprised of a prelate, three lesser nobles, and eight jurists. The great nobles were allowed to be present at meetings, but they had no vote. Furthermore, military, administrative and diplomatic positions were often denied them. While the position of nobles was politically and militarily weakened, their social and economic status was relatively unchanged. On the other hand, while enjoying more security and prosperity, the towns and their residents still lacked political power. Actual political power was now formally in the hands of the joint monarchy and in the wide-spread bureaucracy it established.

The Cortes was the legislative body of the kingdom, and it consisted of thirty-six townsmen, two representatives from each of eighteen towns. After 1480, the nobles and clergy were seldom convened by the king and queen in large groups. Hence, the nobility and the Catholic hierarchy had little influence in the affairs of state. At the same time, the cities and towns lacked the power to resist the demands of Isabella and Ferdinand for money and services. From 1483 to 1497 the Cortes did not meet at all since the government was wealthy.

Large sections of the Iberian Peninsula remained under the control of Muslim chiefs. The work of the Reconquista had been going on for centuries, and Ferdinand and Isabella determined to complete the task. Devout Catholics that they were, Ferdinand and Isabella ordered that all Muslims and Jews be driven from Spain unless they agreed to be baptized and live as Christians. For this supposed act of "charity," they were given the title of "The Catholic Monarchs" by Pope Alexander VI. In 1492, the last vestiges of Muslim domination were destroyed when the Moorish kingdom of Granada fell to the forces of the king and queen.

The Catholic Monarchs had other political and economic reasons for expelling Muslims and Jews whose lands and possessions could be confiscated for the crown. Any debts owed to Muslims or Jews were automatically cancelled. A homogeneous, Christian population would be easier to dominate and control. The Inquisition was established by Ferdinand and Isabella in their kingdom as early as 1478, and some form of Inquisition had been practiced in Aragon from the late thirteenth century. In 1483, the Dominican Friar, Torquemada, was appointed Inquisitor-General by the Pope. His official mission was to root out heresy and purify the Catholic religion of errors in matters of faith. Torquemada had no authority to try Jews or Muslims. Only those who had converted to Christianity or Christians who had converted to Islam or Judaism were technically within his jurisdiction. Former Muslims and Jews who were suspected of practicing their old religion in secret were his primary targets. Estimates of the number of persons killed under the Spanish Inquisition—including those who were burned at the stake or otherwise executed and those who died in prison—range from 32,000 to 125,000 or more. It is estimated that about 170,000 Jews were expelled or fled from Spain because of the orders of Isabella and Ferdinand.

Otherwise, Isabella was considered a kind, gentle person. She would not even watch bull fights since she had an aversion to the sight of blood and suffering. Only on advice of the queen's personal confessors and her advisers did she allow the Inquisition to proceed. Her conscience was clear: she believed that Christian Spain was engaged in a just and holy war. Nevertheless, her approval of the Inquisition and its excesses has left an indelible stain on her memory and reputation.

The king and queen of Spain were involved in a war with the Muslims in Granada. Over the centuries, various rulers in the Iberian Peninsula had fought to rid their lands of the Moors (Berbers, Arabs, and other North Africans). Nevertheless, from the end of the thirteenth century to the latter part of the fifteenth century, peace had prevailed among the Christians and the Moors. In reality, the Moors had contributed much to the Iberian culture with their knowledge of medicine, astrology, and agriculture. Their ideas of art, architecture, and literature enriched the Iberian way of life.

Isabella and Ferdinand vowed they would drive the Muslims and all unbelievers out of their kingdoms. In 1481, they re-commenced the Reconquista. Queen Isabella reportedly helped to plan all the campaigns while Ferdinand led their troops into combat. Before each charge, Isabella reviewed her troops in military armor and on horseback. Eventually, the Christian soldiers took the hills and valleys and every town and city. Spain was now united.

When the rulers entered the city of Granada, they went to the Alhambra, which had been reconsecrated. After Mass was celebrated amid great pomp, the "kings" retired to the Mexuar or receiving chamber. The flag of St. James, Christian patron of the Crusade, now flew over the city, and victory was in their hands.

In early 1492, the Treaty of Granada was signed: Spain now controlled Granada. At first, Muslims were allowed to practice their religion and were exempted from taxation. The Moors were also left with possession of their land, property, customs, and laws. These policies did not last, however, and in 1499, the Archbishop of Toledo ordered the conversion of all Muslims to Christianity. An insurrection soon followed. In 1502, Isabella ordered all Moors to convert or be deported. Since measures were taken to thwart their departure, they were forced to become Christians at least in name. The converts were known as Moriscos.

Isabella realized that many reforms were needed, and she appointed Franciscan Ximenez de Cisneros to reorganize the Spanish Church. The reform included changes in church administration in Spain: dioceses replaced military districts and a strict code of discipline was enforced for priests, monks, and bishops. Conformity to Church law was required of the entire population; rules and practices of the Church in Spain had to conform to laws set down by Rome. The Inquisition was part of the reform.

As the Reconquista came to an end, the two monarchs turned their attention to other matters. They wanted to revitalize Spanish trade. Their neighbor and rival, Portugal, had opened new routes to the east and was benefiting from trading rights with China and India.

About that time an adventurous Genoan sailor known as Christopher Columbus tried to gain financial support for an experimental venture from the city-states of Genoa and Venice. He was convinced that the earth was round, and he believed that by sailing west one would eventually arrive in the Far East. He had also begged for support from the king of Portugal and the two monarchs of Spain. During the wars of the Reconquista, Ferdinand and Isabella were too busy to listen to strange theories of geography. For six years Columbus was denied an audience with the two monarchs. But when they were finally in firm control of all of Spain, they granted Columbus an audience.

Spain was at peace, and the Muslim and Jewish problems seemed to be solved. Ferdinand was skeptical whereas the more imaginative Isabella saw great possibilities. Spain would be so rich she could launch another crusade and defeat the infidels who held the Holy Sepulcher. Columbus was about to bring his ideas to the French and English, when Isabella decided to finance the voyage and give Columbus a share in the profits. He was to receive 10 percent of all the riches that came from his discoveries. Her generous nature expressed itself when she offered to sell her jewels to help finance his exploration, if there was not enough money in the government treasury. "I will assume the undertaking for my own crown of Castile and am ready to pawn my jewels to defray the expenses of it if the funds in the treasury are inadequate."

Columbus maintained that his expedition was God's will because the heathens of the Indies could be converted to Christianity. In August of 1492, Columbus set sail with the *Santa Maria*, the *Nina,* and the *Pinta*. There were eighty-seven men aboard the three ships. They first arrived at San Salvador in the Bahamas. Thinking he had arrived in the East Indies, he called the natives "Indians." Five months later, he returned to Castile, not Aragon. A poet wrote at the time: "To Castile and to Leon, Columbus gave up a New World."

On his return to Spain, he carried not only great treasure but some natives as well. The queen insisted that the Indians be returned and freed in their native land.

She was sympathetic to them and organized the Secretariat of Indian Affairs, which ultimately became the Supreme Council of the Indies. Legislation was passed that protected Indians from abuse and exploitation by the colonists and adventurers. Unfortunately, as we know from later Spanish history, Isabella's wishes were not always carried out.

The royal couple rewarded Columbus with great celebrations, many riches, and the title of "Admiral of the Ocean Seas." His next venture, with seventeen ships and fifteen hundred colonists, brought him to the island of Hispaniola. Still he did not find the spices and riches he sought. On his third trip, he was placed in chains on the island of Hispaniola because of his supposed mismanagement of the settlement. He was brought back to Madrid in disgrace. Isabella ordered him released, but his reputation was badly tarnished. Next, he embarked on his fourth and last voyage. This time he was certain he would reach the Orient. Instead, he reached Honduras, where he and his crew suffered appalling hardships. Finally, he returned to Spain where he died in 1506, a broken hearted, sick, and poverty stricken man.

This era was the inauguration of the "Golden Age" of Spain. Isabella was the major force driving Spain's leadership in the world as a super power. She is often called the "Mother of the Americas," for she truly was a visionary who changed world history forever. Ships laden with raw materials from the new world enabled manufacturing to flourish. Spain exported leather goods, silver, silks, cloth, glass, steel weapons, and many other finished products. Agriculture prospered, and commerce and navigation soared to unprecedented new levels as a result of the great discoveries of the era. Isabella was the initiator of this great trade development that made Spain western Europe's strongest political power.

The influx of wealth funding the treasury for the next two centuries made Spain the dominant world power, ushering in the dawn of the modern era. Internally, Spain was at peace because of the severe but orderly laws by which its people were ruled. Externally, Spain had a world-class army and navy which made other nations shudder.

Isabella is credited with founding a palace school for arts and letters. This tender but tough woman, who built a huge collection of art works, also believed in education for females. She took a special interest in the religious order of the Poor Clares, who ministered to the destitute. Learning

Latin as an adult, she pursued reading and education in her mature life. Great art and literature continued to flourish even a hundred years after Isabella's death.

Isabella and Ferdinand had five children—four girls and one boy. Isabella insisted that the girls be as well educated as her son. Unfortunately, her children did not give her much joy. They all had tragic lives, except for Maria, who became Queen of Portugal and seemed to live a relatively normal life. Isabella's daughter, Isabella (named after her), died in childbirth; John, her only son, died at age nineteen; Joan succumbed to mental illness; and Catherine married Henry VIII. As Henry VIII's first wife, she played a pivotal role in world history that resonates to this day. She was the mother of Queen Mary, the Catholic queen of England, known also as "Bloody Mary."

With Isabella's great religious devotion and piety she seems almost saintly, and there has been a strong movement as recently as the twentieth century to have her canonized. However, Jewish groups protested vehemently against such a proposal because they viewed her as a vicious murderer.

Her portraits do not show her as a beauty with her long nose and down-turned mouth. Often she dressed non-ostentatiously, but when a special celebration was called for, she knew how to bedeck herself in opulence and elegance. Furthermore, her court was known throughout Europe as being one most serious and discrete. Unfortunately, faith and morals were not held by her husband who was a notorious philanderer. Exuding charm and power along with her religious devotion, she was regarded as an almost mystical figure. When southern Spain was restored to Christianity by Ferdinand and Isabella, she was regarded as a saint because of her devotion and sacrifice to God and the Church.

Queen Isabella I died in 1504 in Medina del Campo at the age of fifty-three. This proud-humble, queen-servant now stood before God. Her daughter, Joan the Mad, was her heir to the throne. Isabella requested that her body be wrapped in a Franciscan robe, which she hoped would guarantee her entry into heaven. She requested a simple funeral and stipulated that money be given to indigent girls with no dowries of their own, and that other funds be assigned as ransom for the release of prisoners held by the Muslims. Her simple tomb rests in the Royal Chapel in Granada. Ferdinand her husband rests beside her.

Ferdinand II survived for another dozen years. While still King of Aragon, he could no longer rule as King of Leon and Castile. The husband of Mad Joan, Philip the Fair of Flanders, insisted that his father-in-law be permitted only to act as regent for the future king. Upon Ferdinand II's death, the son of Mad Joan, Charles II, became King of Spain. He was later to become the Holy Roman Emperor, Charles V. Isabella I of Spain stands out as one of the greatest women in world history.

Portrait attributed to George Gower circa 1588, oil on panel, at the National Portrait Gallery, London The portrait was painted to commemorate the defeat of the Spanish Armada, and the original painting was cropped before it was sent to the Gallery. Scenes over the Queen's left shoulder show the fire ships being sent out into the channel, and over the right shoulder the Armada is seen wrecked off the coast of Scotland. (public domain)

CHAPTER NINE

Elizabeth I of England, "Virgin Queen"

"Though the sex to which I belong is considered weak, you will nevertheless find me a rock that bends to no wind."

Elizabeth I was born in 1533, daughter of Henry VIII and his second wife, Anne Boleyn. She was the sixth and last monarch of the Tudor dynasty. When Elizabeth was three, her mother was executed on fabricated charges. The marriage was annulled and Elizabeth was declared illegitimate. But by the third Succession Act of 1543, Elizabeth was named successor to the throne as long as her half-sister Mary left no heirs. However, her half-brother Edward the direct successor of Henry ignored Henry's Succession Act and named Jane Grey his cousin as the legal successor of Henry VIII. Lady Jane was proclaimed queen but was deposed and executed after only a few weeks. Mary and Elizabeth had stood together firmly against her. After the short reigns of her half-brother Edward and half-sister Mary, Elizabeth became queen in 1558 and ruled until her death in 1603 at nearly seventy years of age.

Under Queen Mary I, the daughter of Henry's first wife, Catherine of Aragon, an attempt was made to crush Protestantism and reestablish the Catholic faith. Elizabeth was forced to comply with the edicts set down by Mary, so she appeared to be returning to Catholicism; however, she had no such intentions. In 1554, many uprisings known as the Wyatt Rebellions occurred in England and Wales. Suspected of collaborating with the rebels, Elizabeth was imprisoned in the Tower of London. Many people demanded her execution, but her supporters prevailed upon her sister, the queen, to spare her life. Thus, she was moved from the Tower to Woodstock where she was kept under house arrest for one year. As children of Philip of Spain, any heirs of Mary would surely have confirmed

Catholicism as the national church. That was not to be, for Mary left no heirs. Before her death, Mary recognized Elizabeth as her heir in 1558. With much pomp and ceremony Elizabeth was crowned in Westminster Abbey on January 15, 1559.

John Knox, the Scottish Calvinist preacher, stormed against female monarchy when Mary I was queen in his 1558 work titled *The First Blast of the Trumpet Against the Monstrous Regiment of Women.* The right of women rulers, however, was endorsed by other Protestant theologians including John Calvin, who maintained that female rule was acceptable where it had been established by custom and law. Furthermore, Calvin asserted that God sometimes channeled his authority through female rulers such as Judge Deborah and the prophet Huldah in the Old Testament.

Elizabeth like her predecessors, Henry VIII and Mary I, emphasized the role of God to protect her from danger and to allow her to be queen. She compared herself to Daniel who had been saved in the lion's den. Indeed, religion and queenship were entwined. The monarch idealized as "God's representative on earth" served as a means of binding the people to the throne. However, an unmarried queen with no heir was unsettling for the future of the nation.

Elizabeth took the advice of many advisers including William Cecil and Baron Burghley. She associated with males in order to emphasize male valor. "And I am not afraid of anything," she bragged to the Spanish ambassador. "I have the heart of a man, not a woman." Yet at the same time, she played up her femininity by focusing on her maternal role as mother of her nation.

Realizing that the pope would never recognize her as the legitimate daughter of Henry VIII and rightful heir to the throne of England, Elizabeth supported the Church of England. Through legislation in the House of Commons and House of Lords, she established herself the head of the Church. She titled herself "Supreme Governor of the Church of England." Public officials were all required to take an oath of loyalty to the queen or risk disqualification from office.

In 1552, under the Act of Uniformity, all were required to attend the Church of England and to use a reformed version of the Book of Prayer. Disobedience of the law was not harshly punished early in her reign, but later many priests and supporters of Catholicism, as well as reformers, were executed. The Jesuits in particular were hunted down. The Elizabethan Religious Settlement remained in place throughout her reign and is the foundation of the Church of England today. The strict reform Protestants believed the Acts of Settlement and Uniformity were a compromise, for she refused to end all Catholic practices. In reality, the Church of England reflected her own religious preferences even more than those of Protestant theologians or her advisers. She stopped the iconoclasm (statues, crucifixes et cetera) that was running rampant, especially of funeral monuments.

Elizabeth was well educated and much credit must go to her early period when, under the tutelage of her governess, Catherine Ashley, she learned to write English, Italian, and Latin. Later under William Grindal, she progressed to Greek and French, and still later, she studied under Roger Ascham who held the philosophy that learning is fun. By 1550, she was the best educated woman of her generation.

As a young woman, Elizabeth appeared in her portraits as quite lovely, tall with curly, reddish hair, dark brown eyes, rather thin lips, pale skin, slender hands, and a nose hooked in the middle. She later was portrayed wearing elaborate wigs as her hair turned to gray. Additionally, she was bedecked with jewels and elaborate clothing.

Elizabeth's most influential adviser, William Cecil, believed at first that in the areas of diplomacy and international affairs, Elizabeth would leave policy making to her male advisers. However, Elizabeth made it clear from the beginning that she was going to be the head of state in name and action. She was not just an appendage of her father. The government was to be operated under her name and in cooperation with her Council and Parliament. She immediately appointed members of her family, close friends, and associates of her most trusted adviser Cecil to her Council. She made many decisions during the 1560s and 1570s and prevented legislation from passing that would have barred Mary Queen of Scots from the throne of England. Furthermore, by these decisions, she allowed Mary to live many years before she ultimately ended up on the scaffold in 1587 by her own doing. Mary Stuart had a great following of Catholics who considered her the legitimate heir to the throne of England. After nineteen years imprisonment in a series of castles and manor houses, she was tried and executed for treason. She had been involved in three plots to assassinate Elizabeth.

In addition to her great political skills, Elizabeth radiated a great personal charm. While she often seemed indecisive to her councilors, she was in fact maintaining an air of flexibility, unlike her father Henry VIII. Moreover, she was steadfastly loyal to her courtiers; they did not have to worry about having their heads removed when there was disagreement. More conservative than her father and siblings in politics, she used as one of her mottos: *video et taco* "I see, and say nothing." She was guarded in foreign affairs and only reluctantly engaged in various unsuccessful military campaigns in Ireland, France, and the Netherlands saying, "I do not like wars; they have uncertain outcomes."

Henry VIII appointed himself King of Ireland in 1541, confiscating lands and bribing nobles. When he ran into financial difficulties, the native Irish were able to regain control, and they fought passionately for control of their land. At Henry's death, Mary took more land and sent English settlers to colonize. Now it was Elizabeth's time to handle the Irish matter. Losing some battles against the natives in the 1560s and 1570s, she took a more aggressive policy to prevent Irish expression of unrest. "I feel that I sent wolves not shepherds to govern Ireland, for they have left me nothing but ashes and carcasses to reign over." She further colonized and built military forts to suppress any hint of insurrection. The repercussions of this were felt until the Irish Revolution of 1919 to 1921 and even beyond.

She acted as a mediator between the Spanish and the rebellious Protestants in the Netherlands; in reality, she was aiding the Protestants abroad. In the area of foreign affairs, Elizabeth generally supported those councilors who wished to avoid war with Spain in the 1570s and early 1580s. As a consequence, she did not send troops to fight the Spanish until the Anglo-Spanish War that began in 1585 and continued intermittently to 1604.

The Catholic Mary's death gave Philip II added incentive to go to war against England. He was already enraged because of English attacks on Spanish colonies and shipping lanes. Thus, he sent the Spanish Armada in 1588 to invade England. Spain met a devastating defeat, and the battle was one of England's greatest naval victories. Henceforth, England would become the great colonizer of the New World and rule the seas. Elizabeth pronounced these profound words as she addressed her troops at Tilbury as they were leaving to meet the Spanish:

> My loving people....I have always so behaved myself that, under God, I have placed my chiefest strength and safe gurard in the local hearts and good will of my subjects; and therefore I am come amongst you, as you see, at this time...being resolved, in the midst and heat of battle, lay down for my God, and my kingdom, and for my people, my honor and my blood, even in the dust. I know I have the body of a weak and feeble woman; but I have the heart and stomach of a king, and of a king of England too, and think foul scorn that Parma or Spain, or any prince of Europe, should dare invade the borders of my realm; to which, rather than any dishonor should grow by me, I myself will take up Arms, I myself will be your General.

(Carole Levin. *The Heart and Stomach of a King.* [Philadelphia: University of Pennsylvania Press, 1994]. 144).

Elizabeth used language as an effective tool in her political life. Her famous speech at Tilbury resonates to this day: "Let tyrants fear—I have the body but of a weak and feeble woman, but I have the heart and stomach of a king." By these words Elizabeth attacked the notion that a woman was less suited to lead a nation in wartime. Her confident and intellectual use of language helped make her a shrewd and skilled politician.

The era of Elizabeth led eventually to the foundation of the British Empire in the seventeenth and eighteenth centuries. English merchants were in pursuit of spices to preserve and enhance the flavor of food. In 1577, during Elizabeth's sovereignty, Sir Francis Drake became the first Englishman to circumnavigate the globe. He was gone three years and traveled 36,000 miles making commercial contacts and political alliances. He returned to England with spices, gold, silver, jewels, silks, and porcelains. He fought valiantly and effectively in battle with the Spanish Armada and often acted for Elizabeth as a "privatee" or secretly authorized pirate.

Another great English explorer, Sir Walter Raleigh, commissioned by Elizabeth founded the "Lost Colony" on Roanoke Island, Virginia, in 1585. Because all English ships were needed to fight the Spanish in 1588, no support was forthcoming to the settlers, and the colony disappeared. In 1607, the first permanent English settlement, better funded and organized, was founded in Jamestown, Virginia. An important sailor, Sir John Hawkins, was instrumental in expanding English trade and in strengthening the English Navy. He also expanded the English slave trade.

Elizabeth's public relations trips were often criticized as being outlandishly extravagant, for almost the entire court traveled with her. Toward the end of her reign, her fame and popularity dwindled because of treasury problems, blamed partly on her excessive expenditures. During these excursions, Elizabeth showed herself off not only as the daughter of Henry VIII, but as both king and queen in her own right. The British expressed an obsession with celebrity, not unlike our own time, and Elizabeth brilliantly exploited it. She used rhetoric and theater as propaganda mechanisms to address private and public issues. Her stage management was magnificent. "I have become a virgin. I am married to England," she once said. The "Virgin Queen" represented herself as totally pure in her dedication as ruler of Britannia. Often, she crafted language to describe herself as both king and queen.

Elizabeth's fame was immortalized and even to this day she is heralded as the ruler of the "Golden Age" of Britain. Through her patronage of the literary arts, Elizabeth assisted in the development of modern English. After the defeat of the Spanish Armada in 1588, England's naval supremacy opened a new world of trade. Everywhere her business operatives went they not only brought back new goods but also new words, which were assimilated into English.

Prior to this time, foreign invaders left their new words, such as the Vikings and Normans. Now the English were exporting their language everywhere they sailed and importing new words from South America, Turkey, Spain, Portugal, China, and other exotic places. Modern English bristled with new words from music, art, and architecture. Moreover, Latin and Greek words were also incorporated. Latin had been spoken by the upper classes during the Roman invasions and continued to be spoken by educated monks and clerics. During the English Renaissance, Latin became the language of diplomacy, medicine, philosophy, and technology, and many Latin terms continued to be used in those fields. Although the grammatical structure of English is Germanic, Latin was the language that laid the foundation upon which the English language flowered. As the English borrowed new vocabulary from many other languages, the common people of England now had a fresh, bold language.

It was time to use the new language. Queen Elizabeth wrote poetry and speeches, and she was a brilliant orator. In addition, she translated French and Latin. Many of the educated nobles, writing for pleasure, wove beautiful romantic poetic tapestries that turned language into literature. They expanded the language by inventing words that had never been used before. One of Elizabeth's ambassadors, Sir Philip Sidney, composed love poems that are considered some of the most romantic ever written. Indeed, English was equal to any language in the world. The age is known as the Elizabethan era: the period in which literature and drama flourished under playwrights such as William Shakespeare and Christopher Marlowe.

In London, many playhouses emerged where ordinary people could go and hear elegant language spoken. Shakespeare made full use of the English language with a vocabulary of more than 24,000 words. He bounced simple one syllable words off "high" English multi-syllable words in playful word games. For the first time in the history of England, language provided financial support to the professional writer. Old English was a rough, course language; in the Elizabethan time, English grew into a richer, more expressive language.

In 1566, the government, under Elizabeth's direction, regulated commerce and industry and established a standard coinage system, which replaced the old silver coins that had been debased during the three preceding reigns. Consequently, the economy stabilized, and confidence in the monetary system was restored. In 1566, the Royal Exchange of London was opened, and the merchants that formed the English East India Company received their charter in 1600.

Elizabeth never married and left no heirs; this actually strengthened her political position, for if she had named an heir, she would have been more vulnerable to a coup. By not marrying, Elizabeth avoided the conflict and contradiction that the Queen was ruler, yet that as a wife she was to be ruled by her husband. It appears that the great love of her life was Robert Dudley whom she probably would have married had he not already had a wife. To make matters more complicated, his wife was mysteriously murdered, and both Elizabeth and Dudley were rumored to have conspired to have her killed. Cecil and other advisers warned her to distance herself from Dudley to preserve her reputation and maybe even the throne.

Later, she indicated an interest in marriage with the French Duke of Anjou. However, he was Catholic and most Protestants despised his religion and his French blood. In the end, their religion separated them, and Elizabeth would not allow any compromise on the matter of religion. Another candidate was the Catholic Archduke Charles of Austria who would have brought a great diplomatic advantage to England through an alliance with the Hapsburg dynasty. Charles accepted most of the articles for marriage drawn up by the queen, except the one denying him the right to hear Mass in a private chapel. When these negotiations ended, the question of her marrying seemed to end. She goes down in history as "The Virgin Queen."

The reign of Queen Elizabeth I included a period in history when some of the most important changes in political, economic, cultural, and social life marked the framework for modern England. Refusing the roles of wife and mother, Elizabeth was the first monarch to rule as a constitutional monarch; she shared powers with her advisers and Parliament. She exercised power successfully as a female ruler in the patriarchal sixteenth century, functioning within the same institutional framework and utilizing the same male prerogatives as former monarchs. An astute politician, she exhibited an agility that served her well.

Other great accomplishments occurred during this time: capitalism spread with trade and industry and the beginnings of colonization took place in the New World. The establishment of the Protestant Church of England had both national and international repercussions. The arts flourished as never before with great playwrights, poets, and writers. With the great wave of prosperity and confidence that swept over the nation in every field of endeavor, the Elizabethan era marked one of the richest periods in English history.

Elizabeth I died on March 24, 1603, after a forty-four reign. She was originally buried in a vault with her father King Henry VIII in Westminster Abbey. Later, her successor, James I, had her entombed in the Abbey beneath a magnificent marble effigy along side her half-sister Mary, daughter of Henry and Catherine of Aragon. The effigy stands in the north aisle of the Lady Chapel. Elizabeth believed "The end crowneth the work."

Portrait of Empress Catherine the Great circa 1745, painted by George Christoph Grooth, St. Petersburg, Russia The portrait is in the collection of the Hermitage Museum, St. Petersburg, Russia. (public domain copyright expired)

CHAPTER TEN

Catherine the Great, Prussian Princess to Russian Empress

"Power without a nation's confidence is nothing."

Princess Sophia August Frederika (later known as Catherine the Great) was born on May 2, 1727, in Stettin, a small sovereign state of Germany. She was the daughter of Christian Augustus, prince of Anhalt-Zerbst, and his wife, Johanna Elizabeth of Holstein-Gottorp. Her father was a studious man, whereas her mother preferred an exciting social life at court. Sophia inherited both personality traits.

Sophia was followed by two brothers. At the time of her birth, her father was the military commandant of Stettin. Her parents followed the customs of the time, having her educated by French governesses and tutors. She learned French almost as early as she learned German. Drawing and proper handwriting were emphasized. She did not receive much love and attention as a child from her mother, and her father was frequently away. However, her Huguenot nanny Babet made a lasting impression for the good on her character. Sophia portrayed this mother figure in her later life as one of her great formulating influences.

A devout Lutheran, her father believed in strict religious training for his daughter. He chose an army chaplain to give her strict disciplinarian teachings from the Bible, and this teacher also gave her history and geography lessons. Sophia considered the chaplain an idiot since he could not answer many of her questions. Furthermore, he threatened to beat her when she refused to accept his doctrines. Often, her governess would intervene and spare her the rod. Later in life, she rejected most of her strict religious upbringing, probably due to the fact that it was too strict.

Sophia is quoted as saying: "All my life I had this inclination to yield only to gentleness and reason and to resist all pressure."

In 1739, Johanna and Sophia were invited to visit Eutin, the home village of Johanna's elder brother, Adolph Frederick. It was here that ten year old Sophia first met her future husband Karl Peter Ulrich, Duke of Holstein-Gottorp, when he was eleven. His mother Anna Romanova, the daughter of Peter the Great, died at age twenty when Peter was two months old. Karl Frederick, Duke of Holstein, Peter's father, died when Peter was a young child. Subsequently, Peter was placed in the care of Adolph Frederick. Peter's father was cousin to Adolph Frederick and also Sophia's uncle. Sophia and Peter were second cousins. Relatives of the children were already making plans for a marriage union.

The reigning monarch of Prussia, King Frederick William, greatly influenced Sophia's view of monarchy. The king had come to visit Sophia's family when she was a young child. She clearly noted that he was unpopular, and that most of his subjects rejoiced upon his death. He did, however, make Prussia a prosperous and strong state. Sophia also observed that his successor was greatly loved and admired. A monarch not only needed to get things done but also needed to win the affection of his people.

Frederick, son of Frederick William, claimed responsibility for arranging the marriage between Sophia and Peter, thus aligning Prussia with the northern powers. In fact, a year before, Sophia's mother had already become involved with the marriage agreement. Frederick had sent a portrait of Sophia to the Empress Elizabeth. The portrait by the great artist, Anton Pesne, brought out her most enduring qualities.

By 1840, Russia consisted of no less than eighty diverse peoples from four different races. Its land mass covered millions of square miles. Governing this vast region required a strong central government, and this central control was placed in the hands of the Tsar (Russian word for Caesar), an autocrat with absolute power. Russia was not like any western European country; it had not been influenced by Roman culture, the Roman Catholic Church, or the Renaissance. Indeed, most of the people were illiterate and backward. After a long arduous journey, Sophia and her mother finally reached Moscow. Sophia, with the dreams of an innocent young girl, had entered a new land and culture where she would live and die. But what a glorious, impressive life it would be!

The Empress Elizabeth, Peter the Great's daughter, viewed this intelligent young girl as an appropriate bride for Peter, her nephew and acknowledged heir. Doing all she could do to ingratiate herself to Empress

Elizabeth, Sophia received her approval and the marriage was arranged. She also received the approval of the Grand Duke Peter and the Russian people.

The princess immersed herself in Russian culture, studying the language, religion, traditions, and customs. Her zealous approach to all things Russian earned her the love and respect of the people. From the age of fifteen, she decided to do whatever was required of her to wear the crown of Russia. Trying to convince her to stay in the Lutheran faith, her father, an avowed Lutheran, sent many books to insure her Protestantism. At the same time, Todorsky and other Russian religious advisers convinced Sophia that differences were only in form. Suffice it to say, Lutheranism had to be dropped because it was too Germanic. The crown was worth a conversion. However in reality, there were many dogmatic differences: such as views on transubstantiation, veneration of the Virgin Mary, and the tenet that the Holy Ghost comes from the Father only. For Sophia this was a turning point; she was leaving behind her childhood upbringing and embracing her new religion.

In 1744, she was received into the Orthodox Church in Moscow and in the sacrament of Confirmation was renamed Catherine Alexeyevna, Empress Elizabeth's mother's name. Shortly thereafter, she was formally engaged and was married to the Archduke Peter on August 1745 in St. Petersburg. Catherine sought to become as Russian as possible, believing that in this way she could better rule Russia. She mastered the Russian language and embraced the soul of the Russian people. Perhaps because of her switching from one form of Christianity to another, her dedication to religion proved to be somewhat weak. In the views of many of her contemporaries, Catherine lacked strong religious beliefs.

In many ways, the Empress Elizabeth was a model for Catherine. The Russians did not hold the view that women were inferior and could not be rulers in contrast to what many of the western church fathers thought and taught. Therefore, Elizabeth felt comfortable with her womanhood and her power. However, during Elizabeth's reign Russia remained stagnant because she had done little to improve the country.

Catherine recognized that political change was necessary for Russia to be revitalized. She was greatly influenced by Montesquieu and wanted new schools and universities and more humane laws to protect the populace against unchecked political power. Intellectually curious by nature, Catherine read as many works of Voltaire as she could get her hands on; later she was quoted as saying, "His works formed my mind and spirit." Voltaire believed a just monarchy was the best form of government, and he attacked prejudice and advocated freedom of religion. He believed that individual conscience needed to be respected and everyone in a society must be useful. Catherine admired England and the British constitutional monarchy that she had been introduced to through the writings of Montesquieu.

Catherine's husband was a disappointment. Totally disregarding all decency and the feelings of others, the German prince, Peter, exemplified some of the worst traits of human nature and thoroughly detested the Russians. He had a hideous physical appearance as a result of his bout with small pox. Moreover, he was something of a lunatic enveloped in "corporal's mania," a childish obsession with toy soldiers, uniforms, parades, miniature cannons, toy fortresses, and war games. Catherine wrote that Peter would make cannon firing noises with his mouth and shout orders to his inanimate army. Sometimes, their bed was covered with dolls and toys. On one occasion, with much fanfare he hung a rat that had devoured two of his toy soldiers. These examples demonstrate his low level of maturity and intelligence.

As for siring an heir, there was a major problem. Apparently, Peter suffered from a physical disability that prevented him from having marital relations. It is believed that Catherine and Peter remained virgins for the first eight years of their marriage until his physical problem was addressed. After ten years, Catherine finally bore a son, Paul. Many historians question Paul's paternity; the most accepted theory is that Paul was indeed Peter's son since the child manifested so many of his father's degraded habits. On the other hand, some historians believe Paul was the son of a dashing Russian officer, Serge Saltykov. It appears that nobody, including the Empress Elizabeth, cared about the paternity as long as there was an heir. Peter boasted that he had affairs with many women, but most experts believe this was a lot of hyperbole.

Catherine at times was most unhappy unable to please either the Empress or her husband. For Elizabeth, Catherine was not Russian enough; for Peter, she was not European enough. Peter never identified with Russia but only as a German prince. His leanings were always German, and he wanted Catherine to ally herself with him against Elizabeth and Russia. Peter treated his wife like his sister and showed no sexual interest in her, remaining cold and indifferent.

As a young bride, Catherine was politically astute. She realized that pleasing the Empress was more important than pleasing her husband, for her marriage was from the start tinged with politics. Consequently, she developed a stoic attitude toward life. Her goal was to become Empress of Russia no matter what it took to get there. Bound to a husband she detested and under the control of the Empress Elizabeth, whom she despised, Catherine determined to console herself in the embrace of a series of young admirers. Unimpeded by religious convictions or conventional morality, she engaged in sexual escapades that were the scandal of Europe. When she became empress, her most trusted advisers were also her lovers. Before the palace uprising of 1762, Catherine bore a second son whose paternity could not be connected to Peter. She arranged for this boy to be adopted and raised with the name Alexei Grigorovich Brobrinski. He was the son of Gregory Orlov.

The Russian Church, as did society at large, treated extra marital affairs leniently in contrast to the strict Lutheran church. There is no promise to "love, honor and obey" in the marriage ceremony of the Russian Church. Catherine believed her first duty was to Russia, so it appears that as long as there was an heir, no matter by whom, the problem was solved. After the birth of Catherine's son, Paul, the Empress Elizabeth immediately took the child into her care, for she planned on raising him. Catherine had fulfilled her most important role, that of giving birth to an heir to the Russian throne.

Meanwhile, Peter turned over the affairs of Holstein, his dukedom, to Catherine so he could have the leisure to play his war games. She efficiently ran his kingdom. She had matured beyond balls and party games and started seriously to study Russian history and political theory. At age twenty-six, she was ready to take on the role with Peter of ruling an empire.

Peter relied heavily on his wife. However, when the Empress Elizabeth died in 1762, Catherine realized she would have to defend herself against her husband. He had threatened to get rid of her or to send her to a nunnery. Catherine, being politically aware, forged alliances and used powerful men to cement her position. The power and the crown belonged to Peter, and she wanted a share in that power.

She had great worries about the succession and feared Peter might be disinherited, in which case her position and that of her son's position would be in jeopardy. She met with her friend, Count Alexis Bestuzhev, and prevailed upon him to draw up papers associating her with Peter in the ruling of Russia.

Moreover, her English ambassador friend, Sir Charles Hamsbury-Williams, arranged a ten-thousand-pound loan for her from Whitehall.

The English preferred an Anglophile ruling Russia, instead of Peter or Alexander Shuvalov (military strongman) who had strong alliances with France. Catherine told Sir Charles that she would either perish or reign much like Theodora had stated in A.D. 500. Catherine, in essence, was acting as a secret agent by using English money to insure Peter would not inherit the throne and she would rule as Empress.

Meanwhile she entered into an affair with Sir Charles' secretary, a dashing young Polish officer. For all of the above offenses, including accepting money from a foreign government, bribery, and adultery with a foreigner, Catherine could have been executed. Throughout her long life, Catherine was almost always in charge of her emotions; in this instance, probably because she needed love and was lonely, she chose to follow her heart.

About this time, Peter started an affair with one of Catherine's ladies-in-waiting, Elizabeth Vorontsova. He flaunted his mistress and even kicked Catherine in public. No doubt he was putting on a show. Catherine disassociated herself from Peter and his Lutheran views. Initially, she wanted to come to power as Peter's wife so that she might influence his behavior. With their relationship as it was, this was impossible.

Indeed, Peter led Russia to the brink of disaster. He nationalized all monastery property and destroyed many religious icons; he was offensive to the Russian Church and many clergymen wished his downfall. The fact that Peter was never officially crowned further showed his disrespect to the Church, for the union of church and state in an official ceremony was important in Russian culture. Furthermore, he commandeered the Bishops' horses whenever he needed more horses for his troops.

Russia fought Prussia for six years. At the end of the Seven Years War, Peter adopted a tone towards Frederick that was quite unusual for a defeated leader; he called Frederick "one of the greatest leaders the world has ever seen" and even named a ship after him. Peter always maintained he was Duke of Holstein first and Grand-Duke of Russia second. He gave high ranking positions to two of his Prussian cousins and then appointed them to his war cabinet. The Tsar addressed his troops in German instead of Russian, and it was apparent to everyone that Peter was more German than Russian. He even compelled his soldiers to dress in the blue uniform of the Prussians. This was bizarre behavior. When he decided to wage war against Denmark, an ally that had never harmed Russia, for what Peter termed an outrage that occurred many generations before, the military were ready to resist his excesses. This war would only help Prussia. They decided something had to be done about Peter.

Continuing to be abusive to his wife, Peter offended the national consciousness by leaving with his Holstein soldiers to his summer residence in Oranienbaum. When he left Catherine behind in St. Petersburg, Peter's military removed him from the throne and made Catherine Empress. Not only did the people rally behind her, so did the Russian Church, an important component in the dethronement of Peter. Different versions have come down through history regarding this military coup. Many believe Catherine was in on the plot from the beginning, and that the four Orlov brothers were in on the conspiracy. It was well known that the eldest brother, Gregory, was her lover, and that another brother, Alexis, was also in her high favor. Thus, the Orlov brothers were presumed to have controlled the guards in the scheme to get rid of Peter.

Another view was that there was no need for Catherine to arrange the downfall of her husband. The people of Russia despised him, and she made the populace aware that she would take over the reigns of government if Peter were deposed. Not lacking hubris, Catherine saw herself as the savior of Russia and the Church.

Catherine placed herself at the center of the action, donning the red and green uniform of the Preobrazhensky regiment, who formed her personal bodyguards and declared herself colonel. She mounted a horse and led fourteen thousand men out of St. Petersburg to Oranienbaum to capture Peter. Seizing power, she felt confident she could save Russia from ruin. Artists have often depicted Catherine in this role of military commander: a slim, self-confident figure on top of a magnificent stallion in her colorful army uniform leading her troops. A woman in male military uniform was an inspirational symbol. This new Catherine was quite a contrast to the young girl who had arrived in Russia eighteen years before, penniless and without a dowry.

Peter was arrested and taken to a country house in Ropcha, where after nine days he mysteriously died. The official cause of death was "apoplexy." Realizing they would never be safe as long as Peter lived, the leaders of the revolt had proceeded with their plan to murder him. Subsequently, after seventeen years of unhappy marriage, Catherine at age thirty-three was crowned Empress in a Moscow Cathedral. Catherine was a foreigner, and consequently she took her coronation with the utmost seriousness, taking the best advice she could from history and emphasizing the quasi-priestly role of the monarch. The monarch was the head of both Church and State.

Voltaire and Denis Diderot, the author of the first encyclopedia and a man with whom she corresponded, heaped praise on her as a student of the Enlightenment and great patron of the arts. She admired Voltaire's attacks on prejudice and religious intolerance. Catherine was a disciple of Montesquieu, who espoused a division of political powers, honest laws, and a citizen army.

Catherine bestowed gifts and pensions on her friends, and her ministers enhanced her reputation by their extravagant praise. Diderot extolled her virtues because she did not demonstrate the typical female affectations of modesty and chastity. Her personality was even tempered: she treated her servants with kindness and she loved small children. Ironically, she did not tolerate any scandalous behavior on the part of her ladies of the court. Her passion for writing expressed itself in pamphlets and plays in French and German. Her letters were full of vivacity, wit, descriptions, and sometimes great insights. She was a constant reader of the classics, history, contemporary works, agricultural and geographical books, and reports from explorers and navigators.

Viewing her personal life in her early reign, many conflicts with her role as ruler are apparent. Catherine truly loved Gregory Orlov, and he and Nikita Panin were two of her closest advisers. However, she could not marry Gregory Orlov because his brother Alexis was thought to have been involved with her husband's murder. Later, she lost another lover, Gregory Potemkin, as a result of her placing her royal position ahead of her personal desires.

Many historians believe Catherine married Peter Potemkin in 1774 when she was forty-five years of age at St. Sampson's Church in St. Petersburg. The ceremony was private, and Potemkin's nephew claimed he was one of the witnesses. Shortly afterward, she completed her Fundamental Law on the Provinces further increasing central control over the provinces. In political matters she and her husband did not always agree; for instance, when war broke out between England and its American colonies, Potemkin pleaded the case for Russia's ally, England, but Catherine declined to send troops. Another example was Potemkin's request that a tax on salt be levied that would benefit one of his friends; one of her first reforms had been the removal of taxes on farm goods, so she would not budge. Moreover, she would not let her love for Potemkin interfere with her duty of ruling Russia.

No man ever trumped Catherine's decisions. Catherine recognized that Potemkin was not realizing his full potential and was unfilled by serving her in small matters in St. Petersburg. Thus, she chose to send him as a roving ambassador to different parts of the world. He went to Poland and the Black Sea where he oversaw the building of the great ports of Kherson, Sevastropol, and Odessa. Her political accomplishments with Potemkin were enormous. For example, he acted as conciliator between the different minorities. As in many marriages with a powerful woman and a talented man, Catherine and Potemkin drifted apart. Soon she took a young lover. Yet Potemkin was the great love of her life in her later years. He was her great "knight in shining armor," whether they were ever actually married or not.

There was no cover-up of Catherine's love affairs, and she was believed to have had two husbands, eleven lovers, and many affairs. She preferred the company of men to women because most women were not educated and men held the power. Her love affairs were renowned all over Europe, and she was known as a woman of voracious sexual appetites.

Catherine was beautiful at her coronation. She had glossy, chestnut colored hair, dark blue eyes and a head perched on a long neck, giving the impression of power and pride. Her jewels and magnificent dress enhanced her beauty. She was of medium height, and as she aged became more portly and gray. Almost always she wore a braid. She was witty and loyal to her friends.

Catherine literally brought the Renaissance to Russia where previously there had been few books. She introduced to the Russian people works by Homer, Plato, Horace, Virgil, and Cicero. She sponsored translations of contemporary writers such as Voltaire, Montesquieu, Rousseau, Beccaria, and modern works such as Jonathan Swift's *Gulliver's Travels* and Daniel Defoe's *Robinson Crusoe.* Her belief was that Russia would harbor the souls of many great writers not yet born. How inspired she was! Encouraging young male and female actors and even children of serfs, she founded a drama school. She exerted great influence on the education of Russians. She also delved into ancient manuscripts of Russian history with the scholars of the day, seeking to inspire pride in the Russian people for the origins of their empire. Her literary interests extended to periodicals, and she herself wrote many articles for these publications.

Catherine had the innate sensitivity and intuition of a writer. She wrote children's books for her grandchildren and numerous satirical plays reflecting Russian society. In other works, such as *Notes on Russian History,* she sought to demonstrate to people of other countries that Russians were indeed the equal of Europeans. Speaking four languages and understanding two others, she was fascinated with words. She studied etymology and corresponded with Thomas Jefferson on the roots of Slavic and American Indian words. She believed all words had a common root; this theory was disproven. Toward the end of her life, she wrote her *Memoirs.*

The letters that she wrote to her friend Frederick Melchior Grimm and Madame de Sevigne spanned a period of twenty-two years and constitute one of the finest and revealing correspondences ever written by a woman. Catherine's letters can be read in Moscow today. How fortunate that Grimm did not destroy them as she directed. Motivated by Catherine's example and legacy of literary enthusiasm, numerous books were published and many women were inspired to write. The ground was fertile for the development of some of the world's greatest authors.

Freedom of the press was one of her ideals. However after the Pugachev Revolt in 1774 led to the deaths of many landowners, Catherine changed her attitude about freedom of the press and shut down all magazines. Learning from past history, she realized that opposing political comment often ended up with a change in rulers. Thus, she prohibited freedom of expression in political matters and only allowed freedom of expression on moral and social issues.

She sent out explorers to new lands that had never been explored including the Aleutians and Alaska. At Cook Inlet, she established a fur settlement, the first permanent settlement in Alaska. Her explorers even went as far south as the area that would later become the state of California.

Catherine's winter palace in St. Petersburg, one of her many palaces, consisted of one thousand rooms and had been built for Empress Elizabeth, Peter the Great's sister, and designed by Rastrelli in the baroque style. Catherine added a series of well-lighted rooms that would serve as a picture gallery, now known as the Hermitage Museum and a theater where Catherine's plays and operas could be performed. Observing that countries in Europe were acquiring great works of art, Catherine decided Russia would not be outdone, so she started collecting great works. Her first acquisition in 1776 was Rembrandt's *Return of the Prodigal Son.* Spending money lavishly, she went on to acquire some of the world's greatest paintings, including works of Raphael, Rubens, Titian, Tintoretto, Van Dyck, Lorrin, and many others. From just a few paintings, her collection grew to 3,926 items. Although certainly not an expert in art, she had a natural sensibility and good taste that served her well. The work of art for which she is best remembered is the regal Peter the Great bronze equestrian statue that stands before the Admiralty Building in the center of St. Petersburg, created by the French sculptor Falconet.

In a book she held in high regard, Archbishop Fenelon's *Telemachus*, Catherine was inspired by his words that would stay with her forever: "Be gentle, humble, compassionate and open handed: do not let your grandeur prevent you from mixing kindly with the humble and putting yourself in their shoes." Catherine had personally experienced insults, oppression, and humiliation from Elizabeth and Peter, so she knew what it was like to be the underdog. She saw first hand the exploitation of household servants and serfs. Russian society was structured like a pyramid with the Tsar on top and the gentry, Church, state officials, peasants, and serfs descending below. Because of a shortage of laborers to work the land between 1550 and 1650, serfdom essentially tied the nomadic serfs to the lands where they worked. Wealth in Russia was counted in serfs not land. Clearly, serfdom was virtual slavery, and Catherine believed serfdom was intrinsically evil and contrary to Christian moral principles.

After studying Montesquieu's *Spirit of the Laws,* Catherine decided she wanted to abolish serfdom in Russia. Panin (one of her advisers) believed this was unworkable and would throw society into turmoil. Weighing Panin's counsel, she came to the conclusion that the abolishment of serfdom would have to take place gradually. She planned accordingly to end this human bondage. Notwithstanding the fact that serfdom was by then thoroughly entrenched in the culture, Catherine made many reforms: she opened state schools to serfs; she permitted owners to free their own serfs; she abolished a law that permitted persons who took in orphans and illegitimate children to deem them serfs; and she stopped the practice of making a serf out of a free person who married a serf. By instituting these reforms, Catherine helped the rest of the populace become educated to the value of human dignity.

Catherine wanted to take Russia out of the Middle Ages. She introduced a council of representatives in which grievances at the lowest levels could be heard and addressed. Striving to take Russia out of the stagnation that arose in the reign of her predecessor, Elizabeth, she introduced many European practices such as religious toleration, freedom of the press—within limits—and fair and just laws. Education needed to be stressed because most of the population, even at its highest socio-economic levels, was illiterate. Everyone was to be treated equally under the same laws. She helped the poor and under-privileged by building schools, hospitals, and orphanages. Catherine's era is known as the Golden Age of the Russian Empire. She had smallpox vaccination introduced and was the first in Russia to be inoculated, thus convincing skeptics that it was safe. In 1764, she secularized the Russian Church, adding much land and taxes to state coffers. She established the first school for girls, the Smolny Institute, in St. Petersburg. Moreover, she encouraged career opportunities though limited for females. There were few universities at the time of her reign, so she encouraged students to study abroad.

If the authority of the state was threatened by religion or politics, Catherine could dole out the most severe punishments: mutilation, whipping, and other tortures. This was true especially after she learned of the excesses of the French Revolution. At first the legislative reforms to free the serfs was a major issue, but later Catherine hardened in her approach when she felt that her own position was threatened. All the monarchies of Europe trembled at the stories of the French Revolution.

Catherine was an unsympathetic mother to her son, Paul, and he chafed under her rule. She was first of all the empress and a politician, and she considered Paul a threat to her sovereign position. He became weak, cruel, and unstable, and Catherine considered him good for nothing but siring children. Of particular interest to her was her grandson, Alexander, who succeeded her to the throne, skipping over the unstable Paul. Clearly, she was devoted to the Russian people, and her highest goals were the safety and greatness of her nation.

In foreign policy, Catherine believed that Poland was incapable of self-rule at the time of the first partition in 1772, which was forced on her by Austria and Prussia. Later, in the second partition of 1793, Catherine acted along with the Prussians trying unscrupulously to exploit and plunder the Poles. Like her late husband, Paul III, Catherine believed in a strong alliance with Prussia. When Frederick the Great died, Catherine found herself at odds with his successor, Frederick II. Catherine had hoped that he would lead an army against the new French Republic, thereby leaving Russia free to annex what was left of Poland, but her plans went awry.

For a time, Catherine had a grand scheme to revive the Greek Empire. When the Turks declared war in support of Poland in order to ensure what they believed was a necessary buffer state, Catherine retaliated. Her dream was to plant the double-headed Russian eagle cross in Constantinople. She organized a group of young Greek soldiers, who were to act as the saviors of the Port of Piraeus. Voltaire was thrilled by the notion of a Greek revival.

She sent a fleet under Alexis Orlov into the Mediterranean in 1770, hoping the Greeks of Morea (the Pelopennesian Peninsula) would take up the cause. They did not.

Opposed by the English and French, the Russians then abandoned the Greeks. The Kuchuk-Kainarji Treaty of 1774, however, guaranteed the rights of Christians in the Port of Piraeus and confirmed the claim of the Tsars to be the guardians of the Orthodox Church in the Ottoman Empire.

Her war alongside Joseph II of Austria against the Turks in 1788 was a war of conquest and partition. But in this conflict, she showed weakness in how she administered her army. She paid little attention to the military in peacetime and failed to strengthen it sufficiently before going to war. Another failing was her appointment of her favorites as generals. Nevertheless, she is regarded by historians as a triumphant military leader.

Catherine's successors later joined with the English to support the Greeks in their War of Independence against the Turks from 1821 to 1830. Today Greece stands as an independent nation.

At age sixty-seven, Catherine bestowed public monies and great power upon her lover, Planton Zubov. Encouraged by him, she invaded Poland and urged Prussia and Austria to invade France. By then most of her republican ideas were cast aside. About this time, she succumbed to bad health and made rash decisions: for instance, she permitted Zubov to send his brother, Field Marshall Valerian with his 20,000 man army, on a ridiculous campaign to invade India by way of Tibet and Persia.

She died on November 16, 1796, having reigned more than thirty years. Catherine dominated her empire just as she did her lovers. She wrote that she wanted to bring her people liberty, happiness, and prosperity. Paul, who detested his mother, immediately arranged for his father Peter III's remains to be moved close to the Empress Elizabeth and near Catherine in the great Cathedral of St. Peter and St. Paul. Here all the sovereigns of Russia were entombed except Peter II who was buried in Moscow. This petty act of revenge angered many of Catherine's supporters, and Paul IV's cruelties and reversals of his mother's reforms caused his unpopularity. In 1801, a collection of patriots conspired to place Paul's son, Alexander, on the throne and to have Paul murdered in 1801. Planton Zubov, Catherine's last lover, was one of the conspirators.

Catherine stands as one of the most influential figures of the second half of the eighteenth century. Although she was both gifted and flawed, she tirelessly, triumphantly and tenderly ruled an empire larger than Rome at its zenith. Like Cleopatra, Catherine dedicated her life to her country, employing whatever means necessary to protect and preserve it. It is interesting to see how a woman not born to power achieved such greatness. Catherine laid the foundations for a constitution although it did not get beyond the discussion stage. She had more success in the field of education. Alexander, her successor, was able to found seven universities that he staffed with teachers from schools his grandmother had founded. Catherine also laid the groundwork for the emancipation of serfs even though this was not accomplished during her reign.

The significance of Catherine's life lies in the precedents she set: her tolerance of all religions, the beginnings of sharing power with the lower classes, her plan for a National Assembly, and the social issues she addressed. Perhaps her crowning achievement was the growth of St. Petersburg into an elegant modern city and the magnificent collection of art in the State Hermitage Museum.

Catherine had been impressed by the freedoms of the West; unfortunately, her successors did not follow through on the plans she introduced and hoped someday would come to fruition. Surrounding herself with good advisers, she achieved great goals politically and socially. Never before or after in the history of Russia were advisers generally allowed to express conflicting opinions without the threat of torture, dismissal, or death. Upon taking the throne, her son Paul IV had legislation passed that would ensure his mother would always remain the last female ruler of Russia.

For a time, Catherine cast a great civilizing influence over the Russian people. She once said: "If you can't be a good example, you'll have to be a horrible warning." When World War I occurred, Russians had had enough of their Tsars. The Russian Revolution forced Tsar Nicholas II to abdicate. Because members of the Duma had been elected since 1905, a Provincial Government was formed under the leadership of Kerensky. The Provisional Government wanted to continue to fight against Germany. Many factions disagreed. A Second or October Revolution took place and the "Reds" or Bolsheviks took power. Lenin then negotiated a peace treaty with Germany in March 1918. The "Whites" or Mensheviks rose up against the Bolsheviks and a civil war lasted until 1923. Lenin died in 1924, and Stalin then rose to power to become the Soviet Union's bloodiest dictator and one of the bloodiest dictators in world history. Sadly, Catherine's dreams of bringing new freedoms to Russia in her lifetime or at least in the future died with her and have not yet been revived. Yet what other Russian ruler had such dreams and tried to implement them? At the end of her thirty-four reign, 1762 to 1796, Catherine had catapulted Russia onto the world stage as a major world empire. She deserves to be remembered in history as *Catherine the Great.*

Portrait of Mary Wollstonecraft by John Opie, oil on canvas, circa 1797 in the National Portrait Gallery, London Wollstonecraft was the first person to put in writing *The Rights of Woman* and is known as the "Mother" of the feminist revolution. (public domain)

CHAPTER ELEVEN

Mary Wollstonecraft, "Mother of the Feminist Revolution"

"Women ought to have representation instead of being arbitrarily governed without any direct share allowed them in the deliberation of government."

A few political women have appeared on the stage of history that have thwarted the image of being an extension of either their father, husband or son. One of them is Mary Wollstonecraft. Wollstonecraft wanted to show all women how to validate themselves as women. She is the first woman to declare *in writing* the rights of women as she viewed them, and she stands out in the evolution of woman's political development. As political theorists, men and women are viewed quite differently. Notwithstanding their politics, famous women of all sorts tend to have much more focus on their personal lives than do men. Wollstonecraft's psychological composition has been written about and dissected like a heart in a science laboratory. Her affairs and emotions titillated many and still do.

A pioneering feminist, Wollstonecraft stands alone in a separate genus as a strong, intelligent woman who argued for the rights of women. She believed that just as men are human, so also are women, and both sexes can reason. Wollstonecraft was a writer, philosopher, and feminist who believed that women could combat their inferior status through education; she did not believe in the "natural" superiority of men.

Hers was a cry for sexual as well as political freedom. In the context of her time and even today, the sexual standards applied to men did not and still do not apply to women. In this regard, Wollstonecraft defied the social mores for herself that ruled in her day. She certainly shocked many in her environment, for she lived as she pleased. Hence, she was ignored for more than one hundred years because of her scandalous lifestyle. Her memory was resurrected at the beginning of the twentieth century when the women's suffrage moment took hold.

Mary Wollstonecraft was born on April 27, 1759, in Spitalfields, a working class section of London. She was the second child of seven children. Her grandfather was a wealthy master silk weaver. Upon his death, he left land and other goods to Wollstonecraft's older brother, and she was left nothing. Unstable in financial matters, her father caused the family to move frequently during Wollstonecraft's childhood as he changed occupations. Her Irish mother favored her elder brother who oftentimes ruled the family like a tyrant. The family finances were so dire that frequently the husband would beat his subservient wife in a drunken rage. The situation was often so desperate that Wollstonecraft would position herself outside her mother's bedroom door to protect her.

She was certainly impacted by her father's traumatizing behavior. Later she also took on the role of maternal protector for her sisters, Everina and Eliza. For almost as long as she lived, Wollstonecraft gave them financial assistance. She was also responsible for other members of her family and helped secure positions for her brothers through her contacts as she rose in the literary world. One, in fact, was sent to work in America. Seeing her sister Eliza physically and psychologically abused, Wollstonecraft encouraged her to leave her husband and child. Eliza suffered a nervous breakdown, depending on Wollstonecraft for everything, according to most accounts.

Many authors are critical of Wollstonecraft because of her involvement in her sister's marital problems. This author would argue that because of her father's deficiencies, she viewed all men in the same critical light. Unfortunately at that time, most women who made the choice to leave their husbands entered into a world of poverty and became social outcasts. They could not remarry and few had marketable skills. Until the Divorce Act of 1857, divorce was almost impossible. Abused women could not legally separate from their husbands until parliamentary acts were passed in 1878 and 1895. The man automatically received custody of the child, no matter whether he was an abuser or philanderer. Women could not legally own property nor did they have legal rights to their children. It was a sorry state of affairs that Wollstonecraft observed as the fate of women. She believed the plight of women was unjust. With no education or skills for employment, women were at the mercy of the tribal customs and traditions of a society governed by men.

Influenced by the friendship of Jane Arden, in whose company she was intellectually stimulated, Wollstonecraft blossomed. Arden's father was a self-styled philosopher and scientist who often spoke on the lecture circuit. Wollstonecraft and Arden became great friends, sharing books and often attending lectures together. As some men and women use others to help shape their business or professional lives, Wollstonecraft gravitated to those who would activate her brain, and she did this for the rest of her life. She was like a cannibal nurtured on the brains of intellectuals. Her only formal education was a brief enrollment in a country school. Another friend who greatly helped her shape her life was Fanny Blood, introduced to her by the Clares, who became her substitute parental figures. In Wollstonecraft's later life she attributed her intellectual awakening to Fanny Blood.

With circumstances at home being less than ideal, Wollstonecraft took a job as a companion to an elderly woman living in Bath. The woman proved to be most difficult, so Wollstonecraft left to take care of her dying mother at home. Not wishing to return to her former employer after the death of her mother, Wollstonecraft moved in with the Blood family. During her two year stay with the Bloods, she realized Fanny was more of a traditional woman, and they had different philosophies. Yet Wollstonecraft remained loyal and dedicated to the Bloods for the remainder of her life and even named her first child "Fanny."

Both Wollstonecraft and Fanny Blood dreamed of a female utopia. They planned on renting rooms together where they would support each other emotionally and financially. However, their dream did not come to fruition because of dismal economic times. In order to support themselves in 1783, Wollstonecraft at age nineteen, her sisters, and Fanny Blood together started a school in Newington Green, a dissenting community. Here she discovered herself and identified with the political and religious radical left; the foundations of her political philosophy were born in this setting. Such personages as Erasmus Darwin (grandfather of Charles), Wedgewood, Cadbury, Priestly, and Wilkinson were part of the group. For the rest of her life, Wollstonecraft remained part of this intellectual community.

Shortly thereafter, Fanny Blood married, and her health failed after she became pregnant. Wollstonecraft left her school in 1785 to nurse her friend, but to no avail, and her friend died. The school was unsuccessful, no doubt, because of Wollstonecraft's absence, and Blood's death threw her into a deep depression. At this time, she wrote her first novel, *Mary: A Fiction* based on the life of her friend, Fanny Blood. This was a low period in Wollstonecraft's life, when she felt insecure and lacked self-confidence. She apparently had no connection or attachment to her family, and thus formed strong emotional ties with her female companions and later with men.

Wollstonecraft's next career move was to take the position of governess to the daughters of the Kingsboroughs, an Anglo-Irish aristocratic family. Few opportunities of employment were offered to women at this time. She only stayed a year, and in 1788, she had published another book *Original Stories from Real Life* based on her experiences as governess. Wollstonecraft's story mirrored the lives of many young women who were poor, uneducated, friendless, and unhappy. Her unpleasant experiences as a nanny, her failed attempt to start a school, her affair with a married man who deserted her and her illegitimate child all served to embitter and anger her. From her sufferings emerged the seeds of revolt. Although she would not have recognized the word "feminist," she became the mother of the female revolution.

All the while, she was noting how limited were opportunities for respectable poor women. She decided she would use her writing craft as a way to earn a living. At the time, it was also almost unheard of for a woman to support herself as an author, and it was considered most inappropriate. Soon she wrote another book, *Thoughts on the Education of Daughters*. In the chapter "Unfortunate Situation of Females, Fashionably Educated, and Left Without a Fortune," she decried the regrettable status of these women. She focused on education of the mind instead of the attention in education paid to the externals such as drawing, dancing, manners, and other frippery.

She saw herself the first of a new species and moved to London where Joseph Johnson, the liberal publisher, took her under his wing. There she thrived in the company of the leading intellectuals of England, including the radical pamphleteer, Thomas Paine, as well as William Blake and the liberal philosopher, William Godwin, who would later become her lover. She wrote reviews for Johnson's periodical, the *Analytical Review,* also learned German and French and translated texts. She had the leisure to read extensively and to attend dinner parties with the intellectually elite. Influenced by the writings of Rousseau, she traveled in circles where the spirit of republicanism was unbridled.

Subsequently, she met and became enamored with the married artist Henry Fuseli. After Mary suggested that she, Fuseli and his wife live together, Fuseli rejected her in horror. Wollstonecraft would have allowed his wife to possess his physical side, while Mary would enjoy his intellectual companionship. As a result, she decided to move to Paris to avoid public embarrassment, and also to participate in the events of the French Revolution, which she celebrated in her book, *Vindication of the Rights of Men.* She attacked aristocracy and the monarchy and endorsed republicanism.

This work was counter to the conservative critique of Edmund Burke: in his *Reflections on the Revolution in France,* he staunchly defended the monarchy, aristocracy, and the Church of England. She accused Burke of using sexist language when he referred to the sexes in *A Philosophical Enquiry into the Origins of the Sublime and the Beautiful.* He used "sublime" and "strength" in relation to males and "beautiful" in connection with weakness and femininity. She blasted Burke on his defense of a society established on the passivity of women. According to Wollstonecraft, Burke's political arguments were unnatural, immoral, and impious.

She dedicated *Vindication of the Rights of Woman* to Charles Maurice Talleyrand. An active politician during the French Revolution, he had written a proposal on education with which she did not agree. She opposed his views on educating females and urged him to change the new French Constitution. Sadly, the revolution did little or nothing to improve the condition of women. Believing in a more democratic middle class philosophy, she rebuked Burke for his stands on tradition, custom, and an aristocratic code of manners. Instantly she became famous for her positions, which were similar to Joseph Priestly and Thomas Paine, who also wrote works proclaiming the rights of man.

In 1792, Wollstonecraft wrote her most famous and significant work, *Vindication of the Rights of Woman,* based on some of the same tenets she put forth in *Rights of Men.* She emphasized women's ability to reason and thus should have the same rights as men. Expressing her rage against the "tyranny of men over women," Wollstonecraft outlined all the social ills she had suffered herself: lack of education, no opportunity for fulfilling work, and the sexual double standard whereby a man could be called a "luxurious monster" or "fastidious sensualist," while a woman was labeled a "whore" for the very same act of impropriety. Little culpability applied to the male sex.

Wollstonecraft argued that men exploited women by taking their bodies and letting their minds rust; she also rejected the notion that women should be "gentle domestic brutes." She demanded education for women, opportunities for fulfilling work, and acceptance by men of women as equal companions. Mary pointed out the childishness and stupidity in which many women languished. Few women today would accept the lot of the "fair sex" as it was then decreed by men and as some men argued was directly linked to the word of God.

Wollstonecraft had ignited a flame that took fire in many women and would rage even to this day. A huge outcry came from many men who did not want a change in their dominance. Many cried "scandal." Yet some men agreed with Wollstonecraft and believed they should not have privileges at the expense of women. Wollstonecraft proclaimed: "Make women rational creatures and free citizens, and they will quickly become good wives—that is if men do not neglect the duties of husbands and fathers."

Virginia Sapiro in her book, *A Vindication of Political Virtue,* argued that *Vindication of the Rights of Woman* is not simply an extension of the *Rights of Men,* as some interpreters believe. Sapiro praised Wollstonecraft for extending political analysis of the French Revolution beyond government institutions and public politics to the family and private politics. At the time of publication, there was much divergence of opinion. Horace Walpole referred to Wollstonecraft as a "hyena in petticoats," and he claimed that although he had not read her book, he was attacking her because of her hostility toward Marie Antoinette in the *Rights of Men.* Soon after Wollstonecraft's publication of *Rights of Woman* in 1792, Thomas Paine's *Rights of Men* was published in its second edition. These two republican theorists were linked in Paris. Their close political ties were also recognized in England as both came under fire. Paine was sentenced to prison for seditious libel and burned in effigy. Rumors circulated that the same fate was about to befall Wollstonecraft. The Dissenters were being attacked as radicals and were accused of stirring up insurrection. Persons supporting the French Revolution and democratic ideals were deemed dangerous to society. The right of habeas corpus was withdrawn. Laws of sedition involving practices and meetings were passed. During this time in Europe, all the monarchies were shuddering.

In 1825, the socialist philosopher, William Thomson, published his *Appeal of One–Half of the Human Race, Women, Against the Pretensions of the Other Half, Men.* Thomson supported Wollstonecraft's philosophy and even went further by connecting racial and sexual oppression. He maintained women were "breeding machines" and "domestic slaves" reduced to the "condition of negroes in the West Indies," and that only by gaining political equality could women be free. Thomson wrote:

> Home is the prison house of the wife. The husband paints it as the abode of bliss, takes care to find out of doors for his own use a species of bliss not quite so calm. The house is his house with everything in it, and all fixtures but the most abject is his breeding the wife....Women of England, awake! Women in whatever country ye breathe degraded...awake. Awake to contemplation of the happiness that awaits you when all your faculties of mind and body shall be cultivated and developed....As your bondage has chained down Man to the ignorance and vices of despotism, so will your liberation reward him with knowledge, with freedom and with happiness. (Amazon.com Marie Mulvey Roberts and Tamae Mizuta. *The Reformers: Socialist Feminism.* [London: Routledge and Thoemmes Press, 1995]. 187-192, 196-202).

Wollstonecraft arrived in Paris a month before Louis XVI was guillotined. There she joined a group of intellectual expatriates; she wished to put her philosophical ideas to the test amidst the smoldering revolutionary thoughts that were being expressed. The philosophical ideas articulated by the Enlightenment and espoused in the early days of the Revolution did not apply to women.

Almost immediately, she formed a deep attachment to Gilbert Imlay, an American adventurer. Subsequently, she became pregnant and bore a daughter, Fanny. However, Imlay had no interest in marriage and soon left her. Nevertheless, Wollstonecraft continued to write. Although she was a new mother in a foreign country during a harrowing Revolution, she wrote a history of the early Revolution.

In 1794, while she was in Le Havre, *An Historical and Moral View of the French Revolution* was published in London. For an English Jacobin, (a political club supporting the French Revolution–derived its name from the Dominican Monastery of the Jacobins where members met in Paris) she was a true daughter of the French Revolution. In her book, Wollstonecraft covered the prehistory of the Revolution before 1789 and sought to understand the political violence of the Terror and the corruption of the regime. Her political observations while in Paris evolved into political strategies and policy discussions.

She and Thomas Paine were two of a small group of elite intellectuals who continued to support the Revolution in spite of the Terror. While witnessing the Revolution firsthand during her time in France, Wollstonecraft matured as a writer and thinker of political theory. Her social circle, including English expatriates and Girondin friends, was defined by politics. Wollstonecraft believed the Revolution was a prelude to an enlightened world even though many of her friends went to the guillotine. Virginia Sapiro wrote, "Wollstonecraft could not and would not justify the Terror, but she did try to explain it. Despotism creates violence, and violence of a special kind, because it is based on fear and desperation." She actually witnessed Louis XVI being carried in a cart to his trial; she did not live to see the demise of many of her democratic ideas and ideals in the violence that followed the Revolution.

Wollstonecraft was a true disciple of John Locke (1632-1704), one of the foremost Enlightenment thinkers who greatly influenced Voltaire and Rousseau. He voiced strong opposition to slavery and the aristocracy. He maintained that property is a natural right stemming from labor, and his ideas on natural rights still affect modern liberalism. Positing the theory that at birth the mind is a blank slate (*tabula rasa*), Locke wrote that the importance of education and good experiences cannot be overemphasized.

Moreover, he wrote about the contract between government and the citizenry. If the government fails to carry out its responsibilities effectively, the populace not only has the right but the responsibility to revolt. Locke affirmed that all men are created equal in nature by God. His ideas influenced the American Revolution, the Declaration of Independence, the United States Constitution, and the French Revolution. In his Second Treatise, Locke addressed shared parental power over children, as stated in the Bible that mothers should share authority with fathers. That was quite a novel idea in the 1600s.

Wollstonecraft believed the French Revolution would lead mankind into a more virtuous existence. Reason would prevail in the end even though chaos would reign for a time after the fall of despotism, and this new order would cover most of Europe. Mankind would then emerge from barbarism into a new age. Citizens would engage in the democratic process of government, which would reach down even to the level of families.

Almost always, Wollstonecraft emphasized the need for education of the citizenry along with the rights of men and women. She deemed that women should be included in this vision of republican government. However, many in France believed the words of Cardinal Richelieu: "Intellect in a woman is unbecoming." Dominance and subordination needed to be replaced with democratic ideals that included not just social classes but gender as well. Voices of both genders should be heard in political theory, not just those of men. Wollstonecraft promoted the right of women to own private property, thus entitling them in some societies to demand more rights, such as voting.

Pregnancy and childbirth cost the lives of many women in the eighteenth and nineteenth centuries—in many places in the world it still does. Ignorance and lack of medical care were severe problems. Little did Wollstonecraft realize when she raised the issue of childbearing that she would later die giving birth to her own child.

After the Revolution, Britain declared war on France, and British citizens in France were in danger. Imlay, fearful for his "wife" and child, had her registered at the American embassy as "Mrs. Imlay" even though they were not formally married. Wollstonecraft continued to use the title "Mrs.," so as to lend legitimacy to her daughter, born in 1794 and as well as to avoid imprisonment herself. Many English were guillotined, and Thomas Paine was imprisoned. No matter what their social origin, women who expressed desire for political rights could be declared insane and even executed. Imlay had promised to be in Le Havre when Wollstonecraft's child was born but did not keep his promise. Consequently, with his long absences and failure to respond to her letters, she finally realized that the relationship was faltering. Nevertheless, she left France and followed him to London where he rejected her. When she attempted suicide, Imlay saved her life.

Still hoping for reconciliation, Wollstonecraft entered into a joint business venture with Imlay in which she tried to help him recoup some of his business losses in Scandinavia. Upon her return to England, she had realized their relationship was over, and she threw herself into the Thames in a second suicide attempt but was again rescued. No doubt she was in deep depression, although she claimed her act was rational.

Finally accepting the fact that her ties to Imlay were cut, Wollstonecraft rejoined Joseph Johnson's literary group in London. She met William Godwin, the liberal philosopher, and their relationship slowly developed into a deep and passionate love affair. Wollstonecraft became pregnant again, and the two married in March 1797. When the fact came out that Wollstonecraft and Imlay had not been married, both Wollstonecraft and Godwin were much maligned. Their marriage was short and happy, but it ended tragically a few days after Wollstonecraft gave birth to her second daughter, Mary, on September 10, 1797. Mary Wollstonecraft died at age thirty-eight. Her daughter, Mary Wollstonecraft Godwin, grew up to become one of the most recognized writers in western literature as the creator of *Frankenstein*. She also became famous for her marriage to Percy Shelley, the renowned English poet. However, Mary Shelley suffered much tragedy in her own life: three of her four children died in early life; and her husband Percy Shelley died in a sailboat accident off the coast of Italy. Sadly, Wollstonecraft's firstborn daughter Fanny Imlay committed suicide in 1816. Evidently, Wollstonecraft's death was too much for her to bear; and no doubt she was affected by her mother's periods of instability and melancholia. She grew up far from the good health and high spirits her mother often described her as possessing as a child. She barely knew her father, and her mother's fame and accomplishments no doubt hung over her. Mary, her stepsister, overshadowed her in brains and beauty. In the end, life for Fanny became just too much to bear.

Prior to Wollstonecraft's death, we have few descriptions of what she looked like. We do have a description of what Wollstonecraft looked like after her death written by a friend, Miss Mary Hays:

> Her person was about middle height, and well proportioned; her form full; her hair and eyes brown; her features pleasing; her countenance changing and impressive; her voice soft, and though without green compass, capable of modulation....When unbending in familiar and confidential conversation, her manners had a charm that subdued the heart. (Eleanor Flexner. *Mary Wollstonecraft*. [New York: Coward, McCann and Geoghegan, Inc., 1972]. 128).

While Wollstonecraft was in Paris during the French Revolution, one of her revolutionary admirers, Count Gustav von Schlabrendorf, described her thusly: "A woman of sweetness and grace with a face whose spiritual expression was more beautiful than any classic beauty....There was magic in her look, her voice, her gestures....One of the noblest, most modest and feminine human beings I ever knew!" (Eleanor Flexner: Mary Wollstonecraft. [New York: Coward, McCann and Geoghegan, Inc., 1972]. 180].

The great artist, Opie, painted two portraits of her, one of which is shown in this chapter. The painting does show her determined chin and expressive eyes. Of course, both portraits were stylized with the powered hair in the fashion of the day, which changed after the French Revolution.

Wollstonecraft argued for the education of women throughout her life. She believed that well-educated women would be good mothers and wives, thus contributing to their families, communities, and nations. As an optimistic writer, she argued that educated women should be companions to their husbands as well as wives. Women were not merely ornaments to be traded in marriage. She criticized Jean-Jacques Rousseau, who maintained in *Emile* that women should be educated for the pleasure of men, if they were to be educated at all. Wollstonecraft wrote: "Taught from their infancy that beauty is woman's scepter, the mind shapes itself to the body and roaming around its gilt cage only seeks to adorn its prison." Attacking the attitude that women were somehow just sex objects concentrating on beauty and ornamentation, she encouraged women to develop every human being's gifts of reason and intelligence.

She wished women not to have power over men but over themselves. Mary Wollstonecraft wrote in *Letters Written During a Short Residence*:

> All the world is a stage, though I and a few are there in it who do not play the part they have learned by rote, and those do not, seem marks set up to be pelted at by fortune, or rather as sign posts which point out the road to others, while forced to stand still themselves amidst the mud and dust.

Wollstonecraft surely stood out as a signpost.

Her view, furthermore, was that women who were carried away with their every sensibility were actually committing a disservice to civilization. Believing that reason and feelings could inform each other, she also realized the importance of feelings, as manifested in her own life. Wollstonecraft maintained that women were often held in bondage, like slaves, under the yoke of ignorance. Consequently, society suffered the loss of female talents, wisdom, and knowledge. If women were afforded educational opportunities as young girls, they would be able to use their new ideas and make new better lives for themselves.

Paradoxically, Wollstonecraft did not want to change the order of things in some areas. In the twelfth chapter of *Rights of Woman,* she laid out a specific plan for the education of females. She believed that all children should be sent to a country day school and should, in addition, receive education at home where they would be inspired to love home and hearth. Moreover, she promoted co-education since relationships between the sexes should be the cement of society. She believed that all poor children should go to school until they were nine, at which time the brilliant should be separated from the others and be educated alongside the rich. Her text was addressed toward the middle class, the backbone of society as she saw it. She attacked the aristocracy but did not sympathize with the poor on the matter of education.

Wollstonecraft expressed her observations of human life and her own experiences in her novels. In *Mary: A Fiction,* she described the life of a woman who is forced into a loveless marriage for economic reasons and who finds fulfillment in two relationships: one with a man and one with a woman. At the end of the book, Mary believed she was going to a Utopian state where there was no marriage nor giving in marriage. Even though Wollstonecraft viewed marriage in *Rights of Woman* in a positive light, her novels do not reflect the same viewpoint. Considering her experiences with her father, mother, brother, and sister plus her own relationships with men, and her observations of the condition of women, it is no wonder her feelings were bitter.

Wollstonecraft was provoked by ill treatment into rebellion. In *Maria*, her novel published posthumously, the heroine is committed to a mental institution where she has an affair with a fellow inmate and develops a deep emotional tie to one of her attendants, Jemima, who has the responsibility of watching over her. Both women are mothers but belong to different social classes. This novel was one of the first works of feminist literature, and Wollstonecraft depicted her characters, though poles apart economically, as joined together through their shared experience of motherhood. She clearly argued that women have the same interests in common.

In 1796, Wollstonecraft's *Letters Written in Sweden, Norway and Denmark* were published. They covered a wide range of subjects: sociological observations of the Scandinavian peoples and philosophical questions, such as the search for human happiness, the role of nature, the rejection of material goods, and the role of emotion in understanding. She lauded the domesticity and industrial progress of the Scandinavians. While writing, she engaged in a great deal of reflective thought about the rights of man in relation to the rights of woman and the mechanism of inclusion and exclusion.

A wife was the property of her husband de jure and de facto. She abhorred the fact that women, like slaves who could not own property, were marginalized in society. In this very successful book, her connection with nature was profound. With her emphasis on imagination and emotion, she influenced the Romantic writers William Wordsworth and Samuel Taylor Coleridge. William Godwin, her husband, wrote: "If ever there was a book calculated to make a man fall in love with its author, this appears to be the book."

Needless to say, Wollstonecraft thwarted the moral and sociopolitical conventions of her day as well as the political and nationalistic conventions for British subjects. She argued that tyranny corrupts the oppressor as well as the oppressed. Since there was no feminist movement in the eighteenth century, her writing is all that much more interesting. A woman developing political theory was unthinkable, for the male gender was considered the engine for political thought. It was commonly thought that women did not have the brains to reason. Wollstonecraft included the female gender as she participated in the social process of political theorizing and argument. She stands out in women's history as a bold writer and philosopher, profoundly influenced by Locke's theory that all humans are born equal, and that includes females.

Wollstonecraft was shaped by her family and the historical time in which she lived. Because her personal life was unconventional, she was much defamed; society was more interested in a woman's purity than her politics. The conventional groups in England made a mockery of her life. With the stresses put upon her by society, she bore a heavy burden. At the same time, her intellect was swirling with revolutionary ideas. She was not the perfect heroine. She got an education on her own as best she could; she chose her own men sometimes in error, and sometimes she was insensitive. Nevertheless, she persevered and overcame ridicule and unhappiness by the sheer force of her personality. Today she remains a venerable image, for her ideas about woman's rights and education were a hundred years ahead of their time. This early pioneer for equal rights has left a great legacy in her writing. As the author of the Bible of the Women's Rights Movement—*A Vindication of the Rights of Woman*—Wollstonecraft's ideas will live on and form the basis for much feminist philosophy today and will continue to do so in the future.

Susan B. Anthony 1820-1906 This indefatigable feminist spent over fifty years fighting for women's suffrage. The Nineteenth Amendment is named in her honor. (unknown photographer public domain)

CHAPTER TWELVE

Susan B. Anthony and Elizabeth Cady Stanton, Never Lose Faith.

"Men, their rights and nothing more: women, their rights and nothing less."
Susan B. Anthony

Susan Brownell Anthony was born February 15, 1820, in Adams, Massachusetts. Fortunately, her father, a sixth generation Quaker, believed in equal educational opportunities for girls and boys, which was unusual at the time. Thus, Susan and her three sisters received the same education as her two brothers. Throughout Anthony's life she had the support of her family. Daniel Anthony would sometimes tell his daughter that she was politically wrong but morally right, and he encouraged her to take the high ground.

As a child, Anthony was raised in the Quaker plain-living style where there were neither toys nor music. The grand outdoors was her playground. Both parents provided her with a loving secure abode, and she remained close to her family throughout her life.

Daniel Anthony had a small cotton mill on his property that he staffed with local women; he believed that women should be able to earn their own way. Hence, Anthony was exposed to working women from her childhood. She sometimes worked in the mill filling in for women who were ill. Consequently, at an early age she understood the value of earning a wage. Women comprised 68 percent of employees in cotton mills by the late 1830s.

During Anthony's mother's generation, women were very dependent on men. Now in Anthony's generation, women were earning their own money, albeit a small sum, which they sometimes used to send home or to further their own education. They could now make choices and support themselves. In fact, many of the women in Daniel Anthony's mill were boarders, so with a husband, eight children (two died in infancy), and roomers to care for, Anthony's hard-working mother required the help of her children to manage the household. At that time, there were few women's rights as most rights were exclusively male rights. But with the advent of industrialization, women were gradually coming together outside the private sphere where they could freely express their frustrations.

After the Revolutionary War public schools and Sunday schools started to compete for female students. However, there were no public schools in the South or in the rural areas of the North until after the Civil War. As a result, many females received their only education in Sunday schools. In 1819, Emma Willard presented a plan for women's education before the New York legislature. Her plan formed a syllabus similar to that offered by Amherst, Brown, and Dartmouth but within the confines of domesticity, for men wanted women dependent on them intellectually. In 1821, Troy Female Seminary (first permanent high school for females in America) was founded by Emma Willard in Troy, New York. Teaching was considered a "respectable" profession for women and many of the graduates of Emma Willard's Troy Female Seminary (still operational) spread out to far away places like Illinois, California, and Oregon where they settled, carrying the seeds of female independence. The first public high schools for girls were opened in New York and Boston in 1826. Literacy grew among females. By the time of the Civil War, many of the most well known novelists were women, including Harriet Beecher Stowe and Maria Sedgwick.

In 1826, Daniel Anthony moved his family to Battenville, New York and ran several mills for a local businessman. He rose to be one of the most important men in the community. Believing that females needed to be educated as well as males, Daniel Anthony sent Susan to school and later home-schooled his children and those of the mill workers. Later he hired other teachers, one of whom was Mary Perkins who was trained by the educational pioneer Mary Lyon.

Anthony observed the difference in the status of the female mill workers and teachers. Jobs for lower class women were limited; a step upward was a position as a governess or a teacher. Her father saw to it that she and her older sister were positioned as governesses and later as teachers. Females as teachers received one quarter of the wages males were paid.

Later, advocating higher education for females, her father sent her to join an older sister at a Quaker private boarding school, Deborah Moulson's

Female Seminary in Philadelphia, to enhance her education. There she was exposed to chemistry, physiology, literature, philosophy, bookkeeping, and arithmetic; this was quite an impressive curriculum for any female student, albeit in an atmosphere of harsh discipline. Susan was allowed to attend for only one semester, for a major depression hit the country. When the financial panic of 1837 erupted, her father lost everything, so the girls were removed from school. Daniel Anthony's home, furnishings, business, and store were put up for auction. At this point, Daniel Anthony moved his family to Hardscrabble, New York, and was forced to start over. Whereas Susan taught school before to enhance her self-confidence and character, she now needed to teach as a means of livelihood. With her father's bankruptcy, her life was changed forever. About this time she changed her dress, moving from the plain Quaker dress to "white, blue, purple, and brown plaid complete with a fancy bonnet, and she reported home that rumors went through the village that the schoolmarm was so attractive that 'someone might be smitten and carry her away.'" However, her interests lay elsewhere. (Kathleen Barry. *Susan B. Anthony.* [New York: New York University Press, 1988]. 198). The Anthony family members were strong abolitionists and were also involved in the temperance movement. At age twenty-nine, Susan took up the banners of these causes and proudly marched with them. For the rest of her life she would be a staunch activist for one cause or another. Eventually she dedicated her life to the women suffrage movement and to the cause of justice and equality for all.

To understand the life of Susan B. Anthony one must understand the life of Elizabeth Cady Stanton, for the two were linked. Susan B. Anthony and Elizabeth Cady Stanton forged the way to equality for all women throughout the ages. It was as if they had one brain—two parts becoming one. Stanton was the more gifted writer and philosopher, whereas Anthony emerged as the speech giver, critic, organizer, and the country's first great woman politician. She could veer to the right or left if by so doing she could steer the women suffrage movement closer to its goal.

They could not have been more different. Stanton came from wealth and comfort in upstate New York, and Anthony came from a poor, farm family. Both women shared an independent spirit and strong will. Generally they stood together, but behind the scenes there were often disagreements. Stanton with her outspoken radical views often alienated people, especially religious groups and men; she addressed religious and social oppression as she saw it. On the other hand, Anthony, the politician, tried to cement relations whenever possible.

For instance, Elizabeth Cady in her early life showed her radical streak when she married Henry Stanton; they agreed to have the word "obey" stricken from the marriage ceremony. At the time, this would have been most unusual.

In her later life, Stanton never minded expressing the most radical views, whereas Anthony was more moderate in order to achieve her goals. Moreover, Stanton kept her maiden name for many years; their marriage was to be one of equals. Stanton bore seven children, while Anthony remained a spinster all her life. Because Anthony was unmarried, she was able to intertwine her personal and public life and dedicate her entire life to her causes.

When these two women started their mission to secure women's rights in America, women had no voice in government. A woman could not speak in public nor could she enter a college or university. She could not become a doctor or lawyer, for she was barred from most kinds of profitable employment as well as from education. When employed, her wages were handed over to her husband. A woman could not own property in her own name.

The law in no way protected her; a husband could punish his wife as he saw fit and divorce laws favored the husband. The husband always was awarded custody of the children even when he was the offender. Even in death a man could still be in control because beforehand he could appoint a guardian for his children. A father could contract apprenticeships for his children without the mother's consent.

The earnings of single women were taxed, and they had no representation. "Taxation without representation is tyranny," cried the early colonists. Abigail Adams in 1776 maintained, "We will not hold ourselves bound to obey laws to which we have no voice." (Kathleen Barry. *Susan B. Anthony* [New York: New York University Press, 1988]. 320). (*History of Women Suffrage*, vol.3.2). Even though at a later time married women could own property that they inherited, they could not buy, sell, contract, or bequeath in their own name. Women were forced to live dependent, subservient lives not just by their husbands but also by their fathers or older male relatives. The man of the family was like God directing and telling women what they could and could not do. Economically and legally they were powerless.

Anthony and Stanton found themselves caught up in the temperance and abolitionist movements before the Civil War, although in different areas of New York State. In 1848, the first Women's Rights Convention was held in Seneca Falls, New York. At that time the "Declaration of

Sentiments" was formulated; Elizabeth Cady Stanton organized the meeting. "The Declaration of Sentiments" listed the rights of women just as Thomas Jefferson had listed the rights of men. On the first day of the convention, only women were allowed to attend; on the second day men were invited. No woman in the group felt qualified to chair the meeting, so Lucretia Mott's husband, James, agreed to accept the position.

Stanton, who never before addressed a group, presented the document to a mixed-gender audience. Public speaking for a woman was bad enough, but to a group of men and women (then considered promiscuous), Stanton showed her verve and fortitude. Stanton told her listeners, "Strange as it may seem to many, we now demand our right to vote, according to the declaration of the government under which we live." Sixty-eight women and thirty-eight men signed the document. Two weeks after the first convention, a second one was held in Rochester, New York. By signing the document, Anthony's parents and sister showed their support of her belief that men and women deserve the same rights. However, Anthony herself was not there; she had not yet met Stanton.

Women actually could vote in one state at the end of the eighteenth century. The New Jersey Constitution did not explicitly include females in its voting section but did not exclude them. In 1790, a state election law included the words "he" or "she" when referring to voters. "He" or "she" would only be eligible to vote in the certain township or precinct in which he/she resided, and he/she had to be property owners. Single or widowed women could own property, thus making them eligible to vote. On the other hand, married women could not own property (their property once married belonged to their husbands); they were therefore not eligible to vote. As it turned out later, partisan politics got very dirty, and many more women than eligible came out to vote in one Essex county election, which proved to be a fraudulent election. Fraud and partisan politics have raged since the inception of our republic, even going back to the days of George Washington. Thus in 1807, the New Jersey legislature passed a law allowing only free white males of the state over the age of twenty-one to vote. Supposedly this law, the legislators reasoned, would allow for the order and dignity of the state. Women would have to wait many decades before they would once again have the right to vote.

In 1848, for the first time ever, a Married Woman's Property Act was passed in New York State. It gave women the right to keep inherited property. Previously the law prevented women from inheritance. Women did not even have the right to keep their earned wages nor did they have the right to anything their husbands earned. Elizabeth Cady Stanton was the inspiration behind this act.

Most newspapers in New York poked fun at the whole idea of women acting on their own, but Fredrick Lloyd Garrison extolled the notion of women having their rights. Horace Greeley further argued that the ideas expressed at the convention might thwart custom, but the natural rights of women could not be denied.

Stanton remained close to home because of her family responsibilities, but she was determined to make people think. She authored many articles on temperance, a main issue of the day, as well as on abolition and women's rights.

Perhaps if Anthony had not grown up in a Quaker household, her life might have gone down a different avenue. Egalitarianism, abolition, and temperance were topics of the day in the Anthony household. In 1848, she helped form a local chapter of the Daughters of Temperance. The alcohol issue moved her from the personal to the social arena and helped awaken her political consciousness.

Anthony was attracted to the Unitarian Church which turned outward, whereas the Quaker religion focused more on inward analysis. The Unitarian Church emphasized free will and social responsibility, elements that attracted Anthony. Anthony gave her first public speech in 1849 addressing the issue of temperance. Her world had expanded from her days of teaching, and now she entered the arena of reform where she would spend the rest of her life. Her organizational skills were put to work as she showed other women how to arrange suppers and fairs where their messages could be put forth. She also showed a special talent for fund-raising. In the temperance movement, one of the first expressions of organized feminism, women burst on the national scene.

Anthony's intention was not just to develop followers but to raise the consciousness of women about an issue and to mobilize their spirits. Sometimes she encouraged confrontation when necessary to achieve an end. Everywhere Anthony went, she energized and motivated women to organize and express their feelings in public. Anthony was the strategic organizer. She recognized that women needed to find their own voices but collectively to speak as one voice, if they wanted to get anything done.

By 1850, the issue of slavery over-shone the debate over temperance. The Underground Railway came into force after the Dred Scott Decision of 1857, and Susan and her father did as much as they could to help the slaves escape to Canada. They believed that slavery was inherently evil.

Abolitionists met at the family farm for Sunday dinner and anti-slavery leaders were invited. John Brown, Frederick Douglas, Wendell Philips, William Lloyd Garrison, and others spoke passionately about the evils of slavery. Anthony began to merge the issue of temperance with slavery in her speeches. She compared the plight of southern slave women with women with abusive alcoholic husbands. Both conditions were abominations. White women joined in support of black women while Sojourner Truth, a former slave and Methodist minister, led the charge for black women against the evils of slavery.

Elizabeth Cady Stanton and Susan Brownell Anthony met in 1851 through the introduction of Amelia Bloomer on a street corner in Seneca Falls, following a lecture by William Lloyd Garrison. They soon formed a deep and lasting friendship and launched a Women's State Temperance Society. Anthony had been denied a voice in the Sons of Temperance, so she decided to form her own organization in which men could neither vote nor hold office. The group accomplished little. One of the reasons for the failure was the fact that women did not have the financial power to promote their causes.

Stanton addressed the Albany legislature in 1854 demanding the expansion of the Married Woman's Property Act, which had passed in 1848 along with the right to vote. Anthony had copies of the speech circulated across the state of New York and made sure every legislator had a copy on his desk. Stanton's father threatened to disinherit her if she spoke again in public. Indeed, Stanton stopped speaking in public until after her father's death, but she did write speeches for Anthony and engaged in all kinds of work from her home. Privately, she toiled incessantly with dedication and fervor for the cause of women's rights.

In the meantime, Anthony was busy traveling around New York State giving speeches and distributing pamphlets. She charged twenty-five cents for admittance to her speeches and a small speaker's fee. A few wealthy reformers donated to the cause. Simultaneously, she worked for the anti-slavery movement, and she was hired to set up speaking schedules for abolitionists. With almost manic energy, Anthony crusaded on with her work for justice and equality for women. Anthony argued:

> Woman must have a purse of her own, and how can this be so long as the law denies to the wife all right to both the individual and the joint earnings?...There is no true freedom for woman without the possession of equal property rights, and these can only be obtained through legislation. If this is so then the sooner the demand is made, the sooner it will be granted.

> It must be done by petition, and this, too, by the next legislature. How can the work be started? We must hold a convention and adopt some plan of united action. (Geoffrey C.Ward and Ken Burns. *Not for Ourselves Alone.* [New York: Alfred A.Knopf, 1999]. 73).

In 1860, Stanton addressed the Judiciary Committee and others in the Assembly Room of the state capitol in Albany. Her speech focused on expanding the Married Women's Property Act even further. The next day, the state legislature voted to give women the "right to own property without interference from their husbands, to keep all their earnings, to transact business on their own, to sue and be sued in a court of law, and to share custody of their children." (Geoffrey Ward and Ken Burns. *For Ourselves Alone.* [New York: Alfred A. Knopf 1999]. 91). This monumental event led to the adoption of similar laws by other states. It was the first major landmark in the fight for women's rights.

Divorce was another matter that needed to be addressed; any woman that suggested changes in the marriage laws was vilified and denounced as a destroyer of family values. Only by having the vote, could women have power to make changes. Enfranchisement was the most important issue. Anthony and Stanton believed divorce was an inalienable right, not just in the case of abuse by a drunken husband, as the temperance women's groups maintained. By the legal right to divorce, a woman could act independently whether in the marriage contract or outside of it. Her position on divorce alienated many women, as well as men, who considered marriage a sacred contract "till death do us part."

According to Anthony, most male abolitionists did not understand the basic arguments of the women's rights movement. When the Civil War began, the issue of women's rights became a minor topic and was put on the shelf. Anthony worried that the progress that had been made would now be lost. Indeed, part of what she feared did transpire: the New York legislature in 1862 revoked the statute in the Married Women's Property Act that gave married women shared guardianship of their children jointly with their husbands. A widow's right to property and to the care and protection of minor children was also revoked.

At the insistence of a Republican leader, Charles Sumner, Anthony and Stanton performed grass roots work. With their army of volunteers, they gathered more than one hundred thousand signatures, supporting the amendment freeing the slaves everywhere. In Boston, Anthony organized lectures at which Ralph Waldo Emerson, Wendell Phillips, and William

Lloyd Garrison spoke. During Anthony's lifetime, she traveled thousands of miles and organized hundreds of meetings across the nation.

In 1862, Lincoln issued the Emancipation Proclamation, which freed all slaves in the rebel states, but continued slavery in the border states because they had not seceded. Anthony and Stanton formed the Woman's National Loyal League, rallying women in the anti-slavery movement. They pointed out that women were like the slaves in many ways; they, too, were supposed to know "their place" and to obey. They demanded slavery be abolished everywhere and their rights constitutionally protected. Anthony argued:

> If the right of one single human being is to be discarded by us, we fail in our loyalty to our country...it is not because women suffer, it is not because slaves suffer, it is not because of any individual rights or wrongs, it is the simple assertion of the great fundamental truth of democracy that was proclaimed by our founding fathers. (Kathleen Barry. *Susan B. Anthony.* [New York: New York University Press, 1988]. 173). (*History of Woman Suffrage Susan B. Anthony* Vol.2, 61).

Olympe de Gouges in 1791 wrote and published *Declaration of the Rights of Woman and the Citizen* on behalf of herself and all women of France. It was based on the *Declaration of the Rights of Man and the Citizen.* She posited the view that women could reason and make moral decisions. Therefore, women deserved the same rights as were being extended to men during the French Revolution; woman was different from man, but she was his equal. In her manifesto, she asserted that women had the right to free speech and equality in marriage. They should also have the right to name the father of their children; the right to establish legitimacy for their "illegitimate children;" and the right to enjoy membership in the public and political aspects of life, as well as other rights.

For such public assertions and not staying in her "proper place," de Gouges went to the guillotine in 1793, four years after the start of the Revolution. In 1791 de Gouges wrote in the *Declaration of Rights of Women*: "Women have the right to mount the scaffold; they should have the right to mount the rostrum." Little did she know then that she would mount the scaffold! French women were not enfranchised until 1944. Like Mary Wollstonecraft of the same period, de Gouges a bold, passionate, intelligent woman helped to lay the groundwork for future feminists. Susan B.Anthony, Elizabeth Cady Stanton, Lucy Stone, Lucretia Mott, and others of the American Suffrage Movement of the nineteenth century looked to these women as inspirations on which to draw strength and passion.

The Thirteenth Amendment, first of the reconstruction Amendments, passed in 1865. It abolished slavery everywhere in the United States and in all places within its jurisdiction, except as punishment of a criminal act. Two thousand members of the Woman's National Loyal League circulated petitions and acquired almost four hundred thousand signatures. These signatures were presented to Congress and were instrumental in getting the amendment passed. The women had worked tirelessly to free the nation of the injustice of slavery. After the passage of the amendment, the Woman's National Loyal League dissolved.

When the war ended, Anthony and Stanton believed that, with their stand with the abolitionists, men would stand with them on the matter of female justice. As justice should be the same for blacks and whites, so should it be for male and female. They maintained they were all part of the same movement for justice and equality, but, unfortunately, that was not the case.

Their old ally, Wendell Phillips, proposed that the Anti-Slavery Society remain in place until all freed male slaves (around two million) were enfranchised with the passage of the Fourteenth Amendment. Phillips, furthermore, argued that the two issues could not be on the slate at the same time. It would be difficult enough to achieve enfranchisement for the freed slaves without adding the women's rights issue onto the agenda.

The Republican Party and strong abolitionists of New England saw that enfranchising two million black men would strengthen their party. On the other hand, enfranchising women would not necessarily help the Republican Party. Often throughout history the weaker group in a coalition is cast off when it is seen as not needed. This appears to have been the case with the male abolitionists. After working hard since 1848 for their rights, the feminists were outraged. The black men's rights were considered more important than women's rights. Anthony and Stanton worked feverishly to get signatures on a petition supporting the inclusion of women suffrage in the Fourteenth Amendment. Their efforts were in vain.

Raising the women's ire even more was the fact that the term "male citizens" was to be added to the Constitution as those allowed to vote. Negro Suffrage would exclude all women both black and white. However, abolitionists were not entirely happy with the Fourteenth Amendment, for it did not explicitly guarantee the black man the right to vote. The states held the power of enforcement, but if the state did not comply, its representation could be reduced by federal law. It would take the passage of the Fifteenth Amendment to truly enfranchise the black male. Even then, with poll taxes, the Ku Klux Klan, property requirements, and other restrictions, there was much injustice toward the blacks.

In 1866, Anthony decided to focus exclusively on Woman Suffrage. She founded the American Equal Rights Association when males in Kansas were about to vote on suffrage for both blacks and women in 1867. This was the first time in American history that such equality was to be established in law. Anthony and Stanton campaigned tirelessly in support of the issue. In the end, newspapers, people who had supported the cause financially, and abolitionist friends deserted the suffragettes, and they lost the vote.

There was now a divide in the movement: those who supported the emancipation of black men as well as women and those who wanted only to focus on suffrage for women. In 1868, Stanton became editor and publisher of *The Revolution*, a radical feminist periodical; Anthony was the business manager. Abortion, infanticide, divorce, and prostitution—a shocking list of issues for the nineteenth century, were addressed. Anthony and Stanton were attempting to shape public opinion. But at the same time they continued to press forward with their political agenda.

Anthony was also working on labor issues involving women. During the second part of the nineteenth century, with the spread of industrialization, abuses against workers intensified. Newly arrived immigrants filled the labor pool; slums arose in the large cities; exploitation of workers was rampant. Anthony joined the National Labor Union (NLU) and actually formed two chapters with female members. Karl Marx noted the acceptance of women into the NLU. Anthony believed in labor's right to strike but also supported women taking over men's jobs during strikes. She called for equal pay for equal work, an issue still relevant in the twenty-first century. In addition, she crusaded for better working conditions for women. Along with Augusta Lewis, Anthony addressed the Women's Typographical Union that she and Lewis had founded:

> Girls, you must take this matter to heart seriously now, for you have established a union, and for the first time in women's history in the United States you are placed, and by your own efforts on a level with men and are able as far as possible, to obtain wages for your labor. I need not say that you have taken a great momentous step forward in the path of success. (Kathleen Barry. *Susan B. Anthony.* [New York: New York University Press, 1988]. 255).

Anthony was eventually thrown out of the Union.

Furthermore, Anthony maintained that many educated women were more competent than black and immigrant men. Women's equality and freedom could only be achieved by enfranchisement. Now the Fifteenth Amendment was to be added with still no mention of woman suffrage. Once again women were supposed to support the Republican plan for Reconstruction, and their major issue of enfranchisement was off the table. Insult was added to injury.

When the Fifteenth Amendment passed and went to the states for ratification in 1869, Anthony and Stanton raced to the Midwest to rally opposition to it. Instead, they preferred an amendment that would enfranchise women.

However, the opposition movement was fractured due to Anthony's association with George Francis Train, an outspoken racist millionaire who supported women suffrage and contributed financially to the movement. He was a Democrat, a great orator and a proslavery advocate. Moreover, Stanton was deemed too radical because of the views she expressed in *Revolution,* a journal financially backed by Train. The Anthony-Train alliance was too much for the reconstruction Republicans. Like many women, Anthony thought and stated that the Republicans were no better than the Democrats in supporting women. Horace Greeley, Frederick Douglas, Wendell Phillips, and Theodore Tilton retaliated by attacking Anthony in newspapers all over the country. Anthony and Stanton were now considered radical extremists. Although both women had been fighting for the common cause of Negro rights, they were shocked by the betrayal of their previous colleagues and friends. Kathleen Barry writes:

> Republicans and abolitionists could attack and condemn the women, but it was unthinkable to them that the women could break ranks with the Republicans. But that in effect is what Anthony did while campaigning in Kansas with Train. As a charismatic-leader, Anthony's direction was determined, independent of Republican or abolitionist politics. What infuriated the abolitionists and Republicans is that they could not penetrate or buy off her radical egalitarianism. She refused to accept any group as a priority over any other in the demand for rights. Thus, there were no conditions under which she would abandon the woman's cause. (Kathleen Barry. *Susan B. Anthony.* [New York: New York University Press, 1988]. 218-219).

In 1869, Anthony reconvened the Equal Rights Association in New York City where she hoped the women would come and join together. It was not to be. Frederick Douglas accused Anthony and Stanton of racism for not supporting the Fifteenth Amendment; they accused him of sexism for not including white and black women in the amendment. Anthony's sentiments were printed in the official record: "Not another man should be enfranchised until enough women are admitted to the polls to outweigh those already there." She did not believe in allowing ignorant Negroes and foreigners to make laws for her to obey. (Geoffrey Ward and Ken Burns. *For Ourselves Alone.* [New York: Alfred A. Knopf, 1999]. 120). Consequently, the convention backed the Fifteenth Amendment and did nothing to support a separate amendment on women's rights. Anthony and Stanton were devastated, and they were now alienated from many of their old supporters.

Later that year the two friends, undaunted, formed the National Woman Suffrage Association. The platform included non-support of the Fifteenth Amendment, support for a Sixteenth Amendment, equal pay for equal work, an eight-hour day, and changes in the divorce laws to benefit women. No man was allowed to hold office in the new organization; Anthony and Stanton felt terribly betrayed and wounded by men. To oppose the new Association, the New England Woman Suffrage Association led by Lucy Stone formed another group. Her American Suffrage Association then backed the Fifteenth Amendment, and disavowed any connection to *The Revolution,* Stanton's newspaper.

Lucy Stone and Julia Ward Howe started a rival weekly called the *Woman's Journal.* Male membership was promoted. The split in the woman suffrage movement lasted more than twenty years. Lucy Stone's group concentrated primarily on enfranchisement, whereas Anthony and Stanton concentrated not only on voting rights but on many social issues, which were considered extremely radical at that time such as divorce.

An attorney, Francis Minor and his wife Virginia had already begun a crusade termed the "New Departure" based on the idea that women of all colors were citizens who had the inherent right to vote under the Constitution. They further maintained the right to vote was guaranteed to women under the Fourteenth and Fifteenth Amendments.

Emboldened by the Minor's legal arguments, Anthony and Stanton urged women all over the country to vote in the next general election. Anthony and her three sisters, along with other women, registered in Rochester, New York, at the local barbershop on November 1, 1872. There was much argument, but two out of three poll workers finally agreed to register the women. On election day, Anthony and ten other women actually voted for Grant and the Republican Party because that party's platform promised a morsel offering to the movement. At least women's demands would be given a hearing.

Anthony was arrested on Thanksgiving Day and fined. She refused to pay the fine, stating that the court had no right to interfere with her natural right to vote. Her attorney paid the fine which greatly annoyed Anthony. She wanted the case to go to the Supreme Court. Instead the case was moved to the United States Circuit Court at Canandaigua and was heard before an anti-women suffrage judge. He refused to allow Anthony to testify on her own behalf because he considered all women legally incompetent. "The greatest judicial outrage history ever recorded," wrote Anthony in her diary. She also stated publically, "It was we the people; not we, the white citizens, nor yet we, the male citizens; but we, the whole people, who formed the union."

In 1875, after three years of litigation, the case brought by Francis and Virginia Minor reached the Supreme Court. In *Minor vs. Happersett,* the judges ruled unanimously against Minor; citizenship meant that an individual was a member of the nation and that was all. Furthermore, the states had jurisdiction over who could and could not vote. This, of course, later opened a Pandora's Box for the Southern states to exploit. Anthony and the National Woman Suffrage Association realized they could not succeed in the courts. They would have to work through the states and Congress. An amendment would have to be added to the Constitution.

On July 4, 1876, in Philadelphia a huge crowd assembled for the hundredth anniversary of American Independence. Anthony and Stanton, along with other leaders of the woman's movement, decided to make a showing at the Centennial Exhibition. They would demand their rights as women from the national government. Women at the time could not even rent a room without their husband's permission. Since she was single, Anthony was the only woman there with the legal right to rent a room, so she rented rooms for the other women. Their aim in attending was to present a new Declaration of Rights for Women. Progress had been made since 1848: women were speaking publicly, educational opportunities had increased, and women were entering the workforce in increasing numbers.

However, General Hawley, the president of the Centennial Exhibition, which was to be held in Independence Hall, informed Anthony that she would not be allowed to speak, and that no women would be seated. Anthony arranged a press pass for herself through her brother from his Kansas newspaper; then General Hawley relented and gave just four more seats to the women. The women were furious. Undeterred, Anthony was determined the Women's Declaration would reach the platform of speakers. So, at an opportune moment between speeches, she led the four other women to the stage and presented the rolled up copy tied with a ribbon to the acting president, Senator Thomas Ferry. Then the women distributed copies to all in the hall that wanted them. Outside the hall, Anthony read the document from a bandstand to a crowd that gathered around her:

> And now, at the close of a hundred years, as the hour-hand of the great clock that marks the centuries points to 1876, we declare our faith in the principal of self-government, our full equality with man in natural rights; that woman was made first for her own happiness, with the absolute right to herself...to all the opportunities and advantages life affords for her complete development; and we deny that dogma of the centuries, incorporated in the codes of all nations...that woman was made for man...her best interests... to be sacrificed to his will. We ask our rulers, at this hour, no special favors, no special privileges....We ask justice, we ask equality, we ask that all civil and political rights that belong to the citizens of the United States be guaranteed to us and our daughters forever. (*History of Woman Suffrage.* edited by Elizabeth Cady Stanton, Susan B. Anthony and Matilda Joslyn Gage, Volume 3 (1876-1885). [Salem, New Hampshire: Ayers Company Publishers, 1985]. 31).

Anthony called a National Woman Suffrage Association Convention in Washington, D.C. every year in order to lobby Congress for their cause. In 1878, the issue of women's voting rights came to the floor in the United States Senate, introduced by Senator Arlen Sargent of California in the form of a sixteenth amendment to the Constitution. The bill died in committee and was not brought before the Senate until 1887 when it was again soundly defeated. It was brought before every session of Congress until 1920, when it finally passed.

Anthony was a source of inspiration to women everywhere, never giving up and charging onward, always leading her followers with hope for a better day. Her energy seemed endless and being a spinster she had more time than many of the other women. During these years, Stanton was less visible in Washington. She was tied to her hearth with a family of seven children and a dislike for politics. By this time, Anthony was the symbol and leader of the woman's suffrage movement and the inspiration for other women.

In 1881 at age sixty-six, Stanton retired to her home in Tenafly, New Jersey. Stanton's health became an issue, and her daughter Harriet, also a suffragette, insisted they go to Europe where Harriet lived. From that time on Stanton remained in the background of the movement, for she adapted to living in Europe with her son and daughter in France and England. However, she often traveled back to the U.S.

In 1890, Anthony continued to be active in the movement and was nominated for the presidency of the National American Woman Suffrage Association. But she insisted that the honor fall upon her friend, Elizabeth Cady Stanton, whom Anthony considered to be the true mother of the Suffrage Movement. Since this was mainly an honorary position, Stanton accepted the honor and left the next day for Europe.

Anthony knew she had to rally to the cause the groups of women that were not necessarily in full agreement with her views. Being politically astute, she formed connections with the Women's Christian Temperance Union, the Women's Division of the Knights of Labor, the Women's Conference of the Unitarian Association, the Daughters of the American Revolution, and others. By so doing, Anthony added vast numbers of supporters to her cause.

With their feminine moral sensibilities, women were attracted to the temperance movement in the eighteen-fifties, when they saw their sisters and children often abused as the result of alcoholism. They were also sympathetic to the anti-slavery movement because they saw slavery as oppression, and women too were oppressed. In the twentieth century, however, most women felt little or no connection to the temperance or abolitionist movements. Although women had already started to make inroads into men's domains in the 1880s, Anthony would not live to see the enfranchisement of women across the country. While women were permitted to vote and even were winning some local elections, only Utah and Wyoming fully enfranchised women by the 1880s.

Anthony, five years younger, kept chugging along. She traveled over the West and Midwest, dedicating herself completely to suffrage. Yet progress was still not happening at the rate Anthony desired. After fifty years of struggle, only Wyoming, Utah, Colorado, and Idaho had given women the right to vote near the turn of the century.

In 1883, Anthony traveled to Europe where she talked to the leading feminists in Europe and became involved in women's international issues. From her meetings and discussions, she realized the need for an international council of women. Anthony in 1888 organized a meeting in Washington, D.C. with representatives from all over the world. It was a time for unity, not just for the delegates from various countries; it was also the time for American women in the movement to settle their differences and join forces. Younger women were rising to leadership roles, and a new generation was making its voice heard. Many protestant countries granted women the vote before WWI—New Zealand 1893, Australia 1902, Finland 1906, and Norway 1913. Most Catholic countries did not give women the right to vote until after WWII.

Subsequently in 1890, the two American organizations came together and formed the National American Woman Suffrage Association. Lucy Stone and Anthony resolved to work together for the betterment of the movement. Stanton, the first president, opposed to associating the women's movement with temperance or religion, advocated the right of any woman to present her concerns before the association. Anthony disagreed.

In 1900, Anthony at age eighty handed over the presidency of the NAWSA to Carrie Chapman Catt, who had a short tenure in office. Then the Reverend Anna Howard Shaw, a close friend of Anthony, succeeded Catt. The mantle was passed to the younger generation of women. Now the movement was in full swing. In 1906, Anthony insisted on attending the National American Convention in Baltimore despite her age and fragility. She was thrilled to see many female college graduates and celebrated the progress women had made during the last fifty years.

She prevailed upon the presidents of Bryn Mawr College and John Hopkins University to establish a standing fund to be used to support women's issues. Monetary concerns were always a major problem. At age eighty-six, Anthony attended her last birthday party in Washington and delivered her final speech:

> This is a magnificent sight before me, and these have been wonderful addresses and speeches I have listened to the past week. Yet I have looked on so many such audiences, all testifying to the righteousness, the justice, and the worthiness of the cause of woman suffrage. I never saw that great woman, Mary Wollstonecraft, but I have read her eloquent, her unanswerable arguments on behalf of the liberty of womankind. I have met and known most of the progressive women who have come after her—Lucretia Mott, the Grimke sisters, Elizabeth Cady Stanton, Lucy Stone—a long galaxy of great women....There have been others just as true and devoted to the cause....(Geoffrey Ward and Ken Burns. *For Ourselves Alone.* [New York: Alfred A. Knopf, 1999]. 212).

Elizabeth Cady Stanton died on October 26, 1902, while appropriately preparing to deliver a speech. The relationship between Anthony and

Stanton stands out in history as one of the greatest melding of talents for the advancement of a common cause. Theirs was an emotional and intellectual tie that was almost perfect. Together they birthed ideas that would resonate till this day; their goals are still being pursued.

Susan B. Anthony died on March 13, 1906. More than ten thousand mourners attended her funeral. Anthony forgot her self-identity with the movement; the movement was her identity. This champion gave all of herself, so that future generations of women could forge their true identity. She fought for their collective rights until her last breath. She was buried in Rochester, New York, next to her parents. Finally, the Nineteenth Amendment to the United States Constitution passed in 1920 and is often called in her honor, the Susan. B. Anthony Amendment. This dedicated pioneer and other brave women paved the way in the nineteenth century for the freedoms and rights women enjoy in the twenty-first. It was a long, difficult journey, but persistence paid off in the long run by other women who took up the torch Anthony had carried for over fifty years. "Failure is impossible."

Elizabeth Cady Stanton 1815-1902 Philosopher, editor and writer She held the first famous Women's Rights Convention in Seneca Falls, N.Y. in 1848. (Photograph Library of Congress public domain copyright expired)

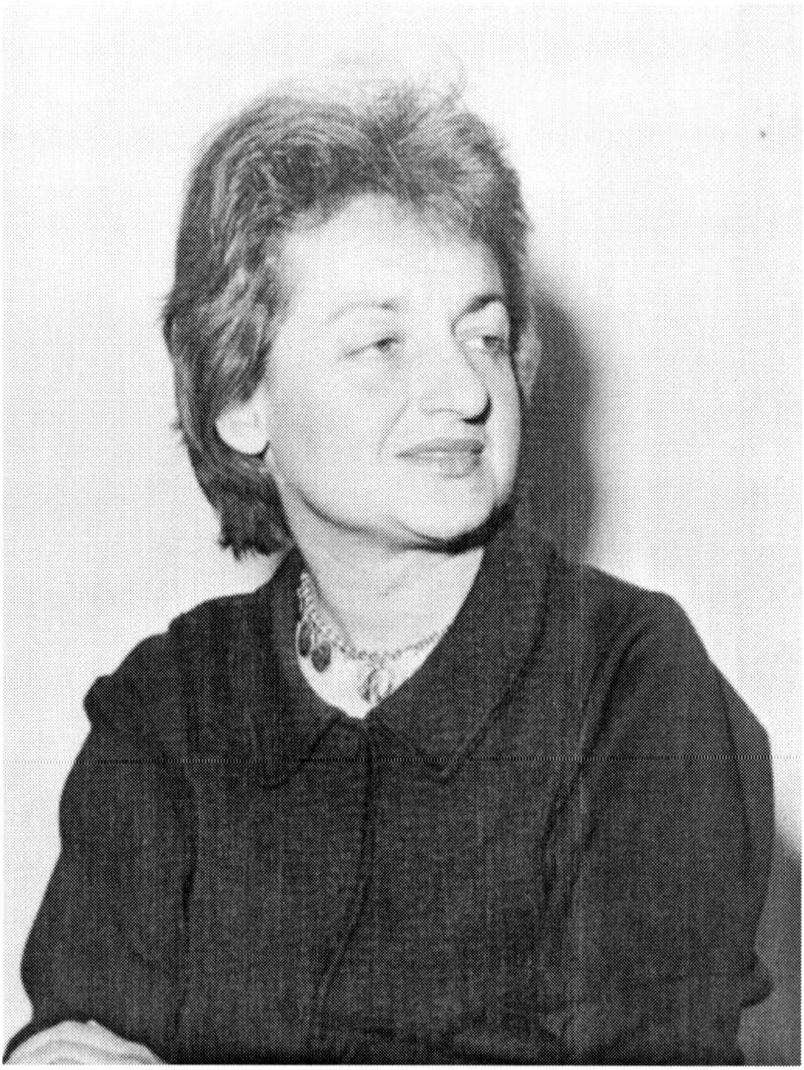

Betty Friedan 1921-2006, author of *The Feminine Mystique*, revolutionized women to change their lives. The book affected women individually and collectively. (Photograph Library of Congress public domain)

CHAPTER THIRTEEN

Betty Friedan, Gloria Steinem, and Phyllis Schlafly

Betty Friedan, Breaking the Barriers

"A girl should not expect privileges because of her sex, but neither should she adjust to prejudice and discrimination."
Betty Friedan

The nineteenth century ebbed away with foundations laid in the women's rights movement. When the Nineteenth Amendment passed in 1920, American women were finally enfranchised. The feminist movement was a social, economic, and political movement that demanded equal rights for women and men. During the later part of the twentieth century, women banded together in a common cause for the passage of the Equal Rights Amendment. This amendment which galvanized women in the 1970s still has not become a reality thus far in the twenty-first century. However, great progress and legal changes within state laws have occurred, perhaps making it not a requirement.

Soon after the passage of the Nineteenth Amendment, the country found itself mired in the Great Depression. Moreover, in the years 1917 to 1945, the country fought two world wars. Not long after that, the United States became involved in a series of more localized wars in Korea, Vietnam, and Central America. The women's movement was not dead, but rather in a dormant stage as the country addressed what seemed like graver issues.

As more and more women participated in the workplace and helped provide a higher standard of living for their families, they soon realized their unequal status. When women had previously joined the work force during the periods of warfare, they discovered their own great capabilities and value. Now they demanded to be recognized for their worth. Many educated and non-educated women found more fulfillment and happiness in the workplace than in the home. So when Betty Friedan's highly influential book, *The Feminine Mystique,* was published in 1963, many women realized that they were not alone in their longing for an identity broader than being simply a wife and mother.

As in the nineteenth century, the racial and gender issues once again came to the fore in the 1960s. Women joined their voices against racial discrimination. With the passage of the Civil Rights Acts in 1964, feminists believed that civil rights belonged to women as well. Mary Wollstonecraft had naively believed that to be true during the French Revolution, when republican rights were extended to men only. Susan B. Anthony was also enraged when the Thirteenth, Fourteenth, and Fifteenth Amendments applied only to black men and excluded women.

The '60s was a period of great social upheaval in the United States—counter-revolution. Many college students engaged in student protests against our involvement in the Vietnam War and against traditional social values. Following the example of the protesters, feminist groups also staged demonstrations, protests, and political lobbying to further their goals.

In 1966, a new organization, the National Organization for Women (NOW) was founded, representing women's social, economic, and political issues. Betty Friedan, Gloria Steinem, Bella Abzug, and Shirley Chisholm were new voices that aggressively campaigned for legislation that would address women's concerns such as abortion rights and labor rights.

A number of smaller organizations were formed to make an impact politically and socially: the National Abortion and Reproductive Rights Action League, the Women's Equity Action League, the Women's Office Worker's League, the Women Organized for Employment League, to mention a few. Just as Elizabeth Cady Stanton had rallied women with the first Women's Conference in 1848, the feminist leaders in 1977 called for a National Women's Conference in Houston, Texas. There they drafted twenty-six proposals that they later submitted to Congress, governors, and legislators, reminding them of their responsibilities and obligations to women. NOW and the National Women's Political Caucus exerted pressure on politicians throughout the country to focus on women's issues and to act on them.

During the '70s, there was much division within the movement. Some women allied themselves with revolutionary groups, seeing themselves as repressed, suppressed, and oppressed. Others identified themselves with the lesbian group and left the women's movement to find fulfillment in the gay rights movement. In addition, the passage by Congress of the ERA Amendment and the *Roe* vs. *Wade* decision by the Supreme Court led to a backlash led by conservative women. Phyllis Schlafly and anti-abortion groups and churches attacked the liberal wing of the feminist movement. Some women resented being perceived as anti-male and did not want to give up the personal security they found in traditional family roles. Camille Paglia, Susan Faludi, and Naomi Wolf expressed the views of the conservatives.

Betty Friedan was the major moving force behind the founding of the National Organization for Women (NOW) and one of the most important feminists of the twentieth century. Betty Naomi Goldstein was born on February 4, 1921, a year after the passage of the Nineteenth Amendment, in Peoria, Illinois. Her father Harry Goldstein, a Russian immigrant, owned a jewelry store, and Friedan was raised in a privileged upper-middle class environment. Of three children, Friedan was the eldest and smartest; she defied social conventions and talked and acted as she pleased.

In grade school, she associated with children from the wealthiest families in Peoria and emerged as one of the leaders and organizers. When Friedan reached senior high school, she felt the sting of anti-Semitism when she was barred from joining the more socially elite of the sororities.

Doted on by her father, Friedan rebelled against what she perceived as her mother's social pretensions. She would not follow in her mother's footsteps; she would be more than wife and mother. Friedan resolved to choose her own path to success and fame. Both parents imparted a sense of social responsibility to their children, especially during the rise of Hitler in the thirties. Her mother wrote a society page for the local newspaper. While still in high school, Friedan started her journalism career. When Friedan's father passed away, her mother went to work full time. Apparently, Friedan was pleased with her mother's happiness at fulfilling herself outside the home.

Experiencing anti-Semitism as a young girl, Friedan sometimes felt isolated from her community. As was true of the many country clubs in the nation, Jews were not allowed membership in the local country club.

The major business tycoons of the day, including Henry Ford and William Randolph Hearst, made certain the walls keeping Jews out of the major halls of business were not breached. Although Jews were assimilated, they were not yet integrated. In Friedan's later life, she attributed this feeling of isolation to her involvement with Jewish and Marxist groups where she and her confederates railed against the injustices of all kinds.

Friedan was a brilliant scholar, majoring in psychology at the all-women's Smith College. She received many academic awards, including a scholarship for outstanding academic performance. Even at Smith, Friedan continued to suffer from others' attitudes of anti-Semitism. Indeed, at the time it was common for elite schools to have quotas for Jews. Her literary career continued, and she was named editor-in-chief of the college newspaper. Friedan took a stand on every issue that she became interested in, making both friends and enemies. She delighted in upsetting the status quo; she was known as a bold and brilliant campus radical.

While at Smith, she took up the cause of the working man. The Labor Movement was the first cause she fervently allied herself with. For the next ten years, she labored with dedication and passion for the rights of the laboring class. In her mind, the economically strong dominated the weak. Ironically, having a chauffeur as a child, Friedan now was on the side of a class that her father struggled so hard to abdicate.

The Smith years brought out talents in Friedan that would be with her for the rest of her life. She wanted to use them to make a difference in the world. Friedan had an ability to attract and organize people wherever she went.

She also developed a strong sense of equality and personal freedom. On one occasion, Friedan visited Harvard and was invited to attend one of the law classes. Walter Hiersteiner, a friend, quoted her as saying: "It's a shame and it's ridiculous that women are not allowed in Harvard Law." During her senior year at Smith, when she was editor of *Scan*, she and some male counterparts were invited to seminars in other Ivy League schools. Friedan quickly noted the difference in the way she and her male companions were treated. The men were treated as the leaders of tomorrow, and she was largely ignored. In 1943, she attended the University of California, Berkeley, on a fellowship for a year. There she became attracted to socialist ideology.

After her father's death when she was twenty-two, Friedan thwarted all the laws of social propriety in the sexual arena. She took as many lovers as she pleased, for this was a time of social experimentation. Like Mary

Wollstonecraft Betty would set her own standards. It seemed she delighted in shaking and shocking.

Although she did not want to live a life like her mother's, she did want to marry. In 1947, she married Carl Friedman and kept her maiden name. Later, she legally changed the name to Friedan. Her first son was born in 1948, and her second son was born in 1952. Feeling a compulsion to have her voice heard, she spoke and wrote about a wide variety of social and moral issues. She began writing professionally for left-wing and union publications, including the Federated Press and EU (United Electrical Workers Union).

The fact that she was fired during her second pregnancy solely because of her condition ignited another flame in her house of fires. Friedan marked this firing as a turning point in her life. It was a case of flagrant sex discrimination. To make matters worse, she was replaced by a man and informed it was "her fault" for getting pregnant. But in 1952, Friedan wisely had had a maternity clause inserted in her contract with the EU. Nevertheless, she was terminated. She was the lead writer for the EU News where she associated with many Communists; many of them were investigated by the FBI. About the only thing Friedan had in common with Marxism was an aim for social justice, although she might have thought differently as a young college student.

When Friedan attended her fifteenth Smith College reunion in 1957, she conducted a survey of her college classmates, focusing on their education, experiences, and contentment with their lives. She was astonished by the results. Using her background in psychology and writing, she started publishing articles about "the problem with no name." Many women, especially housewives, responded positively to her views, and later this theme would be expanded in *The Feminine Mystique.* When her book was published in 1963, Friedan's fame and influence would rise to new heights. As a journalist, she wrote so average people could understand and take some action to change their lives. Many did. Women felt trapped and stereotyped by the media in the '50s; for example, shows like "Leave It to Beaver" and others cast women in roles that greatly limited their capabilities. Friedan raised awareness in women of their restrictions. Friedan wrote at the beginning of her book about the "problem that has no name:"

> The problem lay buried, unspoken, for many years in the minds of American women. It was a strange stirring, a sense of dissatisfaction, a yearning (that is longing) that women suffered in the middle of the 20th century in the

> United States. Each suburban housewife struggled with it alone. As she made the beds, shopped for groceries—she was afraid to ask of herself the silent question—is this all? (Betty Friedan. *The Feminine Mystique.* [New York: W.W. Norton and Company, 2001]. 57).

The book was an overnight sensation, and Friedan was now an important personage. Many historians and sociologists credit her book with significantly shaping American women's view of themselves. Indeed, it signaled the "first wave" of the new women's movement.

With success her personal life changed. Her marriage floundered, and she moved from suburbia New Jersey with her three children to an apartment in New York City. After twenty-two years of marriage, Friedan divorced her husband Carl in 1969. Friedan was not a man-hater as she was often described; she greatly enjoyed the company of men, and they figured prominently throughout her life.

In 1966, Betty Friedan, Catherine East, Pauli Murray, (a black lawyer and first ordained black female Episcopal priest) and twenty-six others founded the National Organization for Women (NOW). Friedan was elected president and Kay Clarenbach chairperson of the board. Betty wrote a five-page document that reflected many of the republican principles of the eighteenth century Enlightenment. There was an echo of Mary Wollstonecraft and the American Declaration of Independence. She wrote:

> The time has come to confront with concrete actions, the conditions that now prevent women from enjoying the equality of opportunity and freedom of choice which is their right, as individual Americans, and as human beings. (Judith Hennessee. *Betty Friedan: Her Life.* [New York, Random House, 1999]. 104).

The primary aim of the organization was to establish laws guaranteeing the equality of men and women. The first legal victories of the organization were the actual enforcement of The Equal Pay Act of 1963 and of Title VII of the Civil Rights Act of 1964. The group then forced the Equal Opportunity Commission to address cases involving sexual discrimination. In 1967, an Executive Order signed by President Lyndon Johnson granted the same affirmative action to women as had been granted to blacks. In 1968, an EOC ruling prohibited sex-segregated help-wanted ads, and the Supreme Court later upheld this ruling.

One example of the discrimination against women was the airlines' criteria for hiring new employees: for certain positions only men could apply; age, height and weight limits excluded many women from becoming "hostesses" or stewardesses. There was discrimination even by local governments in some states, and women were often automatically "excused" from jury duty.

Therefore, the feminist movement struggled with the same issues: sexual harassment, crimes against women, equal pay for equal work, reproductive rights, rights of rape victims, and affirmative action. Banks, stock exchanges, and major corporations also were charged with sex discrimination. Less than 2 percent of women in similar industries in the late '60s were paid more than ten thousand dollars a year.

Friedan and her fellow feminists decided to fight back even harder. At first, Friedan spearheaded a Woman's Strike for Equality in 1970 in New York City that could virtually shut down business and factories and disrupt family life. However, she decided against it. Instead she mobilized a march and public protests in New York City, the likes of which were never before seen in America. Starting at Grand Army Plaza outside the Plaza Hotel, Friedan led fifty thousand women from all over the country down Fifth Avenue in the middle of rush-hour traffic.

The day chosen for the demonstration was appropriately the anniversary of the passing of the Nineteenth Amendment, which enfranchised women. Betty and other leaders of the movement urged women to be politically active and to exert more influence on their state legislatures. They urged women to demand more day-care centers, equal opportunities for education and employment, and changes in state laws on issues such as abortion.

In 1970, even before the march, Friedan announced plans to form the National Women's Political Caucus. Women had to run for public office in order to have the power to make change. Friedan's idea was to have women in both parties form lobbies to exert pressure where needed and to support competent women candidates.

In 1973, *Roe vs. Wade* rocked the nation. All federal and state laws against abortion were overturned. Finally, women had the option of control over their bodies. This was another of Friedan's many triumphs: she had been one of the founders of the National Association for the Repeal of (anti) Abortion Laws.

The issue of lesbianism had fragmented the early feminist movement. At first, Friedan did not want the women's movement to be associated with gay rights. Yet in 1977 at the National Women's Conference, she called for unity, and lesbian women were to be included in the movement. She decried the divisions within the movement that she considered to be weakening its power. Many of the pro-life group left the organization because of disagreements over abortion. But there were no disagreements over the benefits achieved for and by women: they could take out loans in their own name; they could get credit cards in their own name. There were day-care centers everywhere and job training for women who wanted careers. As her legacy, Friedan had opened up the freedom of choice in many areas of women's lives. She died on February 4, 2006, in Washington, D.C. on her eighty-fifth birthday.

★★★

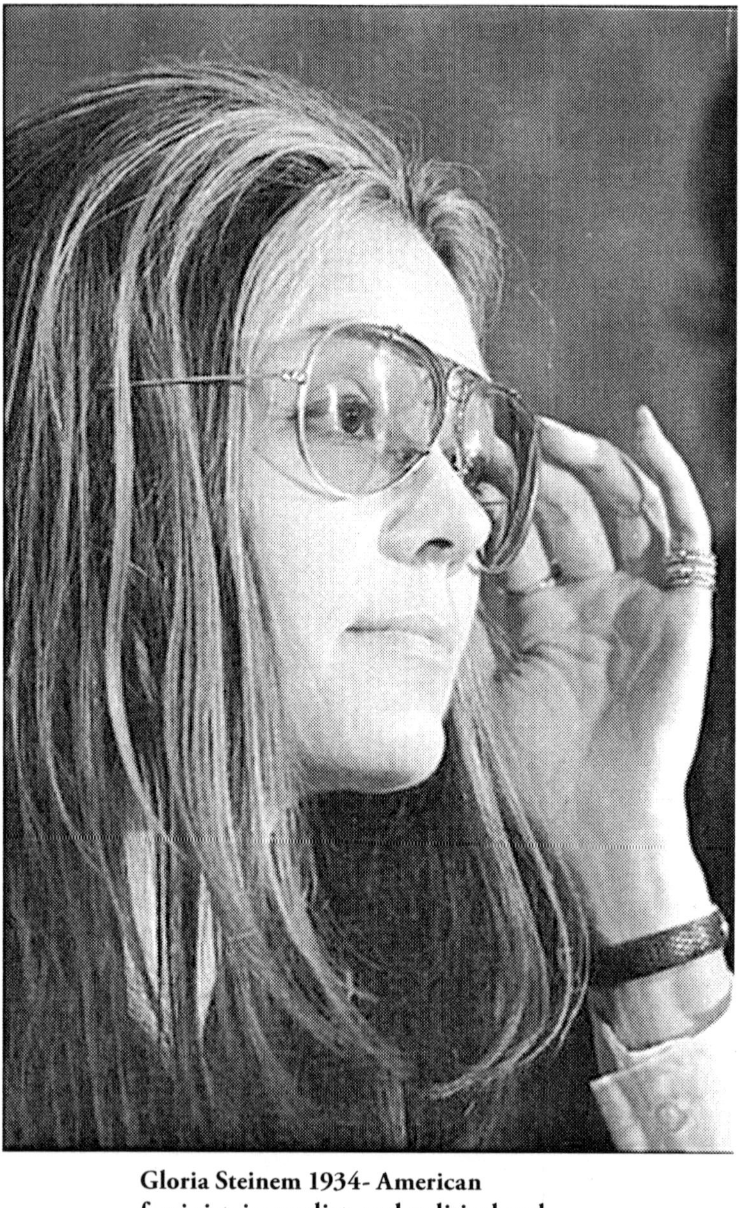

Gloria Steinem 1934- American feminist, journalist, and political and social activist Steinem helped found the National Organization for Women and the National Women's Political Caucus. (Photograph by Warren K. Leffler public domain Library of Congress)

Gloria Steinem, Revolutionary Under Celebrity

Gloria Steinem, another influential activist of the twentieth and twenty-first centuries, was born in Toledo, Ohio, on March 25, 1934. Her father was an antique dealer, and her mother had been a newspaper journalist prior to her marriage. Ruth Steinem, Gloria's mother, had graduated from Oberlin College with honors and even taught calculus at the college level before her mental breakdown. Steinem's grandmother was the well known suffragette, Pauline Steinem, of nineteenth century fame. It is noteworthy that both Friedan's and Steinem's mothers were writers, and the daughters followed in their footsteps. Moreover, they both viewed their mothers as living narrow, unfulfilled lives. They were both Midwesterners and graduates of Smith where they excelled academically.

Because of Steinem's father's occupation, the family traveled much of the time in a trailer collecting antiques. The summers were spent at their inherited resort property on Clarklake, Michigan. Fortunately, the Steinems received monies from the lake properties that at least kept them from poverty. Gloria Steinem's and her older sister's Smith College educations were paid for partly by monies from these properties. Since the Steinems were traveling the country most of the year, Steinem was often home schooled by her mother. Steinem's parents divorced when she was eight. Afterwards, Steinem's mother sank into an incapacitating depression so severe that Steinem had to take care of her. She cooked and cleaned house taking on her mothers' role. They were so poor that they lived at times in rat infested conditions.

Her father's abandonment of the family surely must have soured Steinem's perception of marriage and family life. But she expressed no anger and tried to forget about those difficult times. Fortunately, at age fifteen, she moved to Washington, D.C. to live with her older sister who saw the plight of her younger sibling and took her out of such deplorable conditions. Subsequently, her mother was institutionalized for treatment.

Later, Steinem entered Smith College, where she experienced a new way of life. Like Friedan, she flirted with Marxist theorists her freshman year. Her junior year, she studied in Switzerland and visited other European countries. This experience helped broaden her view of the world. Although Steinem suffered great emotional privation as a young girl, with her Smith

College experience she enjoyed a more sophisticated, luxurious, and intellectual life. For instance, she sailed on the Queen Mary to England for her junior year studies in Switzerland, where she stayed on Lake Lucerne in a room with a balcony overlooking the lake.

During her senior year, she cast about looking for work. Steinem discovered the sexist attitudes at some magazines such as *Time,* which employed women mostly as researchers, not as writers. Steinem's academic counselor advised her that getting into the legal profession would doom her to years of tedious research. She received a degree in government and graduated Phi Beta Kappa and magna cum laude in 1956.

Shortly thereafter, she was awarded a two-year fellowship to study in India. Steinem visited England on her way to India and discovered she was pregnant; she had an abortion that she made public about fifteen years later but did not regret. For her, the experience was a constructive and turning point. Steinem always had male lovers in her younger life and appears to have had a huge libido. She had an aversion to marriage and wanted no children. As a strong force behind the pro-choice movement, Steinem appeared in the documentary film, *I Had an Abortion,* in which she describes the time in her young life when she had an abortion.

Steinem viewed marriage as entrapment. She believed her mother had been trapped by her marriage and her children. Steinem had been trapped by taking care of her mother for six years. Only her father had been free. In Steinem's opinion, marriage meant losing the power to control one's own life. By engaging in no personal commitments, she felt free and would live her life in this manner until she was in her sixties. (Sydney Ladensohn Stern. *Gloria Steinem.* [Secaucus, New Jersey: Carol Publishing, 1997]. 85).

During her time in India, Steinem was struck by the suffering of the poor and the inequities of class and gender. It was a monumental time for her, realizing that Communism in theory was quite different than Communism in practice. She returned to the U.S. with high-minded idealism.

Her writing career began in 1960 when she moved to New York City and started writing magazine articles. One of her most famous articles, "A Bunny's Tale," appeared in *Show* magazine in a two-part series; it dealt with the scant wages and poor working conditions of the Playboy bunnies. Steinem had been hired as a bunny and actually worked in the job for three weeks. She even posed nude for *Playboy* magazine; later on, she expressed regret and humiliation for her action. In 1970, Steinem debated Hugh

Hefner on the "Playboy Philosophy" and the feminist movement. She believed that exploiting women for male entertainment was decidedly an injustice to women.

For a time, her writing career was derailed when editors looked to her for frivolous writing rather than serious articles. To Steinem, the publishing business was as sexist as any other organization where male writers were given the more important assignments, and females were given the less serious reporting jobs. As a freelance writer, she wrote "puff pieces" for *Harper's, Glamour, Ladies' Home Journal, Esquire,* and the *New York Times Magazine.* In 1964, *Glamour* ran a six-page spread describing Steinem's style: clothes, accessories, cosmetics, dark glasses, kohl-rimmed eyes, short skirts, small scarves, straight-slung hair, thin healed shoes, and pale orange Fu-Manchu nails. Yet underneath the celebrity lurked the revolutionary. In 1965, Steinem earned thirty thousand dollars when the median income for men was about six thousand dollars and for women about four thousand. This was a huge amount for a free-lance writer. With her brains and beauty, she was noticed everywhere she went; she was a glamorous celebrity. (Sydney L. Stern. *Gloria Steinem.* [Secaucus, New Jersey: Carol Publishing Company, 1997]. 153).

She helped found *New York Magazine* in 1967, and there she launched her political writing career. She shared a leftist political column, "The City Politic," with Peter Maas. In 1968, Steinem attended the Democratic National Convention in Chicago. She went to the convention as both a campaigner and political writer.

Steinem always aligned herself with Democrat candidates: Adlai Stevenson, John and Robert Kennedy, Eugene McCarthy, and later George McGovern. She fiercely opposed the Vietnam War and was also highly critical of the Gulf and Iraq Wars. Actively working for McGovern's campaign, Steinem wrote pamphlets, raised funds, and served as his press secretary. But in 1972, she differed with McGovern on the abortion plank in the Democrat platform.

Additionally, Steinem supported Caesar Chavez, the leader of the United Farm Workers, and she even participated in the grape-pickers' strike of 1968. She was one of five co-chairs for a huge fundraiser at Carnegie Hall on behalf of farm-workers. Instrumental in getting Chavez on the cover of *Time,* Steinem also wrote an article about him in *Look.* Her fundraising and publicity raised the ire of some, who accused her of being "radically chic" because of her association with Chevez and the Black Panthers.

Possessing great organizational skills and the ability to talk to anyone on any level, she was highly successful in her interviews, fundraising, and other activities. She tried to avoid controversy and to bring people together when they could find common ground. Of course, this was not always possible.

Although Steinem did not join the "sit-down" at the Plaza Hotel, which Betty Friedan had organized, she did cover it in her "City Politic" column.

A group of women stormed the Oak Bar where only men were allowed to lunch. The demonstrators demanded that the bar be integrated since it was a public space. A few weeks before the demonstration, Steinem had been evicted from the hotel by the assistant manager when she went for an interview. She was informed that unescorted ladies were not allowed. A few weeks later when she again visited the hotel for an interview, the same assistant manager repeated the message. This time Steinem refused to leave and instead demanded to know why unescorted men were not also banished. The manager backed down. In her book, *Revolution from Within*, Steinem saw this as a turning point in her life. She had stood for her rights, and the man had backed down! More women needed to stand up for their rights too.

Title VII of the Civil Rights Act of 1964, signed into law by President Lyndon Baines Johnson, prohibited discrimination based on race, religion, national origin, or sex. One result was the establishment of the Equal Employment Opportunity Commission in 1965. Most of the focus was once again on rights of black men. It became obvious that an organization such as the National Organization of Women (NOW) needed to be formed to further address women's rights.

When Betty Friedan, Kay Clarenbach, and the other twenty-six women founded the National Organization of Women in 1966, they believed that women's rights needed to be directly addressed. As women flocked to join NOW, they brought with them all kinds of ideology. Just as the nineteenth century suffragettes left the abolition and racial movements to focus on women's rights, women who had been tied to the anti-war and civil rights movements now focused exclusively on women's rights. Different factions warred with each other. There were also generational gaps. Some radicals left NOW to form other organizations. But in their different ways, they all attacked the tyranny of patriarchal norms that hindered the realization of women's goals.

For the most part, NOW wanted women to be gradually integrated into the society through legal reforms; the radicals wanted immediate changes in society. They had waited too long already. Betty Friedan worked for legal changes in the system and valued family and traditional marriage. She did not want NOW perceived as the destroyer of family life. Steinem sympathized with the radicals. *The Feminine Mystique,* in Steinem's view, was written for bourgeois women, and she generally expressed contempt for them. In her mind, they were children who benefited from their husbands' work, which they themselves did not do and could not do.

In 1971, Steinem joined forces with Betty Friedan, Shirley Chisholm, and Bella Abzug and founded the National Women's Political Caucus. Bella Abzug, a Congresswoman from N.Y., saw herself best qualified to be the leader and shaper of the organization. She and Friedan engaged in a tumultuous battle, for Friedan saw herself as queen-mother of the women's movement. Friedan wanted to include women of diverse backgrounds and political opinions. In other words, she believed that women should support other women for political office, no matter what their views or experiences. Friedan was a liberal but not a radical; her focus was on sexual discrimination. She wanted social change but not social upheaval. The group was to be inclusive: different ideas would be tolerated and Republican women would be welcomed to join.

Bella Abzug, Gloria Steinem, and Shirley Chisholm held a different view: they saw women as an oppressed group and married women as slaves. Abzug maintained that the N.W.P.C. women should be homogeneous in their views, ideas, and goals. Ultimately, the ideological war ended in something of a compromise. Abzug and Steinem set certain criteria for considering candidates for membership. Members were expected to support repeal of abortion and contraception laws and to support the ERA Amendment legislation, equal and fair treatment of women in the workplace, and withdrawal from Vietnam. However, individual chapters could set their own standards.

A huge rift developed between Friedan and Steinem that never was resolved. The press adored Steinem with her attractive looks and pleasant personality; Friedan was seen as abrasive, bellicose, and unattractive and not the appropriate leader of the new generation of women. In 1972, *McCall's Magazine* named Gloria "Woman of the Year." Gloria in her mini-skirts was the glamorous, beautiful, brainy darling of the media. Friedan resented this and believed there would be a huge backlash if the radical women continued their claims of female superiority and attacks on traditional family values. Friedan viewed their attitudes as reverse discrimination. As a result, many women left the movement. Friedan considered herself the founder of the first wave of the new feminist movement and the person who most motivated women to change from just being to doing.

Steinem and the other leaders helped establish NOW chapters throughout the country, encouraging and educating women to run for public office. Using her organizing and public relations skills, Steinem helped increase the number of women delegates both to the Democratic and Republican conventions. The goal of N.W.P.C. was to form a power bloc that would exert influence in the delegations and secure their candidates nominations for political spots. Later, they would work tirelessly for their candidates.

In 1972, Steinem founded *Ms. Magazine,* which covered a vast array of women's issues and other material. Just about any action pertaining to women was covered: incest, abortion, rape, sexual harassment in the workplace, inequities in pay in the workplace, spousal abuse, and political issues. The magazine portrayed lesbianism in a positive way. The publication was a huge success. Some groups, however, were offended by the magazine. In 1980, a coalition of Baptists and Mormons in Contra Costa, California put pressure on the school board to ban the magazine, maintaining it contained too much sex. The magazine was later sold in 1987 to an Australian company, and again in 2001 to the Feminist Majority Foundation.

In 2004, Steinem attacked George W. Bush. She argued that if he were elected in 2004, abortion would be criminalized. He was elected, and her prediction did not come to pass. Her adverse criticism of both Presidents George H. W. Bush and George W. Bush was harsh. Steinem endorsed Hillary Clinton in the 2008 campaign. She publicly reiterated Susan B. Anthony's claim that gender is the most restricting force in American life and criticized the media's sexist coverage of Hillary Clinton. On the other hand, she viciously attacked John McCain's vice-presidential choice, Sarah Palin. She declared Palin unrepresentative of the needs and wants of American women.

In addition to her strong political views, Steinem was also concerned with global, social, and moral issues. Against pornography she wrote:

> Blatant or subtle, pornography involves no equal power or mutuality. In fact much of the tension and drama comes from the clear idea that one person is dominating the other.... Whatever the gender of the participants, all pornography is an imitation of

the male-female, conqueror-victim paradigm, and almost all of it actually portrays or implies enslaved women and master. (Sydney L. Stern. *Gloria Steinem*. [Secaucus, New Jersey: Carol Publishing Company, 1997]. 432).

One of the most important issues that Steinem addressed and highlighted for the public is female genital mutilation. In an article in *Ms. Magazine* (March 1979, p.65) titled "The International Crime of Female Mutilation," she wrote: "The real reason for genital mutilation can only be understood in the context of the patriarchy: men must control women's bodies as the means of reproduction, and thus repress the independent power of women's sexuality." She estimated that more than seventy-five million women in the world had suffered from this abominable mutilation by the time she wrote the piece.

The Redstockings, a radical feminist group, attacked Steinem in 1975 with the charge that she had worked for the CIA in the late '50s and early '60s. The CIA was linked to the National Student Association at this time and was recruiting young people to serve as ambassadors of democratic principles to countries under the yoke of Communist ideology. She admitted working for the CIA financed institution at the time but denied further involvement. In actuality, Steinem's duties included writing news releases for the press and other media and for selecting delegates to interview at the Vienna Communist Youth Conference in 1959. The conference was attended by tens of thousands of youths from around the world. Later, she attended a youth conference in Helsinki. The CIA wanted young American college students to participate in formal and informal discussions regarding U.S. and Communist styles of philosophy.

Steinem worried that attending Communist youth festivals would come back to haunt her; it did. The Redstockings accused her of being a "Mata Hari." She was also attacked from the right by Friedan who accused her of using the movement to further her own ends and not being a true feminist.

Steinem actively campaigned for the Equal Rights Amendment. She has participated in nonviolent demonstrations and protests. Also, she has written articles, speeches, and books promoting equality between women and men. She has been a member of the Democratic Socialists of America, co-founder of the Coalition of Labor Union Women, Choice USA, and the Women's Media Center. Steinem was also one of the co-founders of the Women's Action Alliance, which was founded to help women organize at the grass-roots level.

The objectives of the organization included the Non-Sexist Childhood Development Project Information Services, the Women's Centers Project, the Teenage Pregnancy Prevention Project, the Alcohol and Drug Education Project, the Aids Project, and the Resource Mothers Project. Largely funded by New York City and New York State, the Women's Action Alliance was forced to terminate due to the cessation of funding in 1997.

Steinem addressed the founding Conference of the National Women's Political Caucus:

> This is no simple reform. It really is a revolution. Sex and race because they are easy and visible differences have been the primary ways of organizing human beings into superior and inferior groups and into the cheap labor on which this system still depends. We are talking about a society in which there will be no roles other than those chosen or those earned. We are really talking about humanism. (Sydney L Stern. *Gloria Steinem.* [Secaucus, New Jersey: Carol Publishing Company, 1997]. 238).

Steinem's positions sometimes appear contradictory. She is a staunch advocate for children who have been abused in day-care centers and decries the sexual exploitation of women. But surprisingly, Steinem defended Bill Clinton against charges of sexual misconduct brought by White House volunteer Kathleen Wiley. In dealing with the Clinton impeachment hearing, she gave support in an OP/Ed piece in the *New York Times,* March 22, 1998 that a man may: "(1) uninvited, open mouth kiss a woman; (2) uninvited, fondle a woman's breast; (3) uninvited, take a woman's hand and place it on the man's genitals; and as long as the man retreats once the woman says 'no,' that this does not constitute sexual harassment." In popular culture her defense has become known as the "One Free Grope" theory.

Steinem must have changed her mind about marriage, for in 2000 at age sixty-six she married David Bale, an entrepreneur and human and animal rights activist. Their marriage did not last long, for he died four years later at age sixty-two. One of the foremost feminist leaders of the twentieth century, Gloria Steinem, journalist, social critic, and political activist continues writing and lecturing on women's issues.

★ ★ ★

Phyllis Schlafly 1924- conservative political activist and author
She is known for her well organized opposition to the Equal Rights Amendment. (courtesy of Phyllis Schlafly)

Phyllis Schlafly, Sweetheart of the Silent Majority

In opposition to the liberal and radical left of the women's movement, Phyllis Schlafly stands as a conservative voice who argues that women need not cast off their traditional roles of mother and wife. In fact, she is a political activist and anti-"women's libber" who is largely responsible for defeating the ERA. It may seem ironic that she is so militant in her activities against the feminist movement, when she herself has benefited so greatly from the struggle for equality. Schlafly is a constitutional lawyer, editor of a monthly newsletter, political activist, writer, and public speaker. The mother of six children and married to her husband for forty-four years until his death in 1993, she appears to have "had it all" with family and career.

Schlafly was born August 15, 1924, in St. Louis, Missouri. Her father John Bruce Stewart was a machinist and salesman for Westinghouse, dealing mainly with industrial equipment. During the Great Depression, he was unemployed and did not find work until WWII. Schlafly's mother Dadie Dodge Stewart was the daughter of Ernest C. Dodge, a successful attorney. Her father was a descendant of General Henry Dodge, the Indian fighter, and one of her mother's ancestors was Captain Francois Valle, Revolutionary war hero. Well-educated before her marriage, Dadie Dodge Stewart had received an undergraduate degree as well as a graduate degree. She not only kept her own family going during the Great Depression as a librarian and teacher, she also contributed to her parents' support as well. Moreover, Mrs. Stewart was able to maintain Schlafly and her sister in a private Catholic girls' school by working in the school library on her one day off a week. The girls were encouraged to avail themselves of all cultural activities in the community. Even though they had little money, Dadie Stewart raised her daughters to appreciate the finer things of life.

Schlafly learned her work ethic from her mother. From her father, Schlafly learned a conservative philosophy. Perhaps because John Stewart lost his job during the Depression, he believed FDR's programs were socialist and ineffective.

Schlafly never viewed herself as being in an underclass because of her gender; she believed she could reach the highest heights in a so-called "man's world." Attending a private Catholic girls' school, she acquired the foundations, values, and goals for her future academic successes and life's journey.

Schlafly's parents could not afford to send her to college. She won a four-year full-tuition scholarship to Maryville College where she studied for only one year. Her sophomore year she transferred to Washington University as a day student, working forty-eight hours a week to pay her college bills while carrying a full academic load. In 1942, she took a job at the St. Louis Ordinance Factory, testing guns and ammunition for two years to earn enough money to support herself through the rest of her college years.

Political science became her great passion. At age nineteen, Schlafly received her A.B. degree from Washington University in St. Louis. She was also admitted to the prestigious honor society Phi Beta Kappa. Radcliffe College provided her with a fellowship, and in 1945, she graduated with a Master of Arts degree in government. Since Radcliff was closely associated with Harvard, Schlafly attended classes taught by Harvard faculty and in the company with mostly male students. According to her, she was not deprived because of her gender. She held her ground competitively; professors and other students found her brilliant. Later, in 1978, she earned her J.D. degree from Washington University Law School in St. Louis.

After graduation, Schlafly landed a job in Washington with the American Enterprise Association, but she had to learn to type first. The Association analyzed legislation, collected data, and gave summaries on pending legislation for Congressmen. It also provided speech-writers for speeches and press releases. The Association was conservative philosophically and salaries were paid for by major corporations who wanted to advocate free enterprise to legislators. While in Washington, she took a course in public speaking at the U.N. Club of Languages.

Following her year in Washington, Schlafly returned to St. Louis looking for another job. She was hired by Claude Blackwell, incumbent Democrat Congressman, a strong anti-Communist and great supporter of the capitalist system. However, he was fighting a tough Republican candidate that year. Schlafly was a one-man office: she wrote speeches and press releases and acted as secretary, receptionist, and campaign manager. Blackwell focused on the disillusionment of the populace, particularly returning veterans with the New Deal legacy. He was reelected. While working for Blackwell, she was also working for a bank in St. Louis, researching, speech-writing, and acting as librarian.

Running unsuccessfully in 1952 for Congress as a Republican in a Democrat District, Schlafly made her entrance onto the political stage. The woman who could not find anything positive in the women's rights movement surely had to notice how she was portrayed in the newspapers. For instance, the *Globe Democrat* in Alton, Illinois, referred to her as the "powder puff" candidate; references were constantly made about her blonde good looks. During the campaign, Schlafly blasted Truman's handling of the Korean War, New Deal policies, and unchecked spending. She raged against how the government was handling Communism. Yet she never blamed sexism for her defeat.

In 1956, Schlafly was a delegate to the Republican National Convention, and in 1960, she was an alternate. Moreover, she served as president of the Illinois Federation of Republican Women in 1960 and again in 1962.

It was not until 1964 when she published *A Choice, Not an Echo* during the Goldwater campaign that she came to national attention. In her book, she denounced the Rockefeller-led liberal wing of the Republican Party. Schlafly ran for the presidency of the National Federation of Republican Women but was defeated by a more moderate candidate, Gladys O'Donnell. Schlafly's opponents referred to her as a right-wing extremist. She did not take this lying down. Ironically, she fought like a true feminist, arguing that she was not going to take any dictates from men in the Republican Party. In 1970, Schlafly ran unsuccessfully for Congress against incumbent George E. Shipley. Once again, she did not blame sexism as the cause of her defeat, nor did she in 1952 when she lost that election. Of sexism she said, "I don't think it's an issue. If it is, I think it will even out." Although Schlafly could not get elected, she was highly regarded by Congressmen. That same year, she was the only woman invited by the Senate Foreign Relations Committee to state her views on the U.S. Nuclear Test-Ban Treaty.

The ERA battle began in 1971. Schlafly moved her base from the Republican Party to a "grass roots" movement comprised of conservative Catholics, Jews, Mormons, fundamentalists, Republicans, and Democrats. She was the leader and chief strategist; she set up anti-ERA chapters across the country and allowed them to have local control. She maintained, "Feminism is doomed to failure because it is based on an attempt to repeal and restructure human nature."

Schlafly's most significant accomplishment was her effective leadership against the Equal Rights Amendment in the 1970s. The ERA was first introduced to Congress in 1923 and reintroduced every year until 1972 when it was passed by both houses of Congress. However, Article V of the Constitution specifies that in order for an amendment to become part of the Constitution, three quarters of the states must ratify. A prior law passed in 1919 stipulated that states must ratify within seven years. So, in 1973, with six years to spare and only eight more states needed for ratification, it appeared that passage was not going to be a problem. However, nobody foresaw what kind of power Phyllis Schlafly could and would wield. After Schlafly launched her grass-roots opposition to the amendment, five states voted for ratification, but five states voted to rescind. It was Schlafly's zeal and leadership that led to the defeat of the amendment.

In 1970, the ERA amendment was again presented to Congress, and the Hayden clause that had been part of the amendment for twenty years was dropped. "Nothing in the amendment will be construed to deprive persons of the female sex of any rights, benefits or exemptions now conferred by law on persons of the female sex."(Carol Felsenthal. *Phyllis Schlafly.* [Garden City, New York: Doubleday and Company, 1981]. 236). Although benevolent-sounding, that clause only applied to women and, accordingly, implied an inherent inequality between men and women. Under the revised version of the amendment, certain current laws would be exempt—for instance, the requirement of a man to support his wife and children. With no "grandmother" clause to protect them, women who were stay-at-home mothers would be greatly disadvantaged. Similarly, labor laws that sheltered women from being forced to do heavy lifting, to work overtime, or to forego needed rest time would be abolished.

Furthermore, federal aid to women's colleges would be withdrawn simply because of their designation as women's colleges. Women would share equal financial responsibility with their husbands. Consequently, the traditional home would be threatened since women would have to work outside the home. These and other protections for women long ingrained in our society would be obliterated.

Arguing with a group called STOP (Stop Taking Our Privileges), Schlafly pressed the point that if the ERA passed into law, women could be drafted and forced into combat roles. This proved to be a well-founded argument when in 1981, the Supreme Court by a 6 to 3 margin ruled that Congress could only register men for the draft (Rostker V. Goldberg, 453 U.S. 57, 1981). Furthermore, the anti-ERA group maintained that American women would lose their "dependent wife status" under Social Security and public unisex bathrooms would become the norm. In 1980, the Supreme Court by 5-4 vote ruled that Congress could provide funds for childbirth, but not for abortions (Harris v. McRae, 448 U.S. 297, 1980). This was another victory for the Schlafly conservatives. Many state laws have neutralized their family laws where change is much easier. A constitutional amendment is another story.

Along with her strong stand on the ERA, Schlafly believes in and often argues her views on behalf of the capitalist system. In 1977, she wrote in her book *The Power of the Positive Woman*:

> Progress has been the greatest in those areas where there has been private enterprise without government interference, such as automobiles, airplanes, and computers. There is no ceiling on man's ingenuity and resourcefulness to cope with problems—so long as we operate in the American climate of freedom....Progress has been the least in those areas where government has tradionally undertaken the job, namely the postal service, public schools, and garbage collection. (Carol Felsenthal. Phyllis Schlafly. [Garden City, New York: Doubleday and Company, Inc.] 72)

In 2007, Schlafly in a *Washington Post* article blasted the efforts of those who supported a new version of the ERA. She maintained that the courts would approve same-sex marriages and take away Social Security benefits for housewives and widows.

Over the years, Schlafly has taken stands on a variety of issues. She attacked President Truman for mishandling the Korean War; she criticized the foreign policies of Presidents Kennedy and Johnson; she opposed arms-control agreements between the U.S. and Russia; she blamed the judicial system for interfering with American rights of self-government; she opposed space exploration during the 1960s because she felt the nation needed to focus more on building up its nuclear capability. Furthermore, she argued against the war in Vietnam from the beginning, but once we were in, she demanded victory; she was against a shared currency between the U.S., Canada, and Mexico; she opposed a Supreme Court decision abolishing capital punishment for minors; she protested against gay marriage and abortion. In 1996, she opposed President Clinton's sending American troops to Bosnia. She urged the government to halt illegal immigration. She opposed U.S. membership in the United Nations and the World Trade Organization, maintaining America by submitting to a world organization, is sacrificing its sovereignty. She argued: "The people who want to dissolve or diminish American sovereignty and replace it with global governance never give up. Their modus operandi is to work toward their one-world goal incrementally through United Nations treaties."

In 2008, Schlafly spoke out against President George W. Bush and Mike Huckabee. She describes President Barack Obama as an elitist and master of words. She opposed the stimulus package, arguing the federal government under Obama is turning the U.S. into a socialized state. She strongly opposed federal funding for ACORN. She is an advocate of free markets and free enterprise.

In 2012, with Republicans in charge of the House of Representatives, it appears the Republican Party is moving to the right influenced by the Tea Party movement. A woman of many contradictions, Schlafly continues to be a strong voice for conservatives.

Golda Meir 1898-1976 fourth prime minister of the state of Israel She is known as the Mother of Israel. (Wikimedia Commons)

CHAPTER FOURTEEN

Golda Meir, Mother of Israel

"A leader who doesn't hesitate before he sends his nation into battle is not fit to be a leader."

Golda Meir was born in Kiev in the Russian Empire on May 3, 1898. Today Kiev is in Ukraine. Her father Moshe Mabovitch was a carpenter. Her mother Blume Neiditch was the great influence in her life. There were a total of eight children, five of whom died in childhood; only Golda and two sisters survived. Blume Neiditch had expressed her independence as a young woman, choosing her husband herself, instead of letting her parents arrange a marriage for her as was the Jewish custom at the time. Besides being less traditional, she was also less orthodox than most Jews in this era.

With determination, Meir's mother urged her husband to leave for America not only in order to improve their economic status but to obtain greater freedom as well. In Russia, Jews had to live in designated areas and their children had to attend specified schools. Pogroms (persecutions) were a constant threat to the family, and financial ruin was always around the corner.

At age fourteen Sheyna, Meir's sister, joined the Socialist Zionists, revolutionaries dedicated to the overthrow of the Tsar. The young girl was constantly in disfavor with her mother because she associated with the disciples of Theodore Herzl, who promoted the World Zionist Organization. Herzl believed Jews would never be assimilated into European culture; therefore, a Jewish homeland in Palestine was the only solution to their problems. Zion, the small "mountain" of Jerusalem, was the logical place, for it was the spiritual center of Judaism. Judea had been promised to the Jews by their God Jehovah. The Jews had been expelled from this land two thousand years before. Palestine, as the land was also called, was an ignored province of the Ottoman Empire until after World War I when Jewish settlers from Russia had returned. Jewish settlers had begun establishing villages in Palestine as early as 1878.

Theodore Herzl, a Viennese newspaper correspondent based in Paris, became interested in the Captain Alfred Dreyfus Affair. Because of anti-Semitism and injustices he observed in that case and because of the hostility Jews faced all over Europe, he was motivated to promote the founding of a new Jewish homeland. He founded the World Zionist Organization and hence has been called the "Father of Israel."

During the same time, many Russian Jews, viewing socialism as the answer to their problems, gravitated to the General Jewish Labor Union. Jews had often been mistreated not only by the forces of the Tsar but also by ordinary Christian peasants and workers. Sheyna and her Zionist friends developed a philosophy that merged socialism with Zionism. Blume Mabovitch feared her daughter would be arrested and the family sent to Siberia. Listening to her older sister and her friends who used fiery rhetoric, Meir became interested in a Jewish revolution. Sheyna was Meir's heroine, so Meir tried to impress her big sister and to emulate her political views.

While Moshe Mabovitch was establishing himself in America, Meir's mother supported the family; she continued to do so even after the family was reunited in Wisconsin in 1906. Moshe found work doing odd jobs at the local railroad yard in Milwaukee. Eventually his wife arrived with their children, and she quickly found an apartment over a store where she could start a grocery business. At age eight, Meir often was placed in charge of the store while her mother shopped at the various markets for fresh produce and meats.

Not speaking a word of English and with no established credit, Blume Mabovitch dared to take on the risk of a new business. Of course, Meir's father felt somewhat diminished by his wife's courage and enterprise; unfortunately, he was not a good provider. The strong example of Meir's mother became part of her psychological make-up. From her childhood experiences, she realized that her role in life should expand beyond home and family.

In grade school and high school, Meir showed strong self-confidence and leadership qualities. While still in grade school, she organized a fund-raiser with her newly established American Young Sisters Society. She rented a hall and scheduled a meeting to raise money to pay for her immigrant classmates' books. The fund-raiser was a huge success. It was not to be her last. Instead of reading a formal speech, she spoke from the heart; this would be her winning modus operandi for the rest of her life. Her chutzpah was obvious at age eleven. Meir graduated valedictorian from her elementary school.

Meir's mother encouraged her to leave school and marry at age fourteen. Meir rejected the idea, and in order to escape her mother's domination, she went to Denver, Colorado, to live with her older sister Sheyna Korngold. Sheyna had also fled her parents' home to marry the man of her choice. In her sister's home, the political thoughts and ideologies that were discussed and debated greatly influenced Meir. Zionism, women's suffrage, politics, trade unionism, and even literature were hot themes of intellectual argument.

In Denver, Meir met Morris Meyerson, one of the group who hung around her sister's house. The man whom she would later marry was more interested in the arts than politics, but the two lonely souls drifted together. Morris did not feel the same passion for Zionism that Meir did, and so the two clashed often.

Many of Blume's domineering traits were also present in her daughter, Sheyna. Consequently, at age sixteen, Meir again moved on and rented an apartment of her own; Meir could not take any more of her sister's berating.

Meir's father implored his daughter to return home, promising to allow her more freedom. Subsequently, she went back to Milwaukee and graduated from high school in 1915. Soon thereafter she joined Young Poale Zion, which later became Habonim, the Labor Zionist youth movement. The young radicals discussed the future of Palestine's collective farms, and members were encouraged to move to Palestine. Meir taught Yiddish, Jewish literature, and history to immigrant children. She developed her fund-raising skills while working on the executive committee of Poale; she would auction off lunches to raise money for the early settlers in Palestine. These pioneers were building an egalitarian society in their kibbutzes, where a great new just society would develop.

But first, the Turks, who had treated the Jews cruelly, had to be defeated. In 1916, Ben-Gurion and several other Palestinian leaders who had been expelled from Palestine went to Milwaukee to recruit for the Jewish Legion. The Jews wanted to fight on the side of the Allies so that, when they won the war, the Jews could stake their claim in Palestine.

Meir continued her education at Milwaukee Normal School. However, she soon dropped out. She longed to move to Palestine and live in a kibbutz. Therefore, at age nineteen, she married Morris with the stipulation that they move to Palestine. Their plans to move there immediately after their marriage were thwarted by WWI. Transatlantic passenger service was all but stopped during this time. Nevertheless, she continued to work as a Poale Zionist fund-raiser and public speaker.

In 1917, Arthur James Balfour, the British foreign secretary, made it sound like a tantalizing reality that after the war an independent Jewish nation would emerge:

> His Majesty's Government views with favor the establishment in Palestine of a national home for the Jewish people...and will use their best endeavors to facilitate the achievement of this objective. (Elinor Burkett. *Golda.* [New York: Harper Collins, 2006]. 39).

Interestingly, Balfour seems to promise that his nation would give to a second nation a part of a third nation which it did not own. The Turkish Empire still controlled Palestine. Furthermore, the Balfour declaration was made a year before the war ended. The British people were informed of this generous land grant in 1920. The government explained that the concession was in gratitude to Chaim Weizman, who invented a process of fermenting horse chestnuts into acetone for the manufacture of explosives. Weizman later became the first President of the new state of Israel.

It was understood by all that the rights of communities already existing in Palestine were to be protected. Since the British had interests of their own to protect, their mandate continued for thirty more years. Understandably, tensions and disputes arose between the native Arabs and immigrant Jews. The Jews believed that the British tended to be pro-Arab.

In 1918, Meir at age twenty was elected a Milwaukee delegate to the American Jewish Congress. The Congress was called to develop policy positions to be presented at the Paris Peace Conference. The main purpose of the Congress was to formulate a program safeguarding the civil rights of Jews in Europe. A resolution was passed in favor of the formation of a Jewish homeland. Meir promoted this resolution and convinced many of the wealthiest and most prominent Jews in America to support her dream of a Jewish homeland. Her achievements made her even more dedicated to Zionism. About this time, she discovered she was pregnant. In order to dedicate herself to the cause of a new Jewish state, she had an abortion.

Being a mother and housewife were not compatible with her other goals, at least at this time.

In 1921, Meir and her husband moved to Palestine and joined a kibbutz. Meir's sister, Sheyna, accompanied them. Meir saw herself as building socialism in a kibbutz. She was willing to do anything for the cause. Her menial duties included picking almonds, planting trees, cleaning chicken coops, and running the kitchen. In the collective community, there were no salaries, no money, and no private property. But Meir's organizational skills soon became apparent, and she was selected as a representative to the Histadrut, the General Federation of Labor.

At the time, a group of working women led by Ada Maimon demanded that their organization, the Women Worker's Council, be merged and given positions on the executive board of the Histadrut. The women were disenchanted by the way their goals of equality were being handled. Meir made no effort to voice an opinion on the issue but rather called for unity. Hence, Ben-Gurion, David Remez, and other men in the General Federation of Labor were delighted to accept Meir as a colleague. Years later, Ben-Gurion made the remark that she was the only real man in his cabinet.

In 1924, Meir and her husband left the kibbutz and eventually moved to Jerusalem. There, their two children, a son and daughter, were born. Living conditions were difficult in Jerusalem, and Meir was exposed to the Orthodox Jewish theology that was opposed to Zionism. Jerusalem was oppressive for her. Fortunately, at just the right moment, a friend offered her a job in Tel Aviv.

The Women's Council was still giving the men of the Histadrut a hard time with their perceived unreasonable demands. Ada Maimon was appalled at the lack of progress women were making, so she quit the organization. Meir was hired to fill the vacuum and was seen as someone who would work with Histadrut and yet not stand in the way of the aims and goals of the Council's more important issues. Meir never showed much sympathy for women's issues. Her aims were much larger, for she saw Histadrut as a portal to modern Jewish history. Although her job with the Council was minor, she at least had an entrée into Jewish politics.

Histadrut was a big powerful union, which gave its members the right to sick leave, vacations, paid holidays, decent wages, and the right to strike. Founded by Ben-Gurion, it was the driving force of the Jewish economy and Palestine's largest employer. Highly democratic, Histadrut included blue-collar and white-collar workers, intellectuals, manual laborers, agricultural workers, and members who lived in kibbutzes. The Union established a strong foundation upon which the new nation would be built. Ben-Gurion was already formulating plans for the establishment of the Jewish state, and he needed money. Meir, an American Zionist, would prove her worth as his major fund raiser in the United States, France, England, and other European countries.

Meanwhile, thousands of immigrants were pouring into Palestine, and their needs had to be addressed. Ben-Gurion and his associates faced a myriad of problems: transportation, construction, finance, industrial development, housing, and medical and social issues. The components of a new society had to be painstakingly assembled.

As secretary of the Working Women's Council in 1928, Meir served as envoy to the United States from 1932 to 1934. The organization's primary focus was on agricultural training for immigrant girls, a radical idea at the time. In this new socialist society, women performed exceedingly well in the agricultural sector; in fact they did more than their fair share of the work.

On the issue of women's rights, Meir believed that men and women should be treated with equality. Meir did not view herself as a feminist and was not sympathetic to the feminist movement. Like Phyllis Schlafly, Meir maintained she was never hampered by her gender. However, she did recognize the difficult time many women experienced in balancing a career with their roles of wife and mother. For single mothers, the obstacles are colossal. From her own experiences, Meir empathized with working mothers. When she had to leave her children at home, she was torn between her love for them and her dedication to the state of Israel. Israel won.

She maintained that she did only what her country asked of her. Later in life, however, she expressed many regrets about her failures as a wife and mother. But in a way, she had become a mother to all the children of Israel. Many years before, Meir's mother had told the young girl that she would never amount to anything with her crazy political ideas. Perhaps Meir was trying to prove her wrong.

Whenever possible, her children traveled with her. She journeyed across America giving speeches and pleading for financial support for the fledgling Jewish state. Most wealthy Jews were not in support of the socialist homeland; they had succeeded in America as capitalists and were skeptical of the Zionists.

In 1936, attacks against Jews by Arabs greatly increased: trains were derailed; thousands of trees planted by Jewish agricultural workers were ruined; agricultural fields were destroyed; and attacks against Jewish persons were rampant. Many Jews were killed or injured. Jews needed to protect themselves, but exactly how to do that was a matter of debate. Meir argued against counter-terrorism. She believed the criminals who perpetrated such crimes should be punished, but indiscriminate attacks on Arabs for the sake of retaliation were not acceptable. Meir hoped that Arabs and Jews could learn to co-exist peacefully.

Her sexual affairs with David Remez, a prominent figure in the Labor party, and with Zalman Shazar, third president of Israel, were well known. Meir and Morris gradually grew apart and finally separated in 1928. They legally divorced about ten years later. Meir's life was dedicated to Israel, not to her husband or children. She enjoyed working more in the public arena than in the private one, and she also preferred working with men.

Upon returning from the United States in 1934, Meir was appointed to the Executive Committee of the Histadrut. Soon she became head of the political department. One of her responsibilities was to arrange the pay-scale and conditions for Jewish laborers. She also had to continue traveling to America and Europe to attend Zionist and Histadrut meetings.

The Arabs put pressure on the British to stop the Jewish immigration from Germany. Consequently, the British built Army camps across Palestine. With the rise of Hitler, it became painfully apparent to the British and everyone else that something had to be done about the Jewish homeland. The British set immigration standards; the Jews constantly objected to the limitations; and the Arabs constantly accused the British of being their enemies. By 1937, there were already four hundred thousand Jews in Palestine. In order to study the situation in 1938, the British government set up the Peal Commission; its solution was to partition Palestine into two separate states. Finally the Jews could have a homeland, even though it was not the size of their original "promised land." An international enclave would be established in Jerusalem, and a protected corridor would be erected from there to the sea.

While Jewish immigrants kept coming, the Arab population in Palestine also greatly increased. The Arabs flatly rejected the Peal Commission's proposal and diplomacy failed. Neville Chamberlain called another commission, and the original partition plan was deemed non-workable. As thousands of Jews were being killed by Hitler across Europe, Meir worked feverishly day and night to help immigrants from Eastern

Europe and Germany enter the country legally or illegally. In retrospect, she wrote:

> I have sometimes wondered how we got through those years without going to pieces. But perhaps physical and emotional stamina is mostly a matter of habit, and whatever else we lacked, we did not lack opportunities for testing ourselves in times of crisis....One can always push oneself a little bit beyond what only yesterday was thought to be the absolute limit of one's endurance. I don't recall ever having felt tired then so I must have gotten used to fatigue. Like everyone else, I was so driven by anxiety and anguish that no day (or night for that matter) was long enough for everything that had to be done. (Golda Meir. *My Life.* [New York: G.P. Putnam's Sons, 1975]. 166).

In 1938, President Franklin Roosevelt called together a group of thirty-two nations, the Evian Conference, to discuss the plight of the European Jews under Nazism. Meir was not an official delegate but rather an observer. The representatives of the various nations offered all kinds of excuses why the Jews could not be admitted to their states. Her experiences at this conference convinced her that a Jewish state had to be a haven for Jewish people from around the world. Jews had to be masters of their own fate.

In 1939, Prime Minister Chamberlain again limited the number of new Jewish immigrants to seventy-five thousand per year for five years. After that, no Jews would be allowed to immigrate without Arab consent. New immigrants would not be allowed to purchase land. An independent state could be formed within ten years, but Palestine was not to become an exclusively Jewish State. Of course, the Jews were not going to accept these conditions with thousands of Jews being exterminated and persecuted in Europe. With quotas enforced in almost every country, Jewish refugees had no where else to go. A Zionist Conference was held in Geneva that year. Israeli Jews determined they would reject British proposals on quotas for immigration (White Paper), even if it meant war. Ben-Gurion explained: "We shall fight Hitler as if there were no White Paper, and fight the White Paper as if there were no Hitler." (Golda Meir. *My Life.* [New York: G.P. Putnam's Sons, 1975]. 61).

At the end of WWII, Meir joined in the negotiations with the British for the formation of the state of Israel. The Jews believed they were now going to have a homeland. Following many provocative incidents, the English cracked down on the Zionists in 1946. After Moshe Sharett's arrest, Meir became the chief negotiator between the English and Palestinian Jews. In order to stop the vast migration of European Jews, the British turned

Palestine into an armed camp. Hitler murdered six million Jews during WWII, and the seeming human wrecks, like a fearless, feverish flotilla bobbing in a stormy sea that survived, were looking for a second chance in Israel. The British Navy, Army, and Air Force patrolled the coast of Palestine in an effort to catch illegal immigrants as well as their facilitators. With her great compassion for these desperate souls, Golda would often go down to the shoreline under cover of darkness to help those refugees that made it through.

The British fear was that if the Jews kept immigrating in such huge numbers, the Arabs would wage war. So restricting land ownership by Jews was supposed to deter more immigration. The Jews, however, insisted they had the right to purchase and own real estate. The British viewed the Jewish influx as an extremely destabilizing factor. Consequently, the British government mobilized their military forces, and Palestine virtually became a police state. Of those violent times, Golda wrote:

> One miracle was that the Jews still came, in the face of British gas bombs and truncheons, knowing that some might be killed and that all would be shipped off to detention in Cyprus. But the other miracle was that our own children were with us in the struggle. As to the future, these blows have strengthened our determination to demand that full measure of political independence which can only be attained through the establishment of a Jewish state. (Golda Meir. *My Life.* [New York: G.P. Putnam's Sons, 1975]. 200).

Upon Sharett's release, he went to the United States to attend discussions on the United Nations Partition Plan. Golda was left to head the Political Department until the state of Israel was formed in 1948. She became the de facto leader of Palestine. Since Ben-Gurion was in Paris, many Zionist leaders were locked up, and since Weizman was in his declining years, she faced an enormous confluence of problems. Should she comply with the British or endorse the terrorism advocated by Etzel? She faced opposition from Orthodox Jews and many others who saw her simply as a "smart woman" but certainly not of the caliber to lead a nation. Influenced by David Remez (labor leader) who admired Mahatma Gandhi, Meir chose a middle road of peaceful disobedience. But her power was not strong enough to hold back the terrorist forces of Etzel and the Haganah. The King David Hotel, home to the British Secretariat, the Criminal Investigative Agency, and the British Military Command, was bombed on July 22, 1946. Ninety-one people were killed and hundreds more were injured.

The pressures on Meir were enormous. Terrorists were bombing railroad tracks, robbing banks, and attacking police stations. Immigrant ships were being seized and those aboard sent to camps in Cyprus. Militant Jews blew up the British Officers' Club in Jerusalem and stormed prisons. The Jewish population was divided in their opinions. Some were for resistance to the British; others advocated cooperation and peaceful means. While the Jews wanted Meir to control the British, the British wanted Meir to control the Jews.

President Harry S. Truman put tremendous pressure on the world community to have the United Nations carve out the state of Israel in Palestine. In 1947, Prime Minister Clemente Attlee submitted the matter to the United Nations. The United Nations Special Committee on Palestine (UNSCOP) addressed the issue of the partition of Palestine; Jerusalem would be left an international city. On November 29, 1947, the General Assembly of the United Nations by a two-thirds majority voted to establish the Jewish state. Almost immediately, Arabs started attacking Jews, and the British did little to stop it. The Jews were on their own; they would have to defend themselves by themselves. It was up to Meir to raise funds to buy armaments to defend the Jews against the Arabs. Looking like a "dumpy hausfrau," Meir was, nevertheless, a woman of steel. Her rousing, non-honeyed speeches in defense of Israel electrified her audiences everywhere she went.

When Meir traveled to the United States to raise eight million dollars from the Jewish community, she shocked everyone by raising fifty million dollars. Later as Prime Minister, she spent much time obtaining financial support and military aid for Israel. Ben-Gurion said to Meir upon her return, "Some day when history will be written, it will be said that there was a Jewish woman who got the money which made the state possible." (Golda Meir. *My Life.* [New York: G.P. Putnam's Sons, 1975]. 214). Besides the financial aid she got the military aid. Indeed, without Meir and her Jewish supporters in the United States, there would be no Israel. They kept it alive.

Even before her return, Yasir Arafat and the Muslim Brotherhood were sabotaging roads and blowing up water lines. As soon as the British mandate expired, thousands of non-Palestinian Arabs from other nations crossed into Palestine. Ben-Gurion ordered the Jews to the offensive; they secured Haifa, Tiberias, Jaffa, and other cities. Thousands of Palestinian Arabs fled the area and never returned. Meanwhile, Meir was dealing with the left, right, and middle political and religious factions of Jewry.

It seemed as though there was nothing she could not face. In 1948, four days before the official formation of the state of Israel, Meir, disguised as an Arab woman, traveled to Transjordan for a secret meeting with King Abdullah. Meir pleaded with him not to join the other Arab states in attacking Israel. If Abdullah refused to join the Arab League, the Iraqi army would have a more difficult time crossing into Palestine. Arab leaders were vying with each other for the chance to control all or a part of Palestine. King Abdullah suggested that the Jews drop their demand for unlimited immigration. He offered the Jews representation in his parliament when he took over the country. Meir explained that this was impossible; Abdullah joined the Arab League.

Finally, on May 14, 1948, twenty-four signatories, including two women, attached their names to the Israeli Declaration of Independence. Meir broke down and cried. Ben-Gurion, Israel's first Prime Minister, proclaimed: "By virtue of the natural and historic right of the Jewish people and the resolution of the General Assembly of the United Nations, we hereby proclaim the establishment of the Jewish state in Palestine…." (Elinor Burkett. *Golda.* [New York: Harper Collins, 2008]. 146).

On the night the British mandate ended, the British high commissioner, and all military officially departed. The next day, Egypt, Syria, Iraq, Lebanon, and Transjordan attacked Israel in what has become known as the War of Independence. Immediately, Meir was again dispatched to the U.S. to raise money for armaments; she returned with seventy-five million dollars in financial aid.

Receiving the first official Israeli passport, Golda served as the first ambassador to the Soviet Union in 1948. Russia, the second nation to recognize Israel after the United States, was a staunch supporter of Israel and offered to sell arms to the new nation. No doubt Russia wanted to keep Britain out of the Middle-East. Israel chose to stay neutral during the Cold War for its own advantage. However, Stalin assumed correctly that Israel ultimately would become a supporter of the West.

The safety and welfare of the Jews in Russia was a major concern of Meir. On one occasion when Meir was visiting Russia, she attended a high-holiday service at the Moscow synagogue where thousands chanted her name. This was a tremendously moving experience. The people were there to celebrate the state of Israel, and Meir was the symbol of that state. Moreover, the Israeli government in November of 1948 honored her with her image on the ten thousand shekel banknote, with her portrait on one side and an image of the crowd that cheered her in Moscow on the other.

Meir was later recalled from Moscow after Stalin cracked down on the Jews. It appeared, at least to the Communists, that the Russian Jews were more loyal to Israel and their Jewish heritage than to the Communist state.

Meir was elected to the Knesset in 1949 as a member of Mapai, a powerful left-wing political party. Shortly afterwards, she became Minister of Labor and served from 1949 to 1956. Since she viewed Israel as an egalitarian, socialist state, she instituted many social and economic reforms. She developed public works such as new roads, schools, hospitals, huge agricultural and industrial developments, thirty thousand houses, and two hundred thousand apartments. In addition, she strove to find or create new jobs for seven hundred thousand refugees located in tent cities across Israel. The hardworking Minister of Labor was not just interested in the security and welfare of Jews.

Furthermore, as Labor Minister she saw to it that roads were built connecting Arab villages and that water was piped into their homes. Sympathetic towards Arab women and aware of their sensibilities, she fostered education and trade skills for them, so they could become independent and self-supporting. Researching areas for industrial and agricultural development, Meir plodded on with her dreams for an egalitarian nation.

Ben-Gurion advised Meir to run for mayor of Tel Aviv since he viewed her as the only viable candidate. However, she needed the votes of two men of the religious bloc, and one of them denied her his vote simply because of her gender. Even to this day, the Orthodox religious bloc periodically causes political problems even though Orthodox Jews constitute no more than 10 percent of the population. Meir was furious because of the great contributions she and other women had made to the building of the state. She did consent to remain as Labor Minister, so her work continued.

In 1952, Meir supported the establishment of a social security system: women over sixty and men over sixty-five were to receive benefits; orphans, widows, and widowers were to receive pensions; pregnant women were to receive free medical care, maternity leave, and job security. Labor laws provided mandatory rest periods, vacations, and a minimum wage. Meir's dream of the democratic socialist state of Israel was finally a reality.

In 1953, she sponsored the Bill for Compulsory Service for Women, allowing Orthodox females to serve in hospitals, schools, or other social services, instead of serving in the military. The Orthodox community greatly opposed this measure, deeming it inappropriate for the government to dictate how women were to live their lives.

Arab attacks continued against Israel, causing great consternation. The U.N. proved to be ineffective against the fedayeen (terrorist group) that attacked Jewish settlements. The raiders bombed water lines, tore up roads, and killed and injured innocent women and children. Moshe Dayan, head of Defense Forces, together with Moshe Sharrett and Ariel Sharon retaliated in vicious fashion and promoted extremism against the Arabs. Ben-Gurion wanted to rein in his arrogant young rebels and replaced Sharrett with Meir as Foreign Minister. She served in this capacity from 1956 until her retirement in 1965. Never speaking in opaque terms, the force of her personality and direct tone marshaled much respect and sympathy for the new nation the world over.

She also represented Israel in the United Nations and circled the globe as the spokesperson for her country. The U.N., under Secretary Generals Dag Hammarskjold and U Thank, was never able to prevent war between the Arabs and Jews. Athough at various times a cease fire would be arranged, the hostilities continued. The U.N. seemed powerless to address Israeli and Arab complaints.

In 1956, Egypt nationalized the Suez Canal and refused to allow Israeli shipping to pass. Egypt then signed a pact with Syria, uniting their forces against Israel with the intention of wiping the new nation off the map. Israel could not just lie down and decided to go it alone. Although Britain and France planned to act militarily against Egypt, they did not actually do so.

The Sinai Peninsula, with its great military fortifications and weaponry supplied by Russia, seemed to provide a safe haven for the fedayeen. The Arab forces could easily attack inside Israeli territory and kill Israelis, while the U.S. and Great Britain merely observed.

But the relatively small Israeli army, which consisted mainly of male and female reservists and a few fighter planes, fought back with surprising ferocity and determination. The Arab forces were stunned by the rapidity with which Israel captured the Sinai Peninsula, the Gaza strip, and the strategically important Straits of Tiran.

Within a mere hundred hours, the combined Arab forces were totally defeated. The Israelis, along with British and French troops, took control of the Suez Canal Zone. However, the U.N. demanded that they all withdraw their forces immediately. Since the Israelis had performed a preemptive strike, it seemed to the world that the Israelis were the aggressors, in spite of the fact that Israel was being attacked on a daily basis. The U.N. insisted that Israel give up the occupied land and retreat to the armistice line of 1949. The U.S. and Russia also denounced the Israeli position, fearing that war in the Middle East could throw the world into WWIII. President Eisenhower even threatened sanctions against Israel.

Meir addressed the U.N. numerous times during the several months of peace negotiations. On one occasion she stated:

> And now may I add these few words to the states in the Middle East area, and more specifically, to the neighbors of Israel? Can we from now on, all of us, turn a new leaf, and instead of fighting among each other, can we all, united, fight poverty, disease, and illiteracy? Can we, is it possible for us to put all our efforts, all our energy, for one single purpose…the betterment and progress and development of all our lands and all our peoples? (Golda Meir. *My Life*. [New York: G.P. Putnam's Sons, 1975]. 308).

In the end, Israel retained the right to navigate the Strait of Tiran, and a U.N. Emergency Force occupied Gaza and the Sharem el-Sheikh area of the Sinai. At least for the time being, the fedayeen were under control.

Meir changed her name from Meyerson to Meir in 1956 at the request of her predecessor in the Foreign Ministry, Moshe Sharett, who wanted all members of the Foreign Service to "Hebrew-ize" their last names.

Meir was slightly injured in 1957 when a "mills" grenade was thrown into the debating chamber of the Knesset. David Ben-Gurion and Moshe Carmel were more seriously injured. A mentally disturbed young man who had a grievance against the Jewish Agency was the culprit.

In 1963, Israel was caught lying to the Americans about its nuclear facility Dimona. Meir argued against Ben-Gurion, Peres, Abba Eden, and Dayan about shading the truth. At this time she felt side-lined by Ben-Gurion.

Nonetheless, continuing her diplomatic role, she fostered ties with Africa in order to gain support in the international community. She believed Israeli involvement with the emerging African nations was more than self-interest. Israel's International Cooperation Program rendered much technical, medical and agricultural aid, and knowledge in many other areas to the newly formed African states. Furthermore, she thought Israel could serve as a model for the newly formed nations. In her biography, she wrote:

> Like them, we had shaken off foreign rule; like them, we had to learn for ourselves how to reclaim the land, how to increase the yields of our crops, how to irrigate, how to raise poultry, how to live together, and how to defend ourselves...had been forced to find solutions to the kind of problems that large, wealthy, powerful states had never encountered. (Golda Meir. *My Life*. [New York: Dell Publishing Co., 1975]. 308-309).

In 1960, Meir along with Sweden's Inga Thorsson and Israel's Mina-Ben-Zvi, founded the Mount Carmel International Training Center for Community Services. Thousands of women from Asia, Africa, and South America traveled to Israel to learn first hand about medical services and social services, such as family planning and proper nutrition. The knowledge they gained they took back with them to their respective countries. Many were trained as social workers, and Israeli men and women went to small villages in East Africa where they shared their knowledge in their respective fields. Thus, every life these pioneer men and women touched reflected the universal concerns human beings shared everywhere for their own lives and that of their children.

The wartime Pope, Pius XII, remains even today a controversial figure in history. Many saw him and still view him as not being pro-active enough against the Nazi oppressors. However, after his death, Meir praised his work on behalf of the Jewish people.

In 1967, the head of the Egyptian Army ordered all United Nations forces out of the Sinai. The U.N. troops had been there since 1957 as a reprisal for Egypt's preemptory action against Israel. Egypt immediately began massing troops and military equipment along Israel's borders. King Hussein of Jordan placed his troops under Egyptian control. A new terrorist organization called El Fatah was once again attacking Israeli settlements from the Gaza Strip to Jordon. Under Yasir Arafat, this group became the most powerful element of the Palestine Liberation Organization.

In defiance of the U.N. mandate, Egyptian President Nasser closed the Straits of Tiran to Israeli shipping. The western capitols fell silent. Meir was embroiled with the war ministry in the decisions affecting national security. Clearly, once again she realized Israel would have to go it alone. Moshe Dayan, the military leader, advocated another preemptive strike and eventually Meir supported him. The Israeli Air Force within a few hours knocked out the Egyptian, Jordanian, and Syrian Air Forces. Meanwhile, ground troops captured the Golan Heights from Syria and recaptured the Gaza Strip and Sinai that Israel had returned to the Arabs ten years before.

The old city of Jerusalem now was in Israeli hands. This war was known as the Six Days War; again the Arabs were soundly defeated on all fronts.

In the early sixties, Golda was diagnosed with lymphoma. The tremendous burdens she bore surely affected her health. In order to rest, she retired from the Foreign Ministry. When her health and strength were restored, she returned to public life as Secretary General of the Mapai Party. After the Six-Day War, she successfully kept together the new coalition government when Mapai merged with two other political parties (Rafi and Ahdut HaAvoda) to form the Israel Labor Party. She backed Prime Minister Levi Eshkol in party disputes. When Eshkol died in 1969, members of the Knesset pressured Meir to run for the office of Prime Minister. Meir was elected and served from 1969 to 1974.

Meir had a great vision of peace for the Middle East. She called to Israel many of the world's great leaders, including Richard Nixon, Pope Paul VI, Willy Brandt, and Nicolae Ceausescu. She accepted a U.S. proposal for peace in 1970 that called for an end to the wars of attrition. Israel pledged to recognize and return to its boundaries in the framework of a peace settlement. But she insisted on maintaining control of some strategic areas. Many in Israel wanted to make peace with the Arabs, while others wanted to annex as much Arab territory as they could. Her bargaining chip, to her way of thinking, was the occupied territories.

However, the United Nations and most of the rest of the world did not agree. How could a nation bargain with land seized from another nation? Yet Egyptians were shelling Israeli positions in the Sinai, and Jordan was harboring nests of fedayeen that attacked Israeli villages. The Arabs, and most world opinion, demanded that Israel relinquish land it had taken during the 1967 confrontation before peace treaties were arranged. Meir's argument was that she needed buffer zones to protect her people. The land in the north was needed to protect the Jewish settlements from the Syrians; the Strait of Tiran was necessary for commerce; and land in the south was required for security against Egyptian troops amassed on the Israeli border. The struggle for Israeli and Arab nations' borders goes on to this day.

Additionally, Israel was plagued with internal problems at the same time. Israel had moved from the Zionist socialist state of the founding fathers and mothers to an economy based on capitalism. There was still great disparity between the rich and poor; this was not the society Meir envisioned.

The Munich Massacre at the Summer Olympics in 1972 shocked the world. Meir did not think enough was being done to bring the murderers to justice. So she ordered the Black September and PFLP operatives to track down the assassins. Once again, Israel took matters into its own hands. With her intelligent and grandmotherly approach, Meir often manipulated the younger generation of politicians to do her bidding.

The Yom Kippur War in 1973 was a critical time for Israel. When Meir heard Syrian troops were massing on the Golan Heights, she realized Israel would need to have foreign aid to repel an invasion. Normally it took a cabinet decision to call for full mobilization of the troops, but Meir was granted emergency power. General David Elazar recommended that Israel launch a full scale pre-emptive attack, whereas Minister of Defense and cabinet member Moshe Dayan argued for a more restrained approach. He wanted to call up just two divisions and the Air Force.

Meir agreed with Dayan believing that Israel could not go it alone. However, many thought Dayan was surrendering to the Arabs. If Israel attacked Syria, she feared the U.S., Israel's major ally, would not support Israel. Meanwhile, Meir kept in touch with Washington, primarily with Henry Kissinger. He later informed her that if Israel had engaged in a pre-emptive strike, she would have received no assistance. In the end, Israel won the war but at the cost of twenty-five hundred Israeli lives. Russia once again sent Egypt and Syria planes and military equipment. The U.S. helped, however, by supplying arms and financial aid to Israel.

After the Yom Kippur War, many in the government decried Israel's lack of preparedness before the war. There were calls for Meir's and Dayan's resignations. The Agranat Commission, appointed by the government to investigate the war, cleared Meir of direct responsibility for the war and related activities:

> ...She decided wisely, with common sense and speedily, in favor of the full mobilization of the reserves, as recommended by the chief-of-staff, despite weighty political considerations, thereby performing a most important service for the defense of the state. (Golda Meir. *My Life.* [New York: G.P. Putnam's Sons, 1975]. 452).

The labor coalition broke up in 1974 mainly because of the handling of the war; Meir believed it was time to step down. In 1975, she was awarded the Israel Prize for her outstanding service to the nation. Meir died of cancer on December 8, 1978, at the age of eighty; she was buried on Mount Herzl in Jerusalem.

Meir was a vibrant leader whose entire life was dedicated to politics and the implementation of socialist principles in everyday life. With extraordinary foresight, this dedicated Zionist helped give birth to a nation and guide it through five perilous wars.

Possessed of an iron will, engaging personality, and grandmotherly image, Golda was a brilliant, formidable leader on the world stage. Like Margaret Thatcher, this "iron lady" saw herself as a leader who just happened to be a woman. Her accomplishments and contributions mark her as one of the world's great leaders of the twentieth century.

Indira Ghandi 1917-1984 She was elected third Prime Minister of independent India in 1967, the first woman elected to lead a democracy. (Wikimedia commons donation to Library of Congress by U.S. News and World Report)

CHAPTER FIFTEEN

Indira Gandhi, Democratic Leader of India

"And if I died in the service of the nation, I would be proud of it. Every drop of my blood...will contribute to the growth of this nation and to make it strong and dynamic."

Indira Gandhi nee Nehru was born on November 19, 1917, in Allahabad, United Provinces, British India. She was the only child of Jawaharial and Kamula Nehru. The Nehrus were a prominent Kashmiri Pandit family. Growing up in the Brahmin caste, the highest Indian social class, Gandhi experienced all the luxuries life could offer. Her grandfather, Motilal Nehru, favored all things British, so the young adults in the family were sent to England to be educated at Oxford or Cambridge. However, he followed certain Indian customs such as arranging the marriage of his son, Jawaharial, to Kamula Kaul. Unfortunately, their marriage was not a happy one. Whereas Jawaharial was an Oxford-educated attorney, Kamula was uneducated and childlike. The other women in the Nehru family frequently criticized and ridiculed her. Yet young Gandhi learned much about Indian traditions and the Hindi language from the long hours she spent with her mother. Nevertheless, she was determined she would never let herself be treated as contemptuously as her mother had been. Since her father was often away on business, Indira became greatly attached to her grandfather, who treated her kindly and generously.

In 1926, Kamula Nehru was stricken with tuberculosis. Subsequently, she, Gandhi, and Jawaharlal traveled to a sanatorium in Bex, Switzerland. Gandhi attended a French school there and learned French. This experience was one of the most memorable of her life. It felt like a vacation. She was able to enjoy the love of both parents without the distractions of life in

India. While Kamula's treatments slowed the progress of the disease, she eventually died of tuberculosis in 1936.

Gandhi grew up lonely as she was almost always in the company of adults. A child of the aristocracy did not mingle with lower class children. At an early age, she watched her father and grandfather taken off to jail for civil disobedience.

Her grandfather, Motilal Nehru, was one of the great nationalist leaders. A prominent wealthy lawyer, he was one of the most important members of the Indian National Congress in pre-Gandhi times. He wrote the Nehru report that expressed a future system of government as opposed to the British system. His son, Jawaharial Nehru, was a prominent lawyer who played an important role in the revolutionary movement against the British. He joined with Mahatma Gandhi in finally gaining Indian independence. Later, Jawaharial became the first Prime Minister of independent India.

When Gandhi was about six, she met Mahatma Gandhi (no relation) who was like a "great uncle" and who acted as an adviser to the child. He remained a great influence throughout her life. Mahatma Gandhi advocated civil disobedience, nonviolent protests against British taxes and laws, and boycotts of British imports and schools. Gandhi maintained that keeping people in ignorance was the worst level of poverty. In protest, Indians burned English clothes and books in a symbolic bonfire. Many were arrested, including Gandhi's father. As a child, Gandhi often visited her father, grandfather, relatives, and friends in jail. She often dreamed she was Joan of Arc leading her people to freedom.

During a peaceful civil-disobedience protest against a salt tax imposed by the British in 1930, Mahatma Gandhi led a two hundred and forty mile march to the sea. He and the marchers extracted salt from the sea water in a representative gesture. The women of India, as never before, from every level of society, rose up in defiance. Tens of thousands demonstrated, and Gandhi's mother left her sick bed to join the resistance.

The primary importance of the march to the sea was the symbolism expressed, for with the English monopoly on salt and the salt tax, it seemed to the Indians that the occupiers controlled the pulse of India. Nothing lives without water and salt. It was illegal for Indians to manufacture or sell salt without a government license, thus giving absolute control to the English.

To understand the development of Gandhi's ideas, ideals, and political attitudes, it is necessary to know something about the events that led to

India's struggle for independence from Great Britain. India came under the rule of the British government in 1858 although the English-owned East India Company had effectively ruled there from as early as 1757. In spite of sporadic attempts at rebellion, most Indians had grown to accept British rule. Many Indians served in the British army and were heralded for their loyalty and courage.

Both Gandhi's grandfather and father had been satisfied to work as lawyers within the British legal system where they were granted a degree of self-regulation for Indian subjects. Political parties, for example, were allowed to exist.

An event occurred on April 13, 1919, that changed Indian history forever and certainly changed Gandhi's life. On that day in the holy city of Amritsar in the northern state of Punjab, twenty thousand unarmed people were gathered in a city park to attend a protest and to celebrate the Hindi New Year. At the time, Britain ruled India as a colonial colony. The British General Reginald Dyer marched one hundred and fifty troops into the park and without warning fired on the crowd killing three hundred and seventy-nine people and injuring over fifteen hundred. Thus ended the great love affair between India with Britain, and the Nehrus now focused on the fight for independence.

The National Congress called for protests and acts of civil disobedience. Throughout the land, the Nehrus, father and son, were arrested on several occasions, as was Mahatma Gandhi and many others. In one instance, Gandhi's father had hidden vital secret papers in the family car. A police inspector stopped the car in order to search it, but Gandhi cleverly pleaded with him not to delay them, or she would be late for school. The search was discontinued.

At age twelve, the girl further revealed her astuteness and leadership skills. She became the leader of the "Monkey Brigade," an anti-British children's group that served as spies and couriers. The young people also conducted patriotic flag marches and protests and helped in their national cause in anyway they could.

The British-controlled police frequently harassed and raided the Nehru household. Their goods and animals were frequently confiscated and family members arrested.

Disenchanted with British schools, Gandhi's parents sent her to a series of Indian schools and non-Indian schools, and at times, she had private tutors. In 1934, when Gandhi was sixteen, she was enrolled at the

Visva Bharatic Academy where the famous writer Rabindranath Tagore was headmaster.

With constant threats confronting her and her family, Gandhi had become somewhat shy and introspective, but under Tagore's guidance and instruction, she blossomed. She absorbed his philosophy and gained a love of the arts. She translated one of her favorite poems composed by Tagore into English from Bengali.

If in the storm troubled nights,
they dare not hold aloft the light,
O, hapless me.
Ignite your own heart with the lightening and pain,
and yourself become the guiding light.

After her mother's death, Gandhi at age eighteen attended the progressive Badminister School in Bristol, England. The school focused on liberal ideas of social justice and an egalitarian, democratic philosophy. Upon graduation, she enrolled in Somerville College, Oxford University. But the young student was more interested in politics and world affairs than in her academic studies. She joined the radical pro-independence India League. As a dedicated socialist, she enlisted recruits for the Spanish International Brigade. She even sold some of her jewelry to support the Republicans in Spain. And when Japan attacked China, she boycotted Japanese goods and raised money to help the Chinese.

While at school in England, Gandhi met another Indian student, Feroze Gandhi, who had a former connection to her family. He had helped care for her invalid mother. Feroze Gandhi and Indira shared an interest in socialist and communist theory, and they grew to be very fond of each other spending all their week-ends together. When they both returned to India in 1941, they announced their intention to marry. Gandhi's father objected; he even sought Mahatma Gandhi's help in dissuading the couple. Since Feroze Gandhi was a Zoroastrian–not a Hindu, and of a lower social position, the Nehru family believed the marital union would be a mistake. Gandhi and Feroze were adamant, and they were married in a Hindu ritual ceremony in 1942.

The couple soon joined the "Quit India" resistance movement. These freedom fighters used tactics such as blowing up police stations, railroad lines, bridges, and courthouses. The British retaliated by using tear gas and imprisoning many Indians. While Feroze Gandhi was hiding underground, his wife was sheltering rebels in their home. Eventually, they were both arrested and sent to jail on charges of subversion. They remained in jail from September 1942 to May 1943.

Upon their release, Jawaharial Nehru arranged a job for his son-in-law as managing editor of the National Herald. No doubt, Feroze Gandhi looked forward to a more settled, quiet life. He had hoped that Gandhi would become a traditional Indian homemaker in the tradition of their mothers. Up to that point in their marriage, Gandhi had been involved with Feroze and her own father in revolutionary activities. Then a year after the couple's release from prison, she gave birth to their first son Rajiv. Two years later her second son Sanjay was born.

But along with her new maternal duties, Gandhi continued to work for the freedom of her country and to assist her father and grandfather in their efforts to establish a new independent nation.

When World War II ended, the British faced many internal problems at home. Dealing with India became a problem Britain did not need. Then in 1947, after a long history of rule in India that began in the mid 1700s, Britain decided to sever its ties.

The former colony of India was divided into two separate nations: Pakistan, which became home to a mostly Muslim population and India, a secular democratic nation, composed mainly of Hindus. When the British troops and bureaucrats withdrew peacefully, they left behind a highly incendiary situation.

Six months after independence, the "Father of the Nation" Mahatma Gandhi, was assassinated by a Hindu fanatic. The somewhat hastily and arbitrary partition of the land caused animosity between Muslims on the one hand and Hindus, Jains, Buddhists, and Sikhs on the other. Many thousands were killed in senseless slaughter; both Muslim and Hindu women were raped, mutilated, or killed.

In 1947, Jawaharial Nehru became the first Prime Minister. Since her mother's death in 1936, Gandhi had acted as her father's chief-of-staff, confidant, and special aide. Now she took on the official role of First Lady, in which she could apply the governance, politics, and negotiation she had learned from her father.

Her first rung up the political ladder was her election in 1953 to the Congress Party Working Committee. Next, she served within the Women's Department of the Congress Party focusing on women's interests. She traveled the country informing women of their rights and responsibilities. In 1959, she was only the fourth woman elected president of the Indian National Congress.

For a time, Gandhi and her husband Feroze were members of the Indian National Congress, but they did not agree about their aims for the country. Feroze was later elected to the lower house of the Indian Parliament, Lok Sabha. Never fond of his wife's father, Feroze attacked Prime Minister Nehru and his political friends and allies. As an avowed supporter of Communism, Feroze opposed the anti-communist policies of Nehru and his daughter. It was no wonder that Feroze and his wife were separated.

When Feroze, who was still Gandhi's opponent in the Parliament, had a heart attack, they reunited so she could take care of him. Gandhi withdrew from most political activity until her husband died in 1960 of another heart attack. Then she went back into the public fray with a vengeance. She became an official representative of India, appearing before the United Nations and speaking to the heads of many nations. She was also the personal representative of her father and his trusted adviser.

Jawaharial Nehru died in 1964 after a stroke. He was succeeded in office by Lai Bahodu Shastri. The new Prime Minister selected Gandhi to be the Minister of Broadcasting and Information. The post was very important because so many illiterate Indians relied on radio for news about their society. She distributed inexpensive radios and increased the number of radio stations and the scope of their programs. She even initiated programs on family planning, which encouraged the use of birth control. Overpopulation and a high birth rate were serious problems for India at that time—and still are—as were the rioting and disputes among ethnic groups and regions. Gandhi used the media to try to calm down the fear and anger of the people. Her exposure to the media made her famous and rather popular.

When Prime Minister Shastri died in 1966, Gandhi was ready to take his place. She traveled about the country, campaigning in urban areas and farm villages. She gave hope to the poor and downtrodden who viewed her like a mother ministering to their pain. On one occasion, an irate onlooker hit her in the face with a stone, and Gandhi undismayed continued her speech and went on to win the election.

As new Prime Minister, Gandhi traveled to the United States to seek financial aid for her starving people. President Lyndon Johnson promised her three million tons of grain and nine hundred million dollars in project aid. Fortunately, for Gandhi, the drought soon ended, and agricultural output increased greatly, largely due to government support and innovative methods. Gandhi and her National Congress Party's slogan became

"Abolish Poverty," and they attempted to do so by socialist practices and policies.

In 1969, Gandhi nationalized the banks. Then in 1971, she nationalized the insurance and coal industries. Amendments to the Constitution stressed societal rights over individual rights and exempted the new amendments from judicial review. During this period, Gandhi grew closer to the Soviet Union and further from the U.S. and the west. A massive government program that would provide economic development and direct assistance to the poor failed, due to widespread corruption among government officials at all levels. Only a small portion of the money ever reached the very poor.

Relations between Pakistan and India had never been amicable since partition in 1947. There had been on-going disputes over the border lines, particularly in Kashmir. The dispute continues to this day. There had already been wars between the fledgling nations in 1947 and 1964. In 1971, Prime Minister Indira Gandhi again declared war against Pakistan because of alleged mistreatment of Indians by the Pakistan military in East Pakistan. Moreover, Pakistan had attacked India. The war lasted only thirteen days and India was victorious. A major result of the war was the secession of East Pakistan from West Pakistan and a new government for (West) Pakistan.

To strengthen India against constant threats from both Pakistan and China, Gandhi initiated a secret nuclear program. In 1974, India exploded its first atomic bomb and thereby raised Indian's status as a future world power and enhanced its own security and stability. As a further means of protecting her nation from foreign aggression, Gandhi signed a treaty with the Soviet Union to foster peace, friendship, and cooperation between the two nations. In retaliation the United States, under President Richard Nixon, cut off all economic and military aid to India while continuing its support of Pakistan. In 1972, Gandhi met with the new Pakistani president to sign a formal peace treaty, which guaranteed the independence of Bangladesh, the former East Pakistan, and the return of ninety thousand prisoners of war.

In spite of her great popularity among the poor, Gandhi's government in the 1971 election was accused of corruption and election malpractices. In 1975, the Allahabad High Court found Gandhi guilty of election fraud. Her election as a Minister of Parliament was invalidated, and she was barred from holding elected office for six years. She was entitled to an appeal but that would have to wait for months.

Gandhi's younger son Sanjay organized massive rallies in support of his mother. He forced government employees to attend and used the public transit system to transport supporters to pro-Gandhi demonstrations. At the same time, Gandhi persuaded President Ahmend to declare a national state of emergency. Gandhi maintained that she was denying democratic rights in order to preserve democracy. For two years, Gandhi ruled as a virtual dictator: she forced her opponents out of parliament and many were arrested; broadcasting was placed under the control of the central government and newspapers were censured; freedom of speech and assembly were denied; political organizations were banned; and habeas corpus was suspended. Indira allowed no opposition ministers to remain in power.

The effects of her autocratic behavior were not all bad. Gandhi instituted a twenty-point program designed to pull India into the twentieth century: crime was reduced; price controls were put into effect; homes were constructed for the homeless; schools and clinics were built; fewer people were without adequate food and clothing. The lives of millions of Indians were improved, and India's economy became one of the fastest growing in the world. In addition, she promoted science and technology to the extent that India soon launched its first satellite into space. She used her army to repress ethnic and regional disputes. In international affairs, she maintained good relations with both China and Russia, while continuing a stance of neutrality during the Cold War.

In spite of her good intentions, corruption among government officials was rampant. Gandhi's son, Sanjay Gandhi, extorted money from industrialists to finance his own car company. Sanjay, without official government sanction, engaged in a series of unethical and illegal actions in support of his mother's policies. To control the size of the population, Sanjay ordered the mass sterilization of men, especially Muslims. An estimated number of seven million forced vasectomies were performed. To eradicate slums, he forcibly relocated tens of thousands to vacant land twenty miles away, with the result that many died and many others were left homeless. Government employees such as doctors, teachers, and policemen were paid their salaries only if the required quota of vasectomies was achieved.

Notwithstanding all the chaotic events that took place in India, Gandhi in 1977 allowed free elections; she and her Congress Party were soundly trounced. In the end all charges against her seemed to evaporate, so she decided to rebuild the Congress Party and start over again. She was reelected in 1980 while her son, Sanjay, was elected to the lower house of Parliament, the Lok Sabha. As Prime Minister for the fourth time, Gandhi had made many enemies and had severe problems to face. When Sanjay was killed in a flying accident, Gandhi had to face her problems alone. The masses of the poor were still homeless, hungry, and illiterate. The modernization of factories left unskilled workers, especially women, unemployed and without financial support for themselves or their families. Even middle-class women's situations had not improved in terms of education, careers, or economic opportunity. But by far, the most threatening problem was the discontent of the Sikhs in northwestern India.

The Sikh people believed they were being exploited by the Hindus with the approval of the national government. The radical Sikhs wanted to secede and form a separate independent state. There were numerous public protests and violent clashes. Many radical Sikh terrorists attended the Golden Temple in Amritsar, Punjab. Of course, many moderate Sikhs also worshipped in the temple. In 1984, Gandhi ordered a military assault on the Golden Temple; the attack was called by the code name "Operation Bluestar." Hundreds of innocent civilians, including some women and children, were gunned down in the cross-fire. The holy place itself was severely damaged and stripped of any valuable trappings. In addition, the revered Sikh leader, Jarnail Sigh Birdranwalw, was killed in the battle. Although the rebellious Sikhs were subdued for the time being, Gandhi and her government had earned the everlasting hatred of the Sikhs.

Not unaware that her own life was in constant danger, Gandhi was assassinated on October 31, 1984. The attack was an act of revenge perpetrated by two of her own Sikh bodyguards. Perhaps foreseeing her death, Gandhi once pronounced these words:

> I am here today, I may not be here tomorrow...Nobody knows how many attempts have been made to shoot me...I do not care whether I live or die. I have lived a long life and I am proud that I spent the whole of my life in the service of my peoples. I am only proud of this and nothing else. I shall continue to serve until my last breath and when I die, I can say that every drop of my blood will invigorate India and strengthen it. (Katherine Frank. *Indira.* [London: Harper Collins Publishers, 202]. 490).

Unfortunately, the assassination provoked a new wave of sectarian violence, and thousands of Sikhs were murdered and looting and arson raged across the land.

Soon after Gandhi's death, her body was cremated, and her only surviving son, Rajiv, flew to Karachi and scattered her ashes over the Himalayas as she had requested. As his mother's heir apparent, Rajiv reluctantly became the sixth Prime Minister. His administration, like that of his mother, was marred by charges of bribery, extortion, and corruption of many sorts. Inflation sky-rocketed and the rich were allowed to get much richer and the poor, poorer. Rajiv was assassinated in 1991 by members of the Tamil Tigers Organization. Carrying on the family tradition in politics, Rajiv's widow, Sonia Gandhi joined the Congress Party in 1997 and rose to become party leader in 1998. She was elected to the Lok Sabha or lower house of the Indian Parliament in 1999 and again in 2004 and 2008. In the 2004 election, Sonia Gandhi was unanimously selected to lead a fifteen-party coalition government subsequently named the United Progressive Party. While it was generally expected that she would take the post of Prime Minister for herself, she instead supported Man Mohan Singh for the position. Her supporters said she had carried out an unselfish act of renunciation.

Sonia Gandhi is currently chairperson of the U.P.P. (Uttarakhand Parivartan Party). Under her leadership, the U.P.P. won by a near majority in the 2009 general election. A fifth generation of the Nehru-Gandhi political dynasty is represented by Rajiv's and Sonia's son and daughter-in-law, Rahul and Priyanha.

Indira Nehru Gandhi rose to the highest political heights in Indian history, serving as Prime Minister for fifteen years. She served as the first and last female Prime Minister of India. The fact that India has survived as the world's largest democracy for more than sixty years is testimony to the fact that she laid the foundation and vision for her country. Indeed, the democracy has its flaws but still lives. In spite of corruption, the country still maintains freedom of speech, religion, and press. There still exists a parliament and judiciary. Gandhi was responsible for keeping the Indian people together. She once said: "Have a bias toward action—let's see something happen now. You can break that big plan into small steps and take the first step right away."

Margaret Thatcher 1925- was the first female Prime Minister of the United Kingdom 1979-1990.
(public domain photograph from her autobiography *The Downing Street Years*)

CHAPTER SIXTEEN

Margaret Thatcher, the "Iron Lady"

"I am in politics because of the conflict between good and evil, and I believe that in the end good triumphs."

Margaret Thatcher, nee Roberts, was born in a room over a grocer's shop on October 13, 1925, in Grantham, England. Her father owned the grocery store, and the family lived in an apartment above the shop. There Thatcher spent the first eighteen years of her life. There was no running hot water, and the toilet was outside at one end of the garden. Thatcher and her sister often helped in the shop, where they learned about thrift and hard work.

Religion played a major part in Thatcher's upbringing. Her parents were strict Methodists and much of their cultural and social life revolved around the church. Games were not allowed and dancing was prohibited. On Sundays, Thatcher attended church four different times: Sunday school at 10:00 a.m.; church service at 11:00 a.m.; another Sunday school session at 2:30 p.m.; and finally, 6:00 p.m. church service. Both she and her sister Muriel, who was four years older, were raised in a strict puritanical manner. Thatcher's rebellious feelings were somewhat assuaged when her father told her: "Margaret, never do things or want to do things just because other people do them. Make up your own mind about what you are going to do and persuade people to go your way." (Libby Hughes. *Madam Prime Minister.* [Lincoln, Nebraska: iUniverse.com.Inc., 2000]. 13). Later in life, she adopted more Anglican views and strayed from strict conformity, yet she always retained the basic values she learned in the local Methodist Church in Grantham.

Thatcher's father Albert Roberts was the great inspiration of her life. He was a leader in the local Methodist Church and Rotary Club. He was elected to the Grantham City Council when Thatcher was four-years old. He served thirty-four years on the council and was chairman of the Finance Committee for many years. In 1945, he was elected mayor of Grantham. He frequently involved himself in fundraising for charitable causes, and his grocery store was a sounding board for local chatter regarding political issues. People often came to the Roberts' grocery to hear his conservative political viewpoints as well as to purchase food. He often delivered groceries himself, and these personal contacts further enhanced his political standing in the town.

Since the store was a family endeavor, Thatcher at an early age was exposed to all kinds of social, economic, and political views. As she grew older, she was expected to do more, especially since World War II was underway. Thatcher's father often expressed his views to her and encouraged her to argue her position. In this way, she developed debating skills. He would take her with him to many interesting places. She grew in knowledge and experience, thus laying the foundation for her political career. During the war, the family frequently listened to radio broadcasts from across Europe. Later in life, Thatcher often referred to the wonderful education she received at home as well as at school.

Beatrice Roberts, Thatcher's mother, did not possess the forceful personality of her husband; she was a kind and gentle person interested in domestic issues. She did, however, have a great interest in music and the arts that carried over to her daughter. Thatcher studied piano from age six to fifteen, and she loved appearing in local school plays.

Thatcher's father believed that it was important for his two daughters to attend the right schools and to have correct diction. Consequently, he bought a second grocery store in a better area of town where his daughters would be in a better educational and social environment. Roberts allowed his daughters to read only non-fiction books, primarily biographies and books about politics. Then he would discuss the books with his daughters over dinner or during their free time. He encouraged both girls to argue their points of view whether he agreed with them or not.

The girls were enrolled in the Huntington Primary School where Thatcher excelled in her schoolwork. Although children from the wealthiest families did not attend Huntington, there were children from a broad spectrum of society. Because of her excellent grades, Thatcher was pushed ahead a year; so at age twelve, she was able to take the scholarship examination for the Kesteven and Grantham Girls School. The schools based scholarships on the level of parental income. The students included children from middle class families, and some that had to go to soup kitchens to eat. Some even came from orphanages.

Thatcher's family income disqualified her from scholarship funds, but in the event of her father's death, she would become eligible. Thatcher passed the test with flying colors insuring her at least a middle school and high school education. She was a serious student and stellar debater. Her great power of concentration became apparent to her teachers when during the war German planes sometimes flew overhead, dropping their bombs close by the school. She served as a firewatcher, which occasionally entailed spending nights on a rooftop scanning the skies for incendiary bombs.

Acceptance at Somerville College for Women at Oxford became her goal; she wished to skip her last year at Kesteven. Thatcher was encouraged to enroll as a chemistry major, so she would have a better chance of admittance than in the overcrowded fields of the liberal arts. Ultimately, after a crash summer course in Latin, she was accepted as a full-time student with financial aid if she required it. Oxford had accepted women students only since 1920, so in 1943 it was a great honor for Thatcher, not born to the upper classes, to be accepted at Oxford. Standards were higher for admittance to women's colleges simply because there were fewer of them. Thatcher attended Somerville 1943 to 1947.

One of the first places Thatcher noted class difference was in the eating hall, where tables were arranged according to class. For example, when Indira Gandhi attended Oxford, undoubtedly, she was seated at one of the top tables where daughters of foreign leaders and wealthy families sat. Thatcher sat with the group of middle-class girls who were on scholarships.

During the war, Thatcher hoed potatoes in what once had been the school's hockey-fields. With limited money from her father, she got a job in 1944 dispensing coffee at a local armed forces canteen. Later that same year, she got a job as an instructor at the Grantham Central School for Boys, teaching chemistry, mathematics, and science. She had always longed for a bicycle while she lived in Grantham but never was able to afford one. With funds from her schooling job, she was able to buy one. At Somerville, a bicycle was a necessity to be able to travel the campus.

Professor Dorothy Hodgkin, who later won the Nobel Prize for chemistry in 1964 and the Order of Merit in 1965, was Thatcher's assigned tutor for four years. Professor Hodgkin was a great inspiration to Thatcher.

Joining the Oxford University Conservative Association, Thatcher immediately became involved in campus politics. Women were barred from membership in the Oxford Union, but Thatcher attended many debates there picking up pointers on artful argumentation. Soon Thatcher realized she preferred politics to chemistry. In the mostly male OUCA, she was elected president because of her obvious talents as a speaker and debater; she was only the second woman ever to hold that position.

Hard-working, a great organizer, and socially astute, Thatcher quickly learned how politics works. Many well-known politicians gave speeches and lectures at Oxford, and Thatcher met many of them. She organized dinners and receptions for many of these well-know politicians when they came to speak at Oxford, and she began to be noticed at these functions. It was then that she first entertained notions of becoming an M.P. (Member of Parliament).

While carrying a full academic load, Thatcher was also involved in many extra-circular activities: Oxford Repertory Company, Somerville-Balliol Choir, University Bach Choir, Scientific Society, and Methodist Student Society. While at Oxford, she was introduced to Anglicanism, and she later adopted this religion formerly as her church.

The British Parliament is composed of two houses: the House of Commons, where laws are introduced and passed, and the House of Lords, where seats are inherited or appointed and where bills can be held for a year before being passed to the Queen for her signature. In 1945, one of the Conservative candidates, George Worth invited Thatcher to work on his campaign. Even though Worth lost the election, she gained much experience in the political campaign that year and saw the downfall of Churchill and the landslide victory for the Labor Party. The nation was shocked.

Thatcher was greatly influenced by F.A. Hayek's *Road to Serfdom*, an anti-socialist book that philosophically argued that big government, no matter for what ends or what reasons, eventually leads to Nazi-style tyranny. Her interests expanded from chemistry and politics to economics.

Thatcher graduated from Somerville College with a degree in chemistry in 1947. Along with two other females, she was hired by British Xylonite Plastics in Colchester. These were the first women hired as chemists by the company. Thatcher wanted to study law, her true passion, but she needed to work for the funds to pay for her further education. Notwithstanding the fact that she held a full-time job, she threw herself into Colchester politics.

In 1948, Thatcher was invited by the Oxford Graduates Association to represent them in North Wales at the annual Conservative Party Conference. There, an old friend from Oxford, John Grant, asked her if she would consider having her name put on the slate for Member of Parliament from Dartford. There were twenty-four candidates on the slate and twenty-three were male. She was the youngest and only woman on the short list. All candidates were invited to speak before the selection committee. When Thatcher spoke without notes for forty-five minutes defining the issues clearly and logically, the committee unanimously selected her as their candidate.

At a dinner party held in her honor in Dartford, she met Denis Thatcher, a successful business man ten years her senior. After a short courtship, the two decided to marry. Denis' mother may have felt Thatcher was beneath his social class, and Thatcher's parents were not happy she was marrying a divorced man. Although they were truly in love, Thatcher still placed her political ambitions first. She established residency in Dartford and worked on her campaign. All the while, she held a full-time job as an industrial research chemist. Running in a staunchly labor district, she was defeated but undaunted. She ran again in 1951 and was again defeated.

Margaret Roberts and Denis Thatcher were married shortly afterwards. It appears Thatcher and Denis had a successful marriage in spite of their careers. Early on in the marriage, they agreed to put career and work first. Thatcher often remarked that she never would have been so successful if she had not had her husband's financial and moral support. Denis in turn applauded his wife's domestic skills, especially her cooking.

Thatcher thought women should pursue higher education, so that they could rise to responsible positions in business or the professions. She supported the view that an educated woman in a career was a benefit to her family and society at large. Women could successfully combine marriage and career. Men often attacked this notion, and many women also had prejudicial views against a dual role for women. The idea that the family suffers was a mistaken notion in her mind. It should be noted that Thatcher had a nanny for her children and sent them to the most elite boarding schools at an early age because she had the money and time for her future legal and political career. Thatcher understood that when the children left home, there was a huge gap in a woman's life. Therefore, she believed that a career for a woman was in her best interests.

In 1952, Thatcher began studying law. When she was well along with her pregnancy, she took her first two law exams and passed. Shortly thereafter, she gave birth to twins, Mark and Carol. After delivering the twins, she sent for papers for her final exam while still in the hospital.

A year later, after finishing her schooling, she qualified as a barrister. Thatcher wrote an article testifying to her views on women's abilities: "Should a woman arise equal to the task, I say let her have an equal chance with the men for cabinet posts. Why not a woman chancellor or foreign secretary?" (Libby Hughes. *Madam Prime Minister.* [Lincoln, Nebraska: iUniverse.com. Inc., 2000]. 52).

Thatcher worked for six months in a tax firm but was soon terminated, probably for weak accounting skills. Nonetheless, with her background in economics and tax law, she later made treasury issues her main interest; she even engaged in the Parliamentary treasury debate of 1961. Public sentiment held that Thatcher was in a predominately male arena, and many men in the 1950s frowned on women with a family working.

However, Thatcher was soon hired by another tax firm where she was able to practice tax law. She joined the Society of Conservative Lawyers and was the first woman to serve on the executive committee. Thatcher made great progress, but one great ambition had yet to be fulfilled: election to the House of Commons. That opportunity presented itself when Sir John Crowther decided to retire in 1959. His conservative, wealthy district Finchley, located outside London, was a seat sought by more than two hundred politicians.

Thatcher won her seat in the House of Commons as a Member of Parliament from Finchley in October 1959 just a few days short of her thirty-fourth birthday. By a stroke of luck, she was allowed early on to introduce a bill of her choice to the Parliament. She chose the Public Bodies Bill proposing that the press be allowed to attend local council meetings from which they previously had been barred. Of course, this enamored her to the press, which did not hurt her future political career. She addressed the House of Commons for almost an hour without notes.

Subsequently in 1961, she was appointed Under-Secretary for Pensions and National Insurance by Prime Minister Harold Macmillan and served until 1964. When the Labor Party won control in 1964, Thatcher became a member of the conservative minority leadership.

Ted Heath, under Harold Macmillan, served as shadow chancellor, and in 1964 he started Thatcher on her road to fame. First, she was appointed spokesperson on land and housing. Next, she was appointed number two spokesperson on treasury. In 1967 and in the following eighteen months, she was assigned several jobs in the "shadow cabinet:" social security, housing and land, treasury, energy, and education. Thus, she became a prominent political figure. (Shadow appointees correspond to persons in the minority party in the U.S. appointed to shadow or observe the ones in the majority party who actually are serving in official positions.)

When defending her position, Thatcher was well armed with facts and figures. She did extensive research on any matter she argued, more so than most of the other Members of Parliament. In attacking the opposition Laborites, she used insults and sarcasm in a most effective way.

When the Conservative Party came back into power in 1970, Thatcher became Secretary of State for Education and Science, a cabinet position. Only the second woman to serve in this post, Thatcher was often frustrated when Prime Minister Heath failed to listen to her ideas.

Later on, she humorously remarked to a woman's group: "If you want something said, ask a man. If you want something done, ask a woman." (Libby Hughes. *Madam Prime Minister.* [Lincoln, Nebraska: iUniverse.com. Inc., 2000]. 72). Many in her own party, including Prime Minister Ted Heath resented her comment while most women loved it.

An incident in 1970 almost destroyed her career. Thatcher was fighting for a law mandating children to stay in school until age sixteen. Her education budget was slashed, so she had to take money from another source, and she cut free milk from schools for children aged seven to eleven. Her reasoning was that parents could afford milk for their children, and the job of government was to provide education. She was referred to as the "milk snatcher" by many opposition leaders in the Labor party as well as by Tories. Although she increased charges for student meals, she also increased the level of the parents' income at which children could qualify for free meals. Children whose parents could afford to pay for the meals did not receive them gratis. But many were still angry at her, and while giving a speech, she was hit in the chest by a rock. Characteristically, she kept on speaking. The press was also greatly annoyed with her, and the "honeymoon" was over.

In the Tory Party's plan, emphasis was put on the primary schools as the foundation for advanced learning. Free nursery schools were to be set up in deprived areas in order to help underprivileged children overcome social disadvantages. Education at the secondary level was to be under the management of the local government. The actual running of the schools and their curriculums were set at the local level. To accommodate students who developed at a later age, the local government would determine the age for entry into secondary education, not necessarily at the fixed age of eleven. However school construction, the number of teachers hired, and their salaries were to be controlled by the national government. The central government also had the job of seeing that the local school boards carried out their mission in such a way that every student would have the opportunity to develop his/her talents. Financially disadvantaged children were to be given direct grants based on their academic abilities. Parents would have the right to send their children to independent schools. Emphasis was to be put on attracting, training, and retaining teachers.

One of Thatcher's great legacies is in the field of education, and she made changes in the educational system. She believed in flexibility. During the twenty-five years she was involved with education, she modified rules that no longer applied and matched regulations with new ideas. She maintained that students, parents, and teachers are not all alike, and their needs must be met in different ways. If schools are different, she believed it does not necessarily follow that a school of one kind is worse or better than another. She did not believe in one universal system of education that would apply to all. Instead, she advocated for independent schools operating along side the huge public system. Within the public sector, there were a great number of Church schools between the government supported schools and wholly private schools, and there was a small but significant number of grant schools. Thatcher promoted experimentation and adaptation. She did not want the Conservative government or any government to impose a particular educational system on local authorities.

Soon after she became Prime Minister, she introduced a new program, the Assisted Places Scheme, which allowed gifted children from poor backgrounds to attend private schools. She wanted all children to have the benefits of learning. Many children dropped out of school as early as age eleven to go to work. Thatcher changed that and made it mandatory for children to stay in school until age sixteen.

Until 1987, sixteen-year-olds could register for unemployment payments, which helped families pay for food, shelter, and clothing. Thatcher, however, believed this was costing the government too much money. When their unemployment stopped, more and more teen-agers moved to the big cities where they often could not find jobs and ended up homeless on the streets.

Under Thatcher, the government created a youth training plan in which an employer and the government shared costs of training an individual while providing a salary and a place to live. The apprentice generally was able to earn a living without government assistance. This attitude of self-help reflected her father's training and her own feelings about people helping themselves.

The Conservative Party lost in 1974. Yet Tory leader, Edward Heath, realized Thatcher's value and appointed her to speak on treasury and environmental issues in his shadow cabinet. Summing up her political sentiments in an address to Commons in 1974, Thatcher said:

> Our challenge is to create the kind of economic background which enables private initiative and private enterprise to flourish for the benefit of the consumer, the employee, the pensioner and society as a whole...I believe we should judge people on merit, and not on background....Liberty must never be confused with license and you cannot have liberty without a just law impartially administered. (George Gardiner M.P. *Margaret Thatcher.* [London: William Kimber Publisher, 1975]. 200).

The next year, Thatcher beat Heath in an election for head of her party, and she became the first woman elected to head a minority party in English history. "To yesterday's men," she chirped, "tomorrow's woman says 'hello.'" In one of her first radio broadcasts, Margaret quoted these words of Abraham Lincoln:

> You cannot bring about prosperity by discouraging thrift.
> You cannot strengthen the weak by weakening the strong.
> You cannot help strong men by tearing down big men.
> You cannot further the brotherhood of man by encouraging class hatred.
> You cannot help the poor by destroying the rich.
> You cannot establish sound security on borrowed money.
> You cannot keep out of trouble by spending more than you earn.
> You cannot build character and courage by taking away man's initiative and independence.
> You cannot help men permanently by doing for them what they could and should do for themselves. (Libby Hughes. *Madam Prime Minister.* [Lincoln, Nebraska: iUniverse.com. Inc., 2000]. 80-81).

In 1968, Thatcher led the Tory Party Conference's opposition to equal rights for women. Thatcher believed women already had equal rights. She saw no conflict in her having a family and career and maintained she had encountered no discrimination in her political climb. When asked on one occasion if she attributed her rise to the feminist movement, she responded that women were getting ahead long before Women's Lib was even considered. The fact that she was a woman did not seem to bother or concern her. "I am just Margaret Thatcher. You must take me as I am." (Alan J. Mayer. *Madame Prime Minister.* [New York: Newsweek Books, 1979]. 130). As a result Thatcher was never a darling of the women's movement.

In 1975, Thatcher traveled to the U.S. to address United Nations ambassadors and foreign policy groups. She took a hard-line attitude towards Russia and the Helsinki Accords signed by the U.S. and most European countries in that year. The Labor Party, headed by Harold Wilson, was strongly in favor of détente, and its followers hoped for a lessening of tension between East and West. She believed these nations were naive in their belief that Russia was going to change in its attitude towards human rights.

During World War II Thatcher's sister's pen pal, an Austrian Jewish refugee, had come to live with the family in Grantham. Her stories of life under the Nazis appalled the young Thatcher especially after she read Solzhenitsyn's novel *The First Circle.* A staunch advocate of human rights, Thatcher did not trust the Russians, and she viewed their build up of arms and weapons during the '70s as proof that Russia's goal was world domination.

Later, during the Cold War, Thatcher addressed the House of Commons: "The Russians are bent on world dominance, and they are rapidly acquiring the means to become the most powerful imperial nation the world has seen." Thatcher stated, "They put guns before butter, while we put just about everything before guns." (Libby Hughes. *Madam Prime Minister.* [Lincoln, Nebraska: iUniverse.com. Inc., 2000]. 91). Tass, one of Russia's news agencies, dubbed her the "Iron Lady," and the label has stuck to this day. Cartoonists had a field day, and Thatcher was thrilled! Meanwhile in order to enhance her knowledge of foreign affairs, she traveled to the U.S., China, Japan, and Indonesia.

Politics is often about imagery and symbols. Thatcher hired Gordon Reece, who had helped her in her early political campaigns, to be her full time media adviser. Having worked with many celebrities in television, he was able to transform Thatcher's image. He taught her to lower her voice which was often annoyingly shrill; to give up her garden-variety hats; and to modify her often nervous style of speaking so that she appeared calmer. She learned to present her personal side more often and worked on changing the original image that she was cold and calculating.

Thatcher in October 1975 gave her first major address as leader of her Conservative Party at Blackpool. The country faced huge economic and financial problems. In her speech to rally support for capitalism, she disavowed the socialistic policies espoused by the Labor government. "Thatcherism," as it came to be called, advocated the least amount of government ownership possible, such as fewer government-owned utilities and industries, and more private and individual ownership. She saw capitalism as the answer to Britain's economic woes.

Prime Minister Harold Wilson was replaced by James Callaghan. Neither of these two Prime Ministers took Thatcher seriously, so her friend, Gordon Reece, again came to her rescue. He hired a television advertising firm to remake her image. The aim was to have the public accept her as a woman, wife, and mother while enhancing her credibility as a political leader.

Problems in England were mounting as Thatcher worked on her public persona. Huge numbers of Pakistanis and Africans were moving into the country. Race riots erupted on the streets. Thatcher recommended that immigration be halted. The Labor Party, Christian leaders, and members of her own party were outraged and accused her of being racist and un-Christian; Thatcher stood her ground by arguing some things just had to be done. Although the Labor Party was in office, the country was experiencing monumental labor problems. There were factory strikes; there was uncollected garbage; there were truckers' strikes; there was poor train service; and there were school closings because of lack of fuel. The country was almost bankrupt. Unemployment was rising and labor unions were making more and more demands. Indeed, the country was in a major crisis.

Thatcher called for a vote of no confidence for the Labor party. After a heated battle, Prime Minister James Callaghan called for the Queen to dissolve Parliament. Thatcher acted quickly. Gordon Reece took over her publicity campaign again, and the Conservative Party won by a narrow majority.

Thatcher was now Prime Minister of England. Her first task was to appoint a twenty-two member cabinet to form a new government. By convention, all members came from the House of Commons or the House of Lords. All areas of the country are required to be represented in the new cabinet, so it was quite a daunting task. She chose members who would support her views rather than those with different agendas. Her duties as Prime Minister were vast: she held meetings with foreign dignitaries, business tycoons, and party leaders; every Tuesday and Thursday from 3:15 to 3:30 p.m. members of the opposition party hurled questions at her;

and she met with the Queen every Tuesday night. Speeches, broadcasts, receptions, and endless paperwork often filled her days from early morning to late at night.

Immediately, Thatcher began to implement her new strategies. British Petroleum, British Airways, and other government-owned industries were sold to private companies. She aimed at getting rid of as many socialist programs as possible. Thatcher believed private enterprise would run companies better than government. She proposed lowering the income tax and raising taxes on alcohol, cigarettes, and gas. She also wanted to raise the VAT (value-added tax on all goods and services). Thatcher made huge cuts in the government budget in order to solve the growing trade deficit because England was importing more than exporting. She advocated a reduction in government borrowing, spending cuts across the board except in defense, and strict control of the money supply. Her economic policies provoked outrage in the Labor Party and among many Tories. Still, Thatcher stuck to her programs. There was even talk of a third party being formed by disgruntled members of both parties. She formed an economic committee of those members of her own party who agreed with her. As a result, when the party met for their annual conference at Blackpool, many Conservative Party members were unhappy with Thatcher. To her opponents Thatcher argued:

> I will not change to court popularity....If ever Conservative government starts to do what it knows is wrong because it is afraid to do what is right, that is the time for the Tories to cry Stop. But you will never need to do that while I am Prime Minister. (Libby Hughes. *Madam Prime Minister.* [Lincoln, Nebraska: iUniverse. com. Inc., 2000]. 112).

In 1982, Thatcher was confronted by the most serious crisis of her first term. The Falkland Islands, three hundred miles off the coast of Argentina, had belonged to England for more than one hundred and fifty years. The islanders were mostly English and wished to remain as such. Sheep-raising was the major occupation. Leopold Galtieri, the new president of Argentina, decided to make an issue of the Falklands. Since England is separated from the Falklands by eight thousand miles, Galtieri presumed that the female Prime Minister of Britain would not have the courage to confront the Argentine military. Galtieri miscalculated. When Thatcher heard the Argentine ships were on their way to the Falklands, she immediately called an emergency session with her Foreign Office and Defense Ministry. She also consulted with President Ronald Reagan and

Secretary of State Alexander Haig. Thatcher appealed to world opinion on the premise that Britain was defending the right of a people for self-determination.

Clearly, Thatcher was not going to allow her countrymen to be taken over by Argentina, and she believed the Falklanders had the right to decide which government they preferred. The matter was sent to the United Nations, and the Security Council called for the immediate withdrawal of Argentine troops. Fighting for her principles, Thatcher used her diplomatic skills to secure the approval of world opinion.

However, many members of Parliament were against standing up to Argentina. The "Iron Lady" prevailed. Two British aircraft carriers and small ships were sent to the area. Meanwhile, Argentine ships with military troops had arrived and taken control of the unarmed population. When the two navies confronted each other, the British sank an Argentine destroyer while the Argentines destroyed the British ship HMS *Sheffield.* In all, fourteen ships were damaged and two hundred and fifty lives were lost by the time Argentina surrendered in June 1982.

Not only did this victory restore much national pride to the British, but on a personal level, Thatcher achieved international recognition as a strong, decisive leader. She was highly praised by the military for the way she handled the crisis. Obviously, the British were changing the way they looked at themselves after years of national decline.

Later, Thatcher in a speech in Chenltenham expressed pride in her country with these words:

> And so today we can rejoice at our success in the Falkland's and take pride in the achievement of the men and women of our task force....We rejoice that Britain has rekindled that spirit which has fired her for generations past and which today has begun to burn as brightly as before. Britain found herself again in the South Atlantic and will not look back from the victory she has won. (Margaret Thatcher. *The Downing Street Years.* [New York: Harper Collins, 1993]. 234).

In spite of the popularity Thatcher experienced after the Falklands victory, domestic problems quickly arose again. Thatcher asked the Queen to dissolve parliament and call for a general election in June 1983. Both parties accused Thatcher of failing to fulfill her promises. Many accused her of being too bossy and "teacherish." The public, however, ignored the political attacks and reelected her to a second term.

Another major crisis occurred between 1984 and 1985. Arthur Scargill, President of the National Union of Mineworkers, launched a series of personal criticisms against Thatcher. He had previously brought down the conservative Heath government in 1974 and now was trying to do the same to Thatcher.

Thatcher wanted to reduce Britain's reliance on coal. According to many economists, coal could be imported more cheaply than it could be extracted from coal mines in the United Kingdom. The coal industry was heavily subsidized in 1984. While some coal mines were profitable, many needed efficiency improvements by means of modern mechanizations. In addition, many mines were deemed unsafe, and jobs would have to be cut, if safety and equipment alterations were made. Britain simply could not compete on the world market.

Scargill, a leftist union leader, vowed that he would bring the country to a halt by calling a major strike. The N.U.M. under Scargill called a strike to protest job cuts. The N.U.M., which encompassed coal miners in England, Scotland, and Wales, rallied its members to a nation-wide strike.

However, in many parts of the United Kingdom, members did not join the strike. Violence and riots broke out between the scabs, pickets, and police. Many were killed or injured. Massive poverty ensued when neither the non-strikers nor the strikers received any pay. Thousands existed on handouts wherever they could find them; poverty and hunger were rampant. Welfare benefits were never available to strikers although they had been available to their dependents in former disputes. But now the government was banning spouses and children from receiving benefits. Electricity, steel production, railroads, and engineering were also affected by the strike.

Thatcher was trying to curtail the powers of unions. Scargill's plan to bring the British economy to a halt did not succeed because many of the union members refused to strike. The Queen did not agree with Thatcher and viewed her actions as insensitive to the workers and too costly to the nation. Nevertheless, Thatcher went on implementing her policies and strategies.

Scargill and his cohorts were accused of having ties to Russia and Libya. Thatcher suggested in her autobiography that an official of the N.U.M visited Libya and requested funds from Colonel Gaddafi. Moreover when Scargill and his associates visited Paris, they met with Communist union leaders. Interestingly, funds were received from non-existent Afghanistan trade unions. Allegedly, funds were also received from Soviet labor unions with obvious government support, for such an action could not take place without official sanction.

Thatcher was enraged over the union's ties to a foreign power. Many union members as well as the British public at large were aghast at the Communist connection. Support for the strike was greatly diminished. Referring to the violence and chaos running wild in the land, Thatcher spoke these words:

> The concept of fair play…a British way of saying 'respect for the rules'… must not be used to allow the minority to overbear the tolerant majority. Yet these are the very dangers we face in Britain today. At one end of the spectrum are the terrorist gangs within our borders, and the terrorist states which finance and arm them. At the other are the hard Left operating inside our system, conspiring to use union power and the apparatus of local government to break, defy and subvert the laws. (Margaret Thatcher. *Margaret Thatcher: The Downing Street Years.* [New York: Harper Collins, 1993]. 368-369).

The collapse of the strike was a terrible blow to the N.U.M. As a result, the power of the union was broken permanently. In the long run, the failure of the strike and weakening of the union was seen as generally beneficial to the British economy. The coal industry was privatized in 1994 and is now known as U.K. Coal. In 2009, there remained only four working coal mines. In some of the small villages in northern England, the unemployment rate rose to 50 percent, and some became like ghost towns.

In 1984, while domestic problems raged, Thatcher went to Brighton to attend a major party conference where she was scheduled to make an important address. A bomb planted by the Irish Republican Army was intended to kill her. It exploded in the Grand Hotel where she was staying. Five people were killed and many were injured. The conservative conference went on the next morning as scheduled. Thatcher delivered an inspiring speech, maintaining that terrorists were not going to bring down Her Majesty's democratically elected government.

Thatcher with much emotion stated:

> The bomb attack was an attempt not only to disrupt and terminate our conference. It was an attempt to cripple Her Majesty's democratically elected government.…And the fact that we gathered here now, shocked but composed and determined, is a sign not only that this attack has failed, but that all attempts to destroy democracy by terrorism will fail. (Margaret

Thatcher. *Margaret Thatcher: The Downing Street Years.* [New York: Harper Collins, 1993]. 382).

Thatcher and Irish Taoiseach (Prime Minister) Garret Fitzgerald created an Anglo-Irish Inter-Government Council, which would act as a forum for meetings between the two governments. When Fitzgerald signed the Hillsborough Anglo-Irish Agreement in 1985, the Irish Republic, for the first time in the history of Anglo-control, was given an advisory role in the governance of Northern Ireland. In 1998, the IRA made the historic decision to start decommissioning its forces after an IRA Convention in Donegal. Nevertheless, the distrust between the Catholics and loyalists in Ireland goes on to this day.

Thatcher met with Mikhail Gorbachev in 1987. He strove to make private enterprise more of a reality in Russia where the government tended to control every aspect of life. This meeting raised her image as a leader with other world leaders at a time when she needed public approval. So she selected an early election date in an attempt to win a third term. The Labor party attacked her as a woman, but this tactic backfired. The public was not impressed by such tactics, and Thatcher was elected for a third term, albeit by a slim margin. Thatcher won because the voters believed she had fulfilled many of her goals. More people owned their own homes than ever before, and Britain was on its way to becoming a great nation once again.

Encouraged by the resolution of the "Irish problem," Thatcher took a stronger stand against terrorism. A staunch supporter of Ronald Reagan, she allowed American forces to use British soil to launch attacks against Muammar Gaddafi's forces in Libya. She had greatly appreciated Reagan's support during the Falklands War, but many in both parties rebelled against her support of the attacks. In the middle of her second term, domestic problems were severe. Bankruptcies were rampant, and American companies were buying up English companies in financial straits. Many in England resented the "sell outs" to Americans and other foreigners.

In 1974, Thatcher summed up her vision of the conservative philosophy with these words:

> The Conservative approach is based on a balance between rights and duties, between individuals and society. Its implication for economic policy is that citizens have the duty to support themselves and their families if humanly possible and the right to seek the optimum return for their effort....To encourage perpetual dependence would be the worst service we could do

to them and society alike. (Alfred Sherman. "*The Owner-Occupiers Party.*" Article for *Daily Telegraph,* Speech Margaret Thatcher. London: July 1, 1974).

The Housing Act of 1980 was passed by Parliament, and this legislation gave five hundred thousand government-housing dwellers in the U.K. the right to buy their houses or apartments from their local authorities. This act was one of the most important social events in the U.K. of the twentieth century. As a result, home ownership increased from 55 percent in 1980 to 67 percent in 1990. Now working class tenants were enabled to become property owners.

Thatcher argued that it was absurd to think that it was the government's responsibility to provide housing for a large and growing labor force as well as a majority of manual workers. She wanted to bring private and institutional capital back into the housing sector. Her belief was that it is better to help people maintain self-reliance than state-reliance. She strove to keep down interest rates in order to make ownership more possible. Thatcher believed that housing belonged in the private sector and control belonged at the local level.

In 2010, it appeared that at least part of Thatcher's housing plan had backfired. When the government decided to sell off many of the public housing projects to private ownership, conglomerates purchased these properties and charged high prices for rentals or sales. Thus, Thatcher's plan for privatization went amuck and defeated her plan for lower middle-class citizens to be able to become property owners. Now the government, once again, had to get involved by building or repurchasing housing for lower-income people at taxpayer expense.

Critics accused her of helping only the middle class and doing little for the lower classes. The effects of her anti-union stance can still be felt in northern England where the majority of the two million unemployed live. Another complaint is that she cruelly cut welfare to persons under eighteen. Her focusing on the individual created an air of selfishness and indifference to less fortunate members of society. Some got rich quick while many more languished in misery.

In her later political career, Thatcher had difficulties with the press. For example in 1986, she tried to stop from publication a book titled *Spycatcher,* which revealed much about the British spy system. The author had the book published in Australia, where he was not under the Official Secrets Act. Similarly, in 1988, she banned broadcast interviews with Irish extremists. Her argument was that they should not be given a platform from which to present their views. The press was in an uproar arguing for the right of free speech. One journalist was fined thirty thousand dollars for defying the ruling and for not making known the source of his material.

Britain has no written Constitution or Bill of Rights as the United States does. As a result, certain democratic rights are often difficult to define and to defend. The English "constitution" is loosely based on the Magna Carta and many unwritten ideas that have become English custom and tradition. Parliament is the supreme law-making body and may pass any legislation it wishes. By contrast, in countries with a codified constitution such as the United States, the legislative body cannot pass laws that contradict the Constitution. Abuses perpetrated on individuals or groups by various levels of government can be brought before the High Court in London or the European Commission on Human Rights.

On April 30, 1980, several gunmen attacked the Iranian Embassy at Prince's Gate in Knightsbridge. They held twenty hostages, mostly Iranian staff, but also a British police officer on duty and two BBC journalists who were applying for visas. The terrorists threatened to blow up the embassy and kill the hostages if their demands were not met. Opposed to the ruling government in Iran, these Iraqi-trained militants, members of the "Group of the Martyr," demanded that the Iranian Government release ninety-one political prisoners and that the rights of dissidents be acknowledged by Iran. They further demanded a plane to fly themselves and the hostages out of Britain. The Iranian government had no intentions of acceding to their wishes; the British government refused to tolerate hostage-taking in its domain.

Thatcher perceived the intention of the terrorists as an attempt to show up the weakness of western governments. But the "Iron Lady" would not bow down to such threats and determined to defeat the terrorists. It was the Home Secretary's official duty to take charge. The Home Office, Foreign Office, Cabinet Office and all intelligence, military, and police agencies were called into action. The metropolitan police tried to negotiate with the terrorists on a special line. An imam tried talking to the men to no avail. The terrorists were not allowed to leave the embassy with or without the hostages. If a hostage were wounded, an assault on the embassy would be launched. If a hostage were killed, the S.A.S (Special Air Service) would be called in. As the situation deteriorated, the S.A.S., on Thatcher's orders, was activated. With great professionalism and courage, the S.A.S. assaulted the embassy. All nineteen hostages still alive at the time were rescued. Four gunmen were killed, one was captured and none escaped. Once again, Thatcher proved her mettle and showed the world that she would not put up with terrorists or give them any ground.

Thatcher was the first foreign leader to visit President Ronald Reagan after his inauguration in 1981. Her term in office coincided with his eight years as President. The two formed a political marriage that helped transform the world with their conservative revolution. Together, they confronted the despots who led the Soviet Union. Her alliance with Mikhail Gorbachev, whom she wooed diplomatically, helped bring about the dissolution of the Soviet Union. Reagan once referred to Thatcher as the "best man in England."

In 1990, Thatcher supported President George Herbert Walker Bush during the Persian Gulf War. She believed that if one aggressor succeeds, others will try as well, and if Saddam Hussein was not stopped, his army would march into Saudi Arabia, Bahrain, and Dubai and down the west side of the Gulf. In that way, he could gain control of 65 percent of the world's oil. Thatcher immediately promised military support to Bush. Operation Desert Storm was initiated with U.N. authorization and a coalition of thirty-four nations. Saddam's forces were soon pushed out of Kuwait and back to Baghdad.

On November 22, 1990, Thatcher resigned after serving in the office of Prime Minister for almost twelve years; she had also served for fifteen years as head of her party. Many people, even within the Conservative Party, were irate because of a poll tax she was advocating and because of her lack of support of the European Union. Her opponents in the Conservative Party called for a leadership election. Thatcher did not receive enough votes to stay in power; John Major succeeded her as Prime Minister.

Thatcher certainly thwarted the social rules by entering politics in the 1940s and succeeding so well. She showed that a woman could have both a career and a family. Her conservative politics brought her world attention. She was a middle-class woman who reached great heights through her own talent rather than her parents' position. She had few problems dealing with male politicians, but many male politicians had trouble dealing with her.

Thatcher stood her ground and argued her positions with passion and logic. She was fascinating, fierce, formidable, and feisty. She believed government was at its best when it was minimal, that people were at their best when they were doing for themselves. From her family upbringing, she believed that hard work pays off in the long run, and that all the British inevitably would come to the same conclusion.

The '80s were a period of great economic growth, a financial bonanza, the age of consumerism. Her critics argued that England had become a nation of greed. Through attacks from unions and industry and in spite of public outrage, Thatcher stood strong against the forces of socialism. In her view, the Labor Party was leading the country into socialism, and the Conservative Party was keeping sensible positions in the middle of the road.

"Maggie," as she was called by many, possessed a stiff upper lip and the "bull dog" determination to get things done. Without her intervention, the Falklanders might be speaking Spanish instead of English. She generated a new economy called "Thatcherism." Her age promoted low inflation, free markets, and the small state with little control of money. She supported privatization and curbs on labor unions. She revolutionized higher education and made it easier for more people to become homeowners.

Although Thatcher believed she could have it all, her personal life and her family suffered from a lack of privacy. The twins, Mark and Carol, born in 1953, were sent to boarding school at an early age, as are most children of prominent families in England. Unlike their mother, they were not raised in a strict fashion. Mark did not succeed in higher education; he was more interested in car racing. However, Carol managed to secure a law degree.

Mark has lead a playboy life and been involved in numerous failed and nefarious business deals. While his mother was Prime Minister, he was accused of making arms deals with foreign governments, including Saudi Arabia. In 1995, he moved to South Africa where he and some wealthy friends were arrested for bankrolling a failed coup to take over the dictatorship of Equatorial Guinea. He ended up in jail, received a four-year suspended prison sentence, and was fined approximately five hundred thousand dollars. He is not allowed in the United States, since he is a convicted felon. He married an American from whom he is divorced and has two children living in the United States. Currently, Mark is living in Spain on the Costa del Sol in posh circumstances.

Unlike her brother, Carol Thatcher has been relatively successful and is the author of several books, including *A Swim-on Part in the Goldfish Bowl: A Memoir,* which recounts the decline of Thatcher's health and the onset of dementia in 2008. In addition, she is a journalist and media personality, having won the fifth season of the reality show *I'm a Celebrity-Get Me Out of Here.* She has written biographies of both her parents. Carol has never married and states that she does not believe in marriage for herself; she lives with her partner in London.

Thatcher holds a life peerage as Baroness Thatcher from Kesteven, which entitles her to sit in the House of Lords. Her primary residence is in London. Prime Minister Thatcher once commented: "Standing in the middle of the road is dangerous; you get knocked down by the traffic from both sides." Fortunately for Britain and Thatcher, she was seldom knocked down and never for long.

Benazir Bhutto 1953-2007 at news conference upon her arrival for a state visit in 1989 at Andrews Air Force Base She fought for the modernization of Pakistan and democratic principles. (U.S. federal government photo public domain)

CHAPTER SEVENTEEN

Benazir Bhutto, Pakistani Martyr

"Democracy is necessary to peace and to undermining the forces of terrorism."

In 1947, India threw off the yoke of British colonialism. The idea of a separate Muslim state carved out of mostly Hindu India was first proposed by the poet-philosopher Muhammad Iqbal in 1930. Thus in 1947, the new nation of Pakistan was carved out of the subcontinent of India. However, East and West Pakistan were separated by more than a thousand miles of Indian territory.

Most of the wealth and resources were passed on to India by the British in spite of plans that had previously been agreed upon. Only the backward areas of Sindh, Balochistan, and the North-West frontier came to Pakistan intact. The Punjab and Bengal were divided; Kashmir to this day is disputed territory. Under this arrangement, Pakistan's raw materials were cut off from Indian factories. Furthermore, India controlled the water supplies to Pakistan's eastern canals, and India established a virtual blockade. Millions of refugees fled over the Indian border to escape the retaliation of irate Muslim massacres on both sides of the border.

When Pakistan first gained relative independence, it continued to be part of the British Commonwealth. Pakistan, with its own cultural, religious, and political identity, came into existence under the great leader, Mohammad Ali Jinnah who had worked to establish Pakistan as a nation built on western ideas of parliamentary democracy. Unfortunately for Pakistan, Jinnah soon died, and Pakistan was thrown into an abyss of warring factions divided along ethnic and religious lines. The people of this widespread new nation had experienced democracy, military rule, theocracy, timocracy (political power based on ownership of land), and the bureaucracy of combinations of types of rule at different times and places. It appeared that Pakistan had no clear vision of its own political identity. The confusion continues in parts of this beleaguered country.

When the first formal constitution was approved in 1958, the nation officially became a Republic, and its first president was Iskander Mirza Habbik. In 1958, he abrogated the constitution and established military law. In a bloodless coup d'état, General Ayuk Klan declared himself President. In a regular election in 1965, Ayuk Klan was legally elected President.

Into this political chaos Benazir Bhutto was born in Karachi, Pakistan, to a prominent political Pakistani family in 1953. She was the eldest child of former Prime Minister Zulfikar Ali Bhutto, a Pakistani of Sindhi descent and Begum Nusrat Bhutto of Kurdish descent. Her paternal grandfather was Sir Shah Nawaz Bhutto who settled in the Larkana District before the independence of Pakistan and India. The Bhuttos were an immensely wealthy family with vast land holdings.

From her earliest beginnings, she was reared in a bi-lingual and bi-cultural life. Moreover, she prided herself on her family history with heroic tales of her ancestors during the Muslim invasion of India in A.D. 712. From these anecdotal tales, a family code was passed down: loyalty, honor, and principle. A narrative often told was that of her great-grandfather who took an English lover. When the outraged British officers of the raj demanded her return, the woman was killed by her great-grandfather's military guard. The killing was justified as an "honor killing," since disgrace would have befallen her great-grandfather if his English paramour had been forcibly returned to the English.

In contrast to the eastern influence, Benazir Bhutto was educated at a series of British and Catholic schools. Education was a top priority in the Bhutto household, and the nuns agreed to make no effort to convert her to Catholicism. Most of the people in her country could not read or write. Soon the young girl began to see the differences among people and the ways they were treated. She observed the poverty of the lower classes, and she also began to care for poor people and regard them as human beings, too. With the benefits of a good British and Catholic training, Bhutto was accepted for study in the United States.

The Bhutto children were raised with the idea of gender equality. The two sons and the two daughters were given the best education possible and were expected to attend the best universities. The children were taught that they had a responsibility to repay society for all the blessings they enjoyed.

Z.A. Bhutto, Benazir's father, did not believe that imams should determine the law of the land or that the country should become a theocracy. He believed in a strong military force, which would be under civilian control. (Benazir Bhutto. *Reconciliation: Islam, Democracy, and the West.* [New York: Harper Collins, 2008]. 184).

At age sixteen, Bhutto left her homeland to study at Harvard's Radcliffe College. She delighted in peppermint ice cream, apple cider, Joan Baez, and peace marches against the war in Vietnam. The women's movement was in full swing, and radical changes were being made in American society. She was elected to Phi Beta Kappa and received a Bachelor of Arts degree with honors in comparative governments.

After completing her undergraduate degree, she transferred to Oxford where she studied from 1973 to 1977, focusing on philosophy, politics, international law, diplomacy, and economics. She read John Locke, Jean Jacques Rousseau, and John Stuart Mill, on the nature of society and the State, and on the need to guarantee the rights of citizens. It was there that she began to form her democratic political philosophy.

Drawn to the art of debate, in 1976, she was elected president of the Oxford Union, a prestigious debating society. Little did she know then that one day she would be putting forth her political agenda to millions across Pakistan. While at Oxford, she drove a fancy sports car and was squired around by the sons of the English aristocracy. Meanwhile at home, many riots were occurring and arrests were frequent. Scotland Yard warned Bhutto that her life could be threatened by enemies of her father. But she returned to Pakistan the same year that her father, Zulfikar Ali Bhutto, was elected prime minister. Shortly after her return, her father was imprisoned.

When Z.A. Bhutto won the election in 1970, East Pakistan did not want to continue to be joined to West Pakistan. East Pakistan wanted its independence. Military troops from West Pakistan were sent to restore and maintain order in East Pakistan by order of President Bhutto. The East Pakistanis claimed the election had been fraudulent. They demanded immediate independence from (West) Pakistan. Heretofore, Pakistan had been ruled by military regimes. War broke out in 1971 with India on the side of East Pakistan. Fearing interference from India, the West Pakistani Air Force abruptly attacked thirteen of India's air bases. A thirteen day war ensued in which Pakistan was defeated. Z.A Bhutto, with his daughter by his side, took the matter to the United Nations in New York, where he pleaded for four days on behalf of a united Pakistan. In the end, Pakistan surrendered to India, and the new nation of Bangladesh was created out of East Pakistan. President Bhutto returned to (West) Pakistan in defeat and disgrace; his country was in ruins. Benazir Bhutto returned to Harvard to complete her studies.

In 1972, President Bhutto met in Simla, India, with Prime Minister Indira Gandhi to resolve the differences between the two nations. It was in this place that Indira's father had met with Mohammed Ali Jinnah to carve out the boundaries of India and Pakistan. Benazir accompanied her father as his aide. After much negotiation, the Simla Accord was signed between the two countries. The Simla Accord provided for the return of ninety thousand prisoners of war, for the reestablishment of communications and trade, and for allowing foreign air flights over each of the countries.

Zulifikar Bhutto established a new constitution, which placed the greatest power in the hands of the Prime Minister. Zulifikar Bhutto then shifted positions and became Prime Minister. When Bhutto was elected in 1970, he promised the people democracy and he delivered it. The new Constitution provided for the protection of human and civil rights. Prime Minister Bhutto guaranteed a parliamentary system of civilian government and elections every five years. He started a program of redistributing land to the poor, who had always been excluded in the old feudal system. Bhutto generously surrendered forty thousand acres of his own family's holdings as an example to the wealthy landowners. He also nationalized many industries such as banks and shipping. He urged workers to form unions, which could allow workers a voice in management along with job security, bonuses, and other benefits. In addition, education for the masses, and especially for women, was encouraged. Under Z.A. Bhutto's constitution of 1973, discrimination against women was prohibited. Greater equality for women gradually became a reality. After six years of progress, Prime Minister Bhutto was overthrown by another military coup. He was arrested and put in prison. He was later released, again arrested, and eventually hanged on the trumped-up charge of "murder."

General Zia-ul-Haq took power on July 5, 1977. He was a harsh military dictator, and he was mysteriously killed in 1988.

When Z.A. Bhutto had been Prime Minister, his wife and daughter had both assisted him. At the time he was imprisoned, they rallied to his support traveling around the country giving speeches to the masses. Although the twenty-four year old Benazir was terrified to speak out in public, her charisma and intelligence were evident. When her father was about to be executed, she promised she would continue to fight for his vindication and for democracy for their people.

Benazir Bhutto and her mother were arrested several times and placed under house arrest or in prison. The young woman was even kept in solitary confinement for six months under the harshest conditions. She had to spend several months in a hospital recuperating and was sent back to jail upon her release. Later she had to spend two more years under house arrest. General Zia refused to set her free unless she promised to stay out of politics. She courageously refused.

While Bhutto was languishing in jail or under house arrest, her two brothers had gone into exile and were organizing a group called L-Zulifikar. To fight General Zia's dictatorial regime, the resistance group used terrorist tactics such as hijacking planes and planting bombs. They demanded the release of political prisoners, including Bhutto and her mother. General Zia was convinced that Bhutto and her mother were at least partly responsible for the rebellious plot.

After their long imprisonments, Bhutto's and her mother's health seriously declined. Mrs. Bhutto was allowed to go to Germany in the company of another daughter. In 1984, Bhutto was permitted to leave the country to be treated in London for a severe ear ailment. Free again, she began a campaign against Zia and his illegal dictatorship. She contacted American and British newspapers to tell them of the human rights abuses in Pakistan. Amnesty International took up her cause by describing and denouncing General Zia's political oppression and his many atrocities. Bhutto wrote letters to the United Nations and to members of the British Parliament, documenting stories of how political prisoners like her mother and herself had been tortured. Accordingly, Britain and the United Nations exerted pressure on Pakistan to hold democratic elections.

In 1985, elections were held in Pakistan, but unfortunately, they were not free or honest. General Zia mandated many new restrictions and arrested many of his political opponents and critics. Outdoor political rallies, as well as speeches on radio or television, were prohibited. Although the Pakistan Peoples Party clearly won the election, General Zia again altered the Constitution to allow himself to remain in power. Bhutto continued her crusade in exile and traveled through Britain, the United States, and Europe railing against the continuing tyranny and abuses of the Zia regime. Since the Cold War between the Soviet Union and the free West was going on, the United States, Britain, and European nations were reluctant to put pressure on Pakistan or General Zia. After all, they were allies against the "red menace" of the Soviet Union. Bhutto was horrified to learn that Margaret Thatcher, while visiting an Afghan refugee camp, awarded a certificate of merit to General Zia and declared him "the last bastion of the free world."

Although Bhutto's public denunciations of General Zia's government failed to topple him, they were effective in raising doubts and suspicions from some members of the United States Congress and State Department. Strong voices were raised calling for an investigation into the allegations against the United States' allies in Pakistan. In a quick defensive action, General Zia called for a national referendum to lend legitimacy and credibility to his government. Although only 10 percent of the population voted, they opposed martial law and the Islamization of the legal system. But the General/Prime Minister again made arbitrary changes to the Constitution, which allowed him to retain both offices of General of the Army and Prime Minister of the nation. He also continued to govern under martial law.

When Bhutto's brother, Shah, died in Paris in 1986 of poisoning, under suspicious circumstances, she decided to return to Pakistan to confront General Zia and his supporters directly. She had been organizing and energizing members of the Pakistani Peoples Party living abroad. Now she wanted to strengthen the P.P.P. in Pakistan by combining it with Zia's opponents in the Pakistani Naval Academy to form the Movement for the Restoration of Democracy. This faction rapidly gained support among the Pakistani people. Not surprisingly, the tyrant cracked down brutally on Bhutto and the new M.R.D. She was arrested and imprisoned once more.

About twenty thousand of her P.P.P. and M.R.D. supporters were slaughtered, and a million political prisoners were imprisoned by the military. General Zia's abuses against his own people continued and even got worse. He persecuted members of the press and other media; the hard-gained rights of women were revoked; and Zia and his cronies stole U.S. arms and billions of dollars destined to assist the Afghan people against the invasion by the Soviet Union. Zia also profited from the billions of dollars worth of heroin and cocaine that came in through the refugee camps. To protect themselves against the illegal abuses of General Zia's troops, wealthy landowners and industrialists had to hire free-lance soldiers to form their own militias. Minority religious groups were also threatened or attacked. Zia used Muslim Mullahs to justify his arbitrary actions as "Sharia Law."

In 1984, Zia's Law of Evidence was passed which discriminated against women and demoralized many of them. For example, sexual crimes against women were next to impossible to prove with the requisite that four male witnesses in good standing had to appear in court. Women's testimony in court counted for only half of a man's testimony. Women were banned from appearing as witnesses in a murder case; compensation to the family of a female murder victim was cut in half. Bhutto advocated the repeal of the Zia Law but met with strong opposition. Not until 2006 was Zia Law repealed by Pervez Musharaff.

Eventually due to public protests and the influences of the international community, Bhutto was released and forced to leave the country. At thirty-three years of age, she was an attractive, single young woman. In a traditional arranged marriage, Bhutto and Asif Ali Zardari were married in 1987 in Karachi. After the Muslim ceremony and family celebration, the couple went to the Karachi Stadium where they were joyously greeted and cheered by more than two hundred thousand people. Clearly, Bhutto was still very famous and popular and a serious threat to the Zia government.

In August, 1988, General Zia and a number of his generals were killed in a plane crash; it appeared that the plane was deliberately blown up. A new government with Ghulam Ishag Khan as temporary President was formed. Bhutto quickly returned to Pakistan to take over the leadership of the Pakistani Peoples Party, which had been led by her mother. Although pregnant with her first child, Bhutto waged a relentless campaign. Her party platform declared that all people were entitled to a job, proper housing, adequate food, and a suitable education. She advocated immunizations, electricity for every home, and security within the country. She gave birth to her son, Bilawal, and five days later was back on the campaign trail. Elected co-chair of the P.P.P., she was soon elected Prime Minister at age thirty-five. She was the first woman elected to lead a Muslim state. She wished for the democratization and modernization of Pakistan.

Although now married and a mother, Bhutto was still referred to by the public as Miss Bhutto. She was popular with most of the people but not with Muslim fundamentalists, wealthy business leaders and landowners, and the remaining followers of the late General Zia. However, after only twenty months in office, she and her administration were dismissed on charges of corruption (for which she was never tried) by President Shulam Ishaq Khan. In 1990, Nawaz Sharif was elected Prime Minister and served for three years.

Due to threats of imprisonment or death, Bhutto and her family were forced to leave the country. Prime Minister Sharif, in fact, did start an investigation of charges alleged against Bhutto and her husband, Asif Ali

Zardari. Bhutto and the P.P.P were accused of failing to establish the rules of law and order and of making the economy even worse than it had been. Mr. Zardari and his wife were also accused of graft, extortion, and money laundering. None of the charges was ever proven in court, but Asif Zardari, nevertheless, eventually spent eight years in prison where he claimed to have suffered torture, inhuman treatment, and other human rights violations.

Even in exile, Bhutto continued to speak out against her political enemies in Pakistan. With poetic irony, Nawaz Sharif was also accused of corruption, murder, and malfeasance in office. He and his administration were dismissed by President Khan. At one point, a new caretaker Prime Minister and temporary President were appointed after Sharif and Khan both formally resigned. Accordingly, Bhutto returned home, ran for election as Prime Minister, and was re-elected in 1993. This time it was Bhutto that demanded an investigation into the charges against her predecessor.

But the tide of politics changed quickly in Pakistan. Before long, Nawaz Sharif was back in power. He was re-elected Prime Minister in 1997. Once again he resurrected the old charges and added new ones against Bhutto and especially, against her husband. Two days before the end of the trial, Bhutto and her children left the country. Zardari was retained and sent to prison.

Prime Minister Sharif made a serious mistake when he appointed General Pervez Musharraf as Chief of the Army; for, Musharraf without authorization, started a disastrous war with India and later led a successful coup d'état against Sharif. Musharraf had already been elected President of Pakistan, but he insisted on retaining his status as Chief of the Army. President/General Musharraf changed the constitution to limit any future Prime Minister to two terms in office. Thus, both Bhutto and her enemy, Sharif, would be ineligible to run.

Bhutto claimed that it was illegal for Musharraf to serve simultaneously as President and Chief of the Army. Musharraf promised that if he were re-elected President, he would resign as Chief of the Army. Bhutto still claimed his presidency was unconstitutional and that he should be declared ineligible to run. Musharraf had promised to hold general elections but postponed them until 2007. It is believed that Musharraf and Bhutto had secret negotiations in which he promised to allow her to return to Pakistan in safety, to receive amnesty against all charges, and to be allowed to run for the office of Prime Minister. She in turn would agree not to oppose Musharraf's bid for re-election to the Presidency.

Bhutto returned with members of her family to Karachi in October 2007 and declared her intention to run for parliament (not necessarily for

Prime Minister) in the coming 2008 election. Her return was met not only with great popular acclaim but also by threats and several actual attempts on her life. Amidst great popular approval, Bhutto took part in a ten-hour triumphant parade and narrowly escaped a suicide-bomb attack. After a brief visit to her family in Dubai, she returned to Lahore, Pakistan. She had endured six years of self-imposed exile. More threats and attacks on her life ensued. President Musharraf declared a state of emergency and placed Bhutto under house arrest "for her protection." Bhutto protested, claiming that a free election could not be held under a state of emergency. She demanded that she be allowed to continue her campaign freely with security protection equal to that of the President. Musharaff reluctantly conceded to her wishes.

As agreed when Musharraf was sworn in as President, he resigned from his military positions in 2008 under the threat of impeachment.

On December 27, 2007, Bhutto gave a speech to the Pakistani People's Party, which she had led even in exile. She was enthusiastically acclaimed. Standing up through the open sunroof of her bullet-proof car to wave to her admirers, she was shot at and bombs exploded nearby killing about twenty by-standers. Bhutto was severely wounded and taken to a nearby hospital where she died within hours. She was only fifty-four years old.

Musharraf has been accused of not providing Bhutto with adequate security protection. Moreover, a United Nations Commission in 2010 charged that Pakistan's military-led government failed to protect Prime Minister Benazir Bhutto before her 2007 assassination, and intelligence agencies hindered the subsequent investigation.

Bhutto gave her life for her democratic principles. She lived up to her father's expectations and carried on the legacy of the Bhutto family. Indeed, she stood as a symbol of democracy to the people of Pakistan. She suffered imprisonment, exile, and personal tragedy. Bhutto hoped for:

> ...a world of peace that provides people opportunities to prosper. Each individual is given life once to lead, and each individual deserves a chance to succeed....People need peace and they need opportunity in Pakistan and everywhere else. That's the world I'd like to see. (Mary Englar. *Benazir Bhutto*. [Minneapolis, Minnesota: Compass Point Books, 2006]. 95).

Her life is an inspiration to young women, especially in Third World countries. She advocated freedom of the press and moved toward free markets. Bhutto focused on education, health, housing, sanitation, and infrastructure development. She believed women needed to be literate, so their children would be literate. She believed that women had the right to choose whether they would live life as homemakers or as career women. During her two tenures, forty-eight thousand schools were built, and wireless communications were introduced. She established a Women's Development Bank to give credit to enterprising women. Under her term, she established agencies to educate women in family training, nutritional counseling, childcare, and birth control. (Benazir Bhutto. *Reconciliation.* [New York: Harper Collins, 2008]. 200). This modernization of Pakistan and her social views served as threats to radical Islamists. Unfortunately, she lived in a world where corruption and bribery are a way of life and that continues to this day. In her book *Reconciliation,* which she completed just before her death, she wrote:

> In making the case that much of the Muslim world's future depends on whether democracy can replace authoritarianism and dictatorship, my premise is that democracy weakens the forces of extremism and militancy. And if extremism and militance are defeated, our planet can avoid the cataclysmic battle that pessimists think is inevitable.
>
> ....I believe we must outline what all societies...but specifically Islamic Societies...can do to give democratic governance a chance to succeed. (Benazir Bhutto. *Reconciliation.* [New York: Harper Collins, 2008]. 284).

In her will Bhutto stated that she wanted her husband, Asif Ali Zardari, to take control of the P.P.P. Zardari agreed to run the party but only until their son, Bilawal Bhutto Zardari, could complete his studies at Oxford University. Bilawal was seventeen when his mother died, so although he could assume the title of chairman of the P.P.P., he would be too young to exercise the office. His father took the office of co-chair and was elected President of Pakistan in September 2008 and continues to serve in 2012. Bilawal, whose name means "one without equal," promised to take personal control of the P.P.P. when he completed his education. He graduated from Oxford in June 2010 and will be eligible to run for a provincial or national assembly seat in 2013. Bilawal has taken a strong stand on social issues and minorities, espousing his mother's progressive attitudes. In the meantime, he will be learning the workings of the P.P.P. under the wings of senior provincial leaders. In spite of voices reflecting opposition to the continuance of the Bhutto dynasty in the subcontinent, it appears Bhutto's son has great support, especially from the youth sector of the party and supporters of his late mother.

On May 7, 2011, Osama bin Laden, the elusive emir of the al-Qaeda network, the mastermind of the 9/11 attacks and thousands of murders around the globe, was killed by a group of American Navy Seals in Abbottabad, Pakistan, near an impressive military base comparable to America's West Point where he had been living for about five years. It appears that bin Laden was receiving help and protection from the Pakistani government. The Inter-Services Intelligence seems to support the Taliban with one arm and the anti-terrorist groups with the other.

Of course, President Asif Ali Zardari, Benazir Bhutto's husband, has denied any suggestions that Pakistan has ever been a harbor for terrorism. He blames Osama bin Laden for the murder of his wife, Benazir Bhutto, whom he described as a "democratically elected progressive, moderate, pluralistic, female leader."

The United States has given twenty billion dollars to Pakistan since 9/11, and the American Government seeks to know justifiably where Pakistan stands on the war against the Taliban and al-Qaeda. To most Americans inside and outside of the government, it seems inconceivable that Osama bin Laden could have existed in a fortress without anyone in the government or the I.S.I. knowing about it.

America's relationship with Pakistan is very complicated. We are aware that because of Pakistan's possession of nuclear weapons, terrorists could take control and inflict damage on India, which also has nuclear weapons. These two countries are constantly on the brink of war and have, indeed, fought several wars. The world could be thrust into WWIII! On April 19, 2012, India successfully test-fired a nuclear missile capable of reaching China and Eastern Europe. Not to be outdone Pakistan six days later launched a nuclear intermediate-range missile on April 25, 2012, believed to be able to reach its rival India.

Bilawal Bhutto Zardari will be facing huge domestic and international problems if and when he takes on the mantle of governance. Having two members of his family, his mother and grandfather, killed by political enemies, Bilawal Bhutto Zardari might be expected to seek revenge. Instead, in a conciliatory tone, he announced, "My mother always said, 'Democracy is the best revenge.' " It will be interesting to see what he does and is able to achieve when he assumes the mantle of power and authority proudly worn by his mother, grandfather, grandmother, and father.

Interview with Aung San Suu Kyi born 1945- regarding the grounds for her rejected appeal She stands as a symbolic leader for the oppressed people of Burma. (image by KET.image public domain)

CHAPTER EIGHTEEN

Aung San Suu Kyi, "The Lady of Burma"

"The struggle for democracy and human rights in Burma is a struggle for life and dignity."

Daw Aung San Suu Kyi Aris was released from house arrest on November 13, 2010, after her most recent confinement of seven years in detention. For fifteen of the last twenty-one years, she has been a virtual prisoner in her own home in Rangoon, Burma. Her composite name states briefly who she is or at least where she comes from. Aung San was the name of her father, a Burmese patriot often called "The Father of Modern Burma." Suu was the name of her grandmother; Kyi indicates that her mother was Ma Khin Kyi; and Aris is the family name of her late English-born husband, Dr. Michael Aris, who was a Tibetan history and culture scholar. Daw is a title of respect given to an older or married woman.

Although rarely allowed to leave her prison-home, Daw Suu Kyi is revered almost like a saint or savior by the Burmese people. She is also known around the world as a recipient of the Nobel Peace Prize, and many other honors and because of her autobiography, *The Voice of Hope*. Since it is politically dangerous for Burmese people to speak her name, she is generally called by the simple title: "Daw, the Lady."

"The Lady," Suu Kyi, was born in Rangoon on June 19, 1945, in a time of violent political upheaval. Great Britain had forcibly annexed Burma in 1886, ruling it jointly with another colonial possession, India. In 1942, with the cooperation of General Aung San, Suu Kyi's father, Japan invaded Burma. The "General" hoped to liberate his homeland from British and Indian control with the help of the Japanese. He also looked to Communism as a way to assist his downtrodden people, so he formed the Communist Party of Burma. Japan was defeated in 1945. Two years later in 1947, Aung San was assassinated by Burmese political opponents. Just six months later, Burma was granted independence, but many hard times were to follow.

When Suu Kyi's father was assassinated, she was just two years old. Her mother was forced to take on new political responsibilities, so she had little time to spend with her children. Although the family was Buddhist, Suu Kyi and her brothers were sent to a strict Catholic school since their mother favored strong discipline. There they began to study English. At age eleven, she entered the English Methodist High School. In 1957, she and the family were saddened by the accidental drowning of one of her brothers. Not long after, her older brother was sent to a boarding school in England.

As a prominent figure in the new Burmese government, Daw Kyin Kyi, Suu Kyi's mother, was appointed Ambassador to India and Nepal in 1960. Suu Kyi, age fifteen, went with her. The young girl did not realize that she would not return to her homeland for twenty-eight years. Suu Kyi lived with her mother while continuing her education: first at another strict Catholic School and then at the recently established Lady Shri Ram College at the University of Delhi. Encouraged by her mother, she majored in political science. The motto of the college foretold the young woman's future: "That alone is knowledge which leads to liberation."

In 1964, Suu Kyi and her mother sadly parted: Daw Khin Kyi returned to Burma to become active in national politics; her daughter went to England to study at St. Hugh's College, Oxford University, where she majored in philosophy, political science, and economics. While a student at Oxford, Suu Kyi met her future husband, Dr. Michael Aris. Upon completion of her studies in England, Suu Kyi went to New York to pursue graduate studies. Once there, she became involved with the United Nations Organization, which was then led by a fellow Burmese, U Thant, and she worked at the United Nations for three years before returning to England.

In January of 1972, she married Dr. Michael Aris. Their first son was born in 1973; their second son in 1977. The young wife assisted her husband with his Tibetan research. She also worked as a part-time librarian at the Bodleian Library at Oxford cataloguing and building up the Burmese collection. Then in 1985, she received a scholarship to do research on Burma's independence movement at Kyoto University in Japan. Since her father had solicited Japan's help in "liberating" Burma, and Japan subsequently invaded Burma, Suu Kyi's interest in her native land and in her father, a national hero, was rekindled. When she left Japan, she went to visit her mother in Rangoon and stayed three months.

From Burma, Suu Kyi went to rejoin her husband and children in Simla, India. While there, she wrote three travel guide books on Nepal, Bhutan, and Burma. The family returned to London in 1987. The following year, she received news that her mother had suffered a severe stroke. A dutiful daughter, Suu Kyi returned to Burma immediately.

The political situation had never been stable, neither before nor since the country won independence in 1946. In 1962, General Ne Win seized power and ruled as a virtual dictator. He lacked the ability to meld the various ethnic groups into a united nation. Traditional Buddhists clashed with the ruling communists while ethnic minorities fought among themselves. Many Burmese who had grown up under British rule had grown accustomed to British customs, language, and a congenial way of life. General Ne Win wanted to eradicate all vestiges of English culture: he forbade the teaching of English and ordered that automobile and bicycle traffic no longer follow the British custom of driving on the left side of the road. The government tolerated and even encouraged a thriving trade in opium which was making officials rich. Many warlords and groups of insurgents also profited from the trade, and they used their wealth to spread more violence. As a result, many thousands of Burmese tried to escape into neighboring Thailand and Bangladesh. To protect his public and international image, the dictator took control of the media and exercised severe censorship. In addition, he used the army to pacify the public and to squash protest demonstrations.

Rangoon University students organized a pro-democracy parade and proceeded to march across the White Bridge. The army and the police met them, killed several hundred students, injured many more, and arrested the ones that were left. The lieutenant general who led the army was labeled the "Butcher of Rangoon," and the blood-covered bridge henceforth was known as the "Red Bridge." The White/Red Bridge incident became a symbol of repression and a rallying point for the democratic movement. As the demonstrations continued, common laborers and Buddhist monks joined the ranks of the protesters. The government responded by ordering soldiers to shoot into the crowds of protesters and used torture and inhumane treatment on the imprisoned rebels. Violence continued to spread and soon all Burma was in deep chaos. Suu Kyi wrote:

> In a country like Burma want and fear stalk us all the time. People wake up in the morning wondering which of their friends have been taken into detention by the authorities. People wake up in the morning wondering where their next meal is going to come from. They wake up in the morning wondering what the future of their children will be and worrying about it. Want and fear go together where there are no human rights and where there is no justice. (Justin Wintle. *Perfect Hostage.* [New York: Skyhorse Publishing Company, 2007]. 399).

Suu Kyi followed the worsening political situation. Although she empathized with the demonstrators, she did not know what to do for them. She volunteered to serve as a negotiator between the government and the rebellious demonstrators, but her offer was rejected. Community spokespersons remembered Suu Kyi's father as a great rebel soldier and leader and begged her to take command. She refused. As a devout Buddhist and admirer of Mahatma Gandhi's peaceful protests, she would not condone a violent revolution. Besides, she realized she lacked the desire and the experience to lead a political movement.

Nevertheless, respect and love for her father and a sense of duty toward her native land led her inevitably into her country's new struggle for freedom and democracy. On August 24, 1988, Suu Kyi gave her first political speech in front of fifty thousand demonstrators. To placate the crowds of protesters, the government promised free elections and a more democratic society. The ban on the media was lifted. Newspapers, magazines, and pamphlets were allowed to circulate freely—for a few weeks. Pictures of Aung San, the "Father of Burma" and Suu Kyi's father, were visible throughout the city.

The prestige and popularity of her famous father and mother spread quickly to their daughter. Some Burmese women even saw her as an avatar of the Buddhist goddess of mercy. Willingly or not, Suu Kyi was thrust into the position of leader of a new freedom movement. Meeting with student and community leaders at her house, they formed a new political party called the National League for Democracy (NLD). Suu Kyi was named General Secretary.

When the visas of her husband and children expired, they were forced to leave the country. Because of her commitment to the Burmese people, she needed to remain to fight for their rights. She traveled the country speaking to crowds of ten thousand or more. She spoke to ethnic minorities urging them to forget their differences and unite for a free Burma. She emphasized the ideals of democracy, especially basic human rights.

But as protests continued and more violence spread from the cities to the countryside, the dictatorial government cracked down again. Due to the violence, many businesses had to close and workers were left without jobs. The price of food and gasoline rose sharply. Looting and other criminal acts became rampant, including direct attacks on government offices and the military. After twenty-five years of repression, the people's anger erupted like a volcano.

The dictator, Ne Win, cracked down in an attempt to crush both the anarchy and the insurgents. Thousands were killed and many more were imprisoned. Martial law was imposed and public demonstrations were prohibited. Since Suu Kyi's father had briefly experimented with Communism in his earlier years, many now accused the new National League for Democracy as being a front for Communists.

For a while the N.L.D. ceased its demonstrations and waited patiently for reforms such as new free elections that Ne Win had promised. The police and army, however, continued to harass students and others they assumed were members of the N.L.D. When Suu Kyi, along with family members and supporters, went to visit the Martyrs' Mausoleum to honor her heroic father, the group was intercepted by soldiers and Suu Kyi was forced to return home at gunpoint. She was warned to stay at home and not to interfere in Burmese politics. Even her telephone lines were cut. In protest, like her model Mahatma Gandhi before her, she went on a hunger strike.

But in August 1989, Suu Kyi decided it was time to openly resist the oppressive government. She began actively campaigning again. Despite harassment by the military, huge crowds came to hear and cheer her. Still advocating non-violence, the young female leader accused General Ne Win of illegally using the military for his own selfish purposes. He retaliated by placing her under house arrest again, thereby preventing her from making any public campaign appearances. In addition, her supporters continued to be harassed, arrested and imprisoned, and the media were allowed to print or broadcast only what government censors allowed. Confident that he and his political party would easily win, he allowed the election to take place.

To General Ne Win's shock and disappointment, Suu Kyi and her National League for Democracy won. That meant that she would become a member of the national legislature with the likelihood of becoming either president or prime minister. General Ne Win was not about to let that happen. He claimed that his military regime had been recognized as legitimate by the United Nations and many foreign governments. Accordingly, he was not "legally" required to turn over power and authority to civilians. To demonstrate his good faith, he would allow the drawing up of a new constitution, but his army would set the guidelines. Furthermore, he promised that any new constitution would have to be approved by the people in a national referendum. Of course, the delegates to the constitutional convention would be selected by the General's own political organization, the S.L.O.R.C. (State Law and Order Restoration Council).

While Suu Kyi was once again placed under house arrest with military guards to guarantee her isolation, her fellow members of the N.L.D. met to discuss their political aims and strategy. The members were divided in their opinions: some wanted an all-out armed rebellion; others advocated waiting to see if the government officially would keep their promises. But on August 8, 1990, Buddhist monks decided they would wage their own peaceful protests; many students and ordinary people turned out to support them. More government brutality ensued: two monks and two students were killed, and many more were beaten. The religious leader of the monks released them from their normal duties. General Ne Win responded by shutting down three hundred and fifty monasteries. Armed troops forcibly entered the monasteries to arrest monks and any civilians they might be harboring. In addition, the New Ministry for Religious and House Affairs was set up to take control of the monks, and the government deprived head monks of their spiritual authority and arbitrarily replaced them. The new head monks and the monks under them had to promise not to oppose the military regime. Those who refused would no longer be allowed to wear their saffron robes.

Still pretending to be the democratic ruler of a free nation, General Ne Win promised new elections. But first he had all those who were elected to parliament in the previous election arrested, including Suu Kyi who was already imprisoned in her own home. The government had passed a decree giving itself the right to detain suspects for five years without formally charging them. When charges were brought against prisoners, the military court could find all sorts of reasons to declare them guilty as charged. Suu Kyi's words resonated: "It is not power that corrupts, but fear of losing power that corrupts."

Since Suu Kyi had been educated in Christian elementary and secondary schools and had spent so many years out of her native land, she had not been steeped in Burmese tradition or in the Buddhist religion.

In her enforced confinement, she began to study Buddhist sacred texts and even to practice daily meditation. Instead of showing anger toward the soldiers guarding her, in true Buddhist fashion, she treated them with kindness and affection. The guards had to be replaced regularly to prevent them from becoming too friendly with their prisoner. Even in her isolation, rumors of the harsh treatment the government provided her made her even more popular with the people of Burma.

Her fame and reputation were growing around the world as well. During her imprisonment, her husband worked tirelessly to reveal the despotic conditions in Burma and especially the unjust treatment of his wife. Newspaper and magazine articles were written about her; her picture even appeared on the cover of *Time* Magazine. Radio and television programs featured her story. Her courage and endurance became famous.

Then awards and prizes started to come in: an Honorary Fellowship from her Alma Mater, St. Hugh's; the Rafto Prize for being "an outstanding human rights advocate;" and the Parliament of the European Union awarded her the Sakharov Prize for Freedom of Human Thought. India awarded her the Jawaharial Nehru Peace Prize. And best of all on Oct. 14, 1991, Suu Kyi received the Nobel Prize for Peace, which included a monetary award of over one million dollars. In accepting the Nobel Peace Prize for his mother, her son, Alexander Aris, announced that the money would be used to set up a health and education fund for the Burmese people. Ironically, the military junta that ruled the country claimed that her generous act was performed to avoid paying taxes. Found guilty of the charge by a military court, she was sentenced to additional years of house arrest.

The overt cruelty and injustice of the Burmese government led the United Nations Assembly to pass a resolution condemning the military regime and demanding Suu Kyi's release. Russia and China opposed the resolution, so it failed to pass. But many world leaders such as Vaclav Havel, Jimmy Carter, George W. Bush, Barack Obama, and several Secretary Generals of the United Nations have demanded her release over the years. With so much foreign pressure, the military junta ruling Burma in 2011 promised new free elections, but since Suu Kyi was under house arrest, she was not permitted to run for office. Many of her supporters in the N.L.D. boycotted the election.

Without intending to do so, Suu Kyi has been thrust into the position of being a symbolic leader for the oppressed people of Burma (now known as Myanmar). She is also a symbol of their hope for eventual freedom from a twenty year dictatorship. But on and off for the last fifteen years, Suu

Kyi has been kept in isolation under house arrest in her island home. The dictatorial military regime has declared her a traitor and evil criminal while her supporters view her as a saintly heroine. Since she has chosen to remain in Myanmar to help her people rather than live outside the country with her husband and children, she has been considered a bad wife and mother by some traditional women both in Burma and abroad. However, her late husband and children understood her dilemma and supported her cause from afar. They labored to demonstrate her innocence and the dictatorial tactics of the current military regime to the world community. Lovers of freedom around the world clamored for her release.

Now that she is free again, Suu Kyi wonders how long her freedom will last. In early 2011, the Myanmar Parliament convened for the first time in more than two decades, bringing about a new constitution that technically ends a half-century of military rule. However, while Myanmar officials tout a transition to democracy, most of the seats are occupied by the all-powerful military.

In 2001 on Suu Kyi's fifty-sixth birthday and also Women of Burma Day, she sent a message disseminated by the N.L.D. to the women of Burma:

> According to a number of psychologists, women are better able than men to cope with crisis situations. We should use this ability to bring about peace and progress to our country, and to better the conditions the world over. There is a great need for our women of Burma to use their capabilities to bring democracy and human rights to our country. It is no longer possible even for housewives to keep out of politics, because politics has invaded the traditional domain of housewives. The root cause of upward spiraling commodity prices, greatly increased charges for electricity and rising costs of education and healthcare is a political one. (Justin Wintle. *Perfect Hostage.* [New York: Skyhorse Publishing, 2007]. 398).

Suu Kyi's National League for Democracy registerd in 2011 as a political party; she announced her intention to run for parliment in forthcoming elections.

In 1997, President Bill Clinton issued an executive order banning most new development of resources in Burma. He justified taking these steps based on the military junta's severe repression of the democratic opposing forces. Many of the democracy supporters were held in prisons for long terms and others have suffered torture or simply just disappeared. The sanctions against Burma are specified in certain U.S. laws based on various functional issues such as the use of child soldiers, drug trafficking, human trafficking, money laundering, failure to protect religious freedom, violations of workers' rights and suppression of political expression. Burma remains the world's leading producer of opium and heroin.

Secretary of State Hillary Clinton visited Burma and Suu Kyi on November 30, 2011. She was the first American senior official to visit Burma in over fifty years. Clinton praised Suu Kyi for her pro-democracy stand and dedication to her country. Clinton expressed the view that she saw "a flicker of hope" that the candle will be ignited into a movement of change in a program of democratization and respect for human rights. Her visit suggests that the U.S. and Burma appear to have opened a door to press ahead with rapprochement.

In January 2012, the Burmese government released over six hundred political prisoners in a gesture of good will towards its new policy of human rights. In March 2012, Suu Kyi announced she would definitely be a parliamentary candidate in the upcoming election. She was elected to the Parliament in April 2012 along with forty-three members of her National League for Democracy Party who will lead the small opposition bloc. On May 8, 2012, she received her first passport in twenty-four years. "The Lady" plans on visiting her two sons in England; Oxford University, her Alma Mater; Norway where she received the Nobel Peace Prize; and the United Nations in New York City.

In the words of Vaclav Havel, fellow recipient of the Nobel Peace Prize and former president of Czechoslovakia, "She is an outstanding example of the power of the powerless." And so she is. Now that she is released from house arrest "The Lady" will continue to agitate for the freedom and the rights of her people.

Nancy Pelosi 1940- She was the first female elected Speaker of the House of Representatives and the first woman to lead a political party in the U.S. Congress. (U.S. Congress image public domain)

CHAPTER NINETEEN

More Women of the 21st Century: Nancy Pelosi, Hillary Clinton, Angela Merkel, Gloria Macapagal-Arroyo

"Being the first woman speaker and breaking the marble ceiling is pretty important. Now it's time to move on."
Nancy Pelosi

Nancy Pelosi was the first female Speaker of the House of Representatives and consequently the first woman to lead a majority party in the United States Congress. She was, and still is, a very powerful woman. However, she lost her position as Speaker after her party (Democrat) lost their majority in the House of Representatives as a result of the November, 2010 election.

Pelosi comes from a political family. She was born on March 25, 1940, in Baltimore, Maryland, the only girl and youngest among six children. Her father Thomas D'Alesandro was politically active in "Little Italy" where the family lived. They were so active that when Pelosi was seven years old her Italian Democrat father was elected Mayor of Baltimore. Pelosi was able to observe at first hand the way politics and politicians worked in Baltimore. She saw her popular father ingratiating himself with voters at all sorts of social gatherings: weddings, picnics, spaghetti suppers, church functions, and funerals. Visitors were always welcome at the D'Alesandro home. Pelosi's mother usually had a pot of soup ready when desperate citizens stopped by to ask for favors such as jobs or financial assistance. Women would often come begging for leniency for their wayward sons who had gotten in trouble with the law. Since Baltimore was the closest city on the direct route from Washington, D.C. to New York and New England, many famous national figures stopped at Mayor D'Alesandro's home where Pelosi had the opportunity to meet and observe them. To mention a few: Harry Truman, Spiro Agnew, Jimmy Carter, and Ronald Reagan visited the prominent mayor. Those opportunities and her admiration for her father sparked Nancy's ambitions toward a future in politics. When her father ran successfully for the U.S. Congress, Pelosi wanted to assist her dad with his political career; she wanted to be a politician, too. But that was not to be for a good while yet.

Mrs. Annunciata D'Alesandro insisted that her only daughter should receive a good strict Catholic education. So Pelosi went to the Institute of Notre Dame where she met fellow students from different races and ethnic groups. A diligent student, she made good grades and excelled on the school's debating team. Next, she went on to Trinity College, a prestigious liberal arts Catholic college in Washington, D.C. Not surprisingly, the prominent mayor's daughter majored in political science. While taking a course in African history at nearby Georgetown University, Nancy met Paul Pelosi, and they were married on September 7, 1963.

The newly-weds went to live in New York City where Paul worked in the banking industry. Within the next six years, Pelosi gave birth to four girls and one boy. Eventually the family moved to Paul's hometown, San Francisco. Paul had little interest in politics, but his older brother did. He was well known in the local Democrat organization, and he urged Nancy Pelosi to get involved. Still busy raising her young children, she started in a small way by chairing fund-raising events for the community and for Democrat candidates. Her passion and involvement with city and state politics grew until finally she declared herself a candidate for Congress in 1987. She was not quite forty-seven years old. She won the election and joined the 100th Congress at a time when only twenty-four of the four hundred and eleven representatives were women.

As the representative of San Francisco, a city with a large gay population, Pelosi was concerned about the spreading plague of the HIV/AIDS virus. Accordingly, she sponsored a number of legislative proposals to provide medical and financial support in the fight against HIV/AIDS. As a result, by the time Pelosi became Speaker of the House in 2007, the federal government was spending more than twenty billion dollars a year on HIV/AIDS research, prevention, and treatment. She also staunchly defended the rights of the gay and lesbian community by opposing the Defense of Marriage Act in 1996 and later the Federal Marriage Amendment.

But Pelosi was also concerned about national and international issues. She successfully opposed President George W. Bush's attempt to reform social security but supported his No Child Left Behind legislation. Her "Pelosi Amendment" addressed environmental issues abroad and at home. She has long been a strong advocate of affordable housing for the poor, national parks (especially in California), civil rights, and the reform of health care. In fact, one of her greatest legislative victories was the passage of the Patient Protection and Affordable Care Act of 2010 (more commonly referred to as "Obama Care"). Although Pelosi remains a Roman Catholic, she is a supporter of women's "right to choose," which maintains the legality of abortion. So in 2003, she voted against the Partial Birth Abortion Ban Bill. Her reason was that the federal government has no right to intervene in a person's private, personal decisions.

In international affairs, Minority Whip Pelosi accused President Clinton of "catering to murders" in failing to confront China for its human rights abuses; she advocated revoking China's preferred trading-partner status. On the other hand, Pelosi congratulated George W. Bush when he awarded the Congressional Gold Medal to the Dalai Lama in 2007. Not only did she oppose George H. W. Bush's invasion of Iraq in 1990 to 1991, she also opposed George W. Bush's invasion of Iraq in 2003 and his troop surge in 2007. She also strongly criticizes the use of torture by the C.I.A. or the U.S. military on detainees in Guantanamo or elsewhere. Pelosi has been a constant defender of human rights of individuals and peoples around the world: China, Tibet, Burma (Myanmar), Rwanda, Sudan, Somalia, and wherever she observes injustice and oppression.

Pelosi was charged with abusing her privilege of military plane usage for her own personal desires when serving as Speaker of the House. In 2011, she and other Congressional leaders were charged with insider trading. Pelosi has denied both accusations. On April 4, 2012, the Stock Act was finally signed by President Obama, which takes at least the first step in curtailing the abuses of insider trading by members of Congress.

When Pelosi attended her first meeting in the White House as Speaker of the House, she realized this meeting was unlike any meeting *any* woman had ever attended at the White House. She writes:

> The president, always gracious, welcomed me as a new member of the leadership.

> As he began the discussion, I suddenly felt crowded in my chair. It was truly an astonishing experience, as if Susan B. Anthony, Elizabeth Cady Stanton, Lucretia Mott, Alice Paul, and all the other suffragettes and activists who had worked hard to advance in government and in life were right there with me. I was enthralled by their presence, and then I could clearly hear them say: 'At last we have a seat at the table.' (Nancy Pelosi. *Know Your Power.* [New York: Doubleday, 2008]. 124).

In 2010, the Republican Party won a majority of seats in the House of Representatives, so Pelosi is no longer the Speaker of the House. Since she was easily re-elected as a U.S. Representative from California, she will continue to be a leader of the Democrat Party. As sixtieth Speaker of the House, she was the highest-ranking female politician in American history.

Addressing the issue of women in high places, Pelosi wrote:

> Raising a family is challenging. I want women to know that the skills I acquired as a mother and homemaker have been invaluable to me. These same skills—so often undervalued—are transferable to many other areas in life, including the United States Congress.

> If women can learn from me, in the same way I learned from the women who came before me, it will make the honor of being Speaker of the House even greater. May the examples I share with my life help others to know their power. (Nancy Pelosi. *Know your Power.* [New York: Doubleday, 2008.] 2).

In spite of the diminishment of her stature and power, Nancy Pelosi will continue to be a formidable power in American politics for the foreseeable future. In January 2011, she was elected Minority Whip.

★ ★ ★

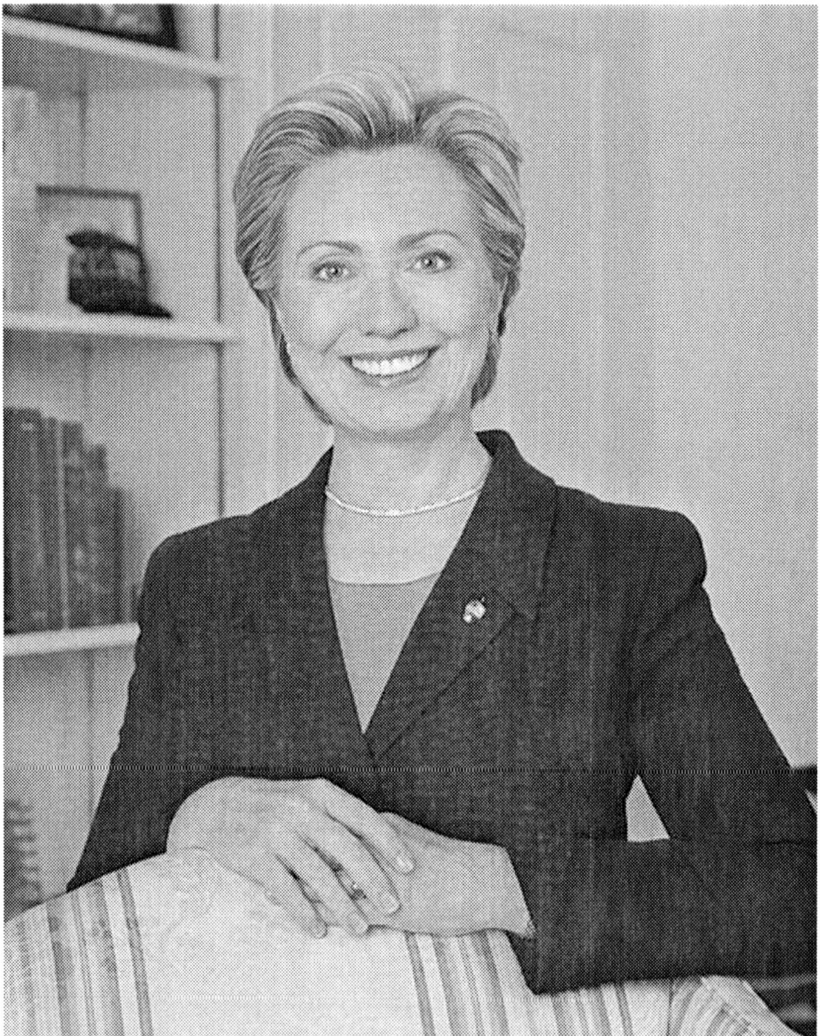

Hillary Clinton 1947- She is the 67th United States Secretary of State and former First Lady of the U.S. (Wikimedia Commons official portrait U.S. Congress public domain)

Hillary Clinton (nee Rodham) was born on October 26, 1947, in Chicago, Illinois. She was the eldest of three children, followed by two brothers, Hugh and Tony. Her childhood was spent in Park Ridge, Illinois, a Chicago suburb. Clinton's father, Hugh Rodham, was a successful entrepreneur who was a conservative Republican. On the other hand, her mother, Dorothy Rodham, was a home-maker and a dedicated Democrat.

Dorothy Rodham greatly influenced her daughter. She was a devout Methodist who stressed social obligations in the up-bringing of her children. When Hillary was introduced to Reverend Don Jones, these attitudes were reinforced and she read religious philosophers and helped the needy by babysitting the children of migrant farm workers. Another influence was meeting the Reverend Dr. Martin Luther King, Jr. during his visit to Chicago on a speaking tour. Her mother encouraged her to read, to speak her mind, to stand up for herself, and to pursue her goals.

While in her school years, Hillary exhibited strong qualities that would remain with her for the rest of her life. In a speech she delivered in Washington, D.C., on March, 20, 2012, to praise the legacy of female aviator Amelia Earhart and to emphasize our ties with the Pacific Island nations, Hillary noted that when she was thirteen years old, she wrote to NASA for an application to become an astronaut. Her answer from NASA: females were not allowed in the program. She was a serious student and was involved in almost all school activities. She rewrote the student assembly constitution and in the eleventh grade became a class vice-president. Already a stellar debater in high school, she was more interested in politics than boys. One of her heroes was Margaret Chase Smith, the first woman elected to the House of Representatives and then to the U.S. Senate.

Possessing ambition, intelligence, idealism, belief in public service, and reliance on financial independence, Hillary set off for Wellesley College at age seventeen where she majored in political science and minored in psychology. There she stood out as a natural leader. In 1968, she was elected president of the student body. She entered Wellesley as a Republican and graduated as a Democrat.

Graduating with highest honors in 1969, Hillary gave the first commencement address in the history of the school. A natural communicator, she was a progressive on the Wellesley campus, bringing about many movements for change.

Next, Hillary moved on to Yale Law School where she was one out of twenty-seven women among two hundred and thirty-five law students. She focused on issues relating to children, especially the poor and disadvantaged.

For a summer she worked with Marian Wright Edelman, a civil rights attorney who headed the Washington Research Project based in Washington, D.C. This group later became known as the Children's Defense Fund. In 1973, Hillary graduated from Yale Law School with a Juris Doctor (J.D.) degree after writing her thesis on the rights of children. She soon took a full-time position with the Children's Defense Fund as a staff-lawyer.

In 1974, Hillary was chosen as one of forty-three lawyers to work on the legal staff of the House Judiciary Committee, which was preparing legal documents resulting from the Watergate scandal involving wire-tapping and burglary. President Richard Nixon's involvement all but forced him to resign. After President Nixon left office on August 9, 1974, the legal staff broke up.

While at Yale Law School, Hillary met and fell in love with another law student, William Clinton. Young, idealistic and ambitious, they both were eager to change the world. Bill and Hillary were married in 1975 and set up housekeeping in Fayetteville, Arkansas, Bill's home state. The young couple agreed that they would focus on Bill's political career first. Clinton actively supported Bill's campaign for the office of Attorney General of Arkansas. When he won the election in 1976, Clinton joined the Rose Law Firm. The next year, she co-founded the Arkansas Advocates for Children and Families. Later on, President Jimmy Carter appointed her Chair of the Board of Directors of the Federal Legal Services Corporation, which provided free legal services to the poor. Clinton was making a name for herself; She was twice listed among the hundred most influential lawyers in America.

When Bill Clinton ran for governor of Arkansas in 1978, Clinton helped plan and manage his campaign, and when he became Governor, Clinton became an influential First Lady. In that position she led a task force to reform the education system in Arkansas, which was then the poorest in the nation. She also gave birth to a daughter Chelsea.

Bill lost his bid for re-election in 1981, but with his wife's untiring assistance he was re-elected in 1983 and remained in office until 1992. As in all of her husband's campaigns and during his time in office, Clinton traveled around the state giving speeches on her husband's behalf. She was also his closest political adviser. At one point, she led a committee on urban health-care reform.

During their time as Governor and First Lady of Arkansas, the Clintons moved onto the national scene. With Clinton at his side, Bill Clinton became prominent in the New Democrat movement that opposed the policies of George H. W. Bush, who was elected President in 1984. As chair of the National Governors Association in 1986 to 1987, Bill Clinton became recognized as a new national leader. In 1988, he gave the opening address at the Democratic National Convention when he nominated Michael Dukakis. Only three years later, Bill Clinton announced that he was a candidate for the presidency.

As always, Clinton stood by her man even though she was aware of his marital infidelities. There were also rumors and charges of the couple's involvement in the Whitewater real estate venture and of favoritism by Governor Clinton toward the law firm in which his wife was a partner.

When her husband became the forty-second President, Clinton, as First Lady, also stepped into national and international prominence. Assigned the daunting task of reforming the health care system in the U.S., Clinton drew a great deal of public attention and opposition. Her complex health-care bill was defeated in Congress in 1993. Next, she turned her focus to the cause of women's rights around the world. In 1995, Clinton spoke at the U.N. World Conference on Women in Beijing, China. One by one, she addressed many of the atrocities committed against women and even against baby girls: the starvation and murder of infants simply because they are female; the sale of young girls into slavery or prostitution; rape as a tactic of war; genital mutilation; enforced sterilization and abortion as a means of population control; and physical and psychological violence committed against girls and women. She stated: "In too many instances, the road to globalization has also meant the marginalization of women and girls. And that must change."

Clinton echoed Mary Wollstonecraft in the eighteenth century when she proclaimed:

> If women have the chance to be full and equal partners in society, their families will flourish. And when families flourish, communities and nations will flourish....If there is one message that echoes forth from this conference, let it be that human rights are women's rights. And women's rights are human rights, once and for all. (Michael Burgan. *Clinton.* [Minneapolis, Minnesota: Compass Point Books, 2008]. 62).

In 1998, Clinton traveled to Seneca Falls, New York, to commemorate the hundred and fiftieth anniversary of the first Women's Rights Convention in America. She addressed an audience of sixteen thousand with these words, for she wondered what the brave men and women who signed the declaration

> ...would say if they learned how many women failed to vote in elections? They would be amazed and outraged....One hundred and fifty years ago, the women at Seneca Falls were silenced by someone else. Today, women—we silence ourselves. We have a choice. We have a voice. The future, like the past and present, will not and cannot be perfect. Our daughters and granddaughters will face new challenges, which today we cannot even imagine. But each of us can help prepare for that future by doing what we can to speak out for justice and equality, for women's rights and human rights, to be on the right side of history, no matter the risk or cost. (Hillary Clinton. *Living History.* [New York: Simon and Schuster, 2003]. 462).

In spite of the ignominious defeat of her health-care proposal, Clinton persisted in her efforts to make a difference especially in the lives of children. In 1997 and 1999, she was instrumental in promoting the State Children's Health Insurance Program, the Adoption and Safe Families Act, and the Foster Care Dependence Act. At last, Clinton had demonstrated her formidable legislative skills to the public. As her husband's political career was winding down, Clinton decided to concentrate on her own political future. After establishing legal residence in New York State, she ran for Daniel Moynihan's senate seat when he retired. With Moynihan's advice and support, Clinton became a U.S. Senator in 2001. Her initial focus was in the areas of education, health, labor, and public works.

But when the World Trade Center was destroyed on September 11, 2001, everyone's focus changed. Clinton supported George W. Bush's war against the Taliban in Afghanistan and his attack on Iraq in 2003. However, she opposed many of Bush's domestic policies as well as his policies on foreign affairs. As both wars dragged on, Clinton decried the Bush administration's lack of an exit plan and the ineffective military plans to win decisively the wars and establish lasting peace.

In 2007, Clinton declared her candidacy to become the first female President of the U.S. In the primary, she won more delegates and more state primaries than any of the few women candidates before her. Clinton explained her vision for the country:

> I am running for president because I believe if we set big goals and if we work together to achieve them, we can restore the American dream today and for the next generation. (Michael Burgan. *Clinton.* [Minneapolis, Minnesota: Compass Books, 2008]. 95).

During her campaign, she spoke about the growing distance between the rich and the poor. She championed minority groups: Blacks, Native

Americans, and Hispanics. She promised to reform health care and education and promised to create new jobs by providing tax incentives to large companies. Most important of all, she promised she would bring home American troops from Iraq and Afghanistan. Despite her energetic campaign, Clinton lost the Democrat Party's nomination to the freshman senator, Barack Obama, from Illinois. Recognizing her many personal and political talents, the new President gave her a position in his cabinet as Secretary of State.

An outstanding example of a successful independent woman, Clinton has also shown herself to be a loving, supporting, forgiving wife, and devoted mother to Chelsea. She has been an energetic and effective First Lady both of Arkansas and the United States. She served two terms as an efficient legislator in the U.S. Senate, and currently serves as an extremely busy and capable Secretary of State. At age sixty-four, more can be expected of her on the national and international scene for years to come. In a speech to the Council on World Affairs in 2009, Clinton offered her assessment of the challenges and opportunities the United States faces in the second decade of the twenty-first century: "We are determined to channel the currents of change toward a world free of violent extremism, nuclear weapons, global warming, poverty, and abuses of human rights and, above all, a world in which people in more places can live up to their God-given potential."

In 2011, Clinton was instrumental in accomplishing the mission in the overthrow of Muammar Gaddafi during what is commonly called the period of the "Arab Spring." To build support for the mission in Libya, Clinton had to rally support from the Arab leaders behind the mission, persuade Congress that other countries would bear most of the cost and mollify the Pentagon by arranging for a quick handover of military command to NATO. All of this took months. The action proved that the U.S. could form new alliances as well as retain old ones, a necessary factor for future international relations. Clinton said:

> As we look at how we manage the "Arab Spring," we are trying to influence the direction, with full recognition that we don't have ownership and we don't have control. And there's a lot that's going to happen that is unpredictable. But we want to lead by our values and our interests in ways that, regardless of the trajectory over the next decade, people will know that the U.S. was on the side of democracy, on the rule of law....And that will, I hope, be a strong antidote to the voices of fatalism or extremism. (Massimo Calabresi. "Head of State." *Time.* November 7, 2011 28-33)

Clinton also formed joint ventures with numerous organizations, funding sixty-seven programs aimed at preserving the rights of women. These programs will offer a new platform against repression in other countries and promote both security and development. At present, she continues to serve energetically and effectively in the powerful position of Secretary of State.

★ ★ ★

Angela Merkel current Chancellor of Germany, the first woman elected to that position She is the second woman to chair the G8* after Margaret Thatcher. She has worked diligently to save Europe's and the world's economy. (public domain)

Angela Merkel, nee Krasner, was born on July 17, 1954, in Hamburg, Germany, on the free side of the Iron Curtain. But as an infant she and her family moved to Communist controlled East Germany. Her Lutheran minister father was given a pastorate position in Quitzow, a small town about fifty miles north of Berlin. Later the family moved to the larger town of Templin where Merkel and her two younger siblings grew up. Pastor Kasner believed that religion and socialism could co-exist and that socialism would benefit society at large. Accordingly, he had a good relationship with the Communist regime; the family was allowed two cars and received permission to travel freely between East and West Germany. Nevertheless, daily life was difficult for the family. Merkel's father was poorly paid, so Frau Kasner worked as a teacher of English and Latin. Yet, since the schools tended to advocate atheism, the three Christian children often felt discriminated against. Perhaps her schoolmates' taunting derision led Merkel to concentrate on her schoolwork; she excelled in science, mathematics, and languages, and later, she majored in physics at the University of Leipzig. From 1978 to 1990, Merkel did research in the new field of Physical Chemistry at the Academy of Sciences in Berlin. She received a doctorate in science based on her thesis on quantum chemistry.

As a student in a socialist country, Merkel studied Marxist-Leninist Socialism and had to join the Free German Youth Movement. But her political philosophy leaned heavily toward democracy. Nevertheless, she was cleverly able to work within the Socialist society as a student leader. Shortly after the fall of the Berlin Wall, Merkel joined a liberal group called the Democratic Awakening, which advocated the reunion of the two Germanys. The gifted young student soon became spokesperson for the organization, which achieved its goal when East and West Germany were reunited on October 3, 1990. In the post-reunification general election of 1990, Merkel was elected to the Bundestag (lower house of Parliament) at the young age of thirty-four. Her party affiliation was the Christian Democratic Union (CDU). As a Christian and a believer in democracy and an anti-Communist, Merkel wanted to rebuild a new Germany based on capitalism and a free-market system.

While still a graduate student, Angela Kasner met and married a fellow science student, Ulrich Merkel. They divorced in 1982 having produced no off-spring. As a young single woman, she loved to go dancing, to wear blue jeans, and to listen to rock music. Although Merkel remarried another science colleague, Professor Joachim Sauer, she chose to retain the name

Merkel, since she was already well known under that name. Both Merkel and Sauer loved walking, hiking, and music and shared much in common. Like her first husband, Sauer prefers to remain in the background. They have no children.

In 1991, Chancellor Kohl appointed Merkel to his cabinet as Federal Minister for Women and Children. At age thirty-seven, she was given real power to make real change: she allocated federal grants to university students and particularly to women and provided job training for disabled women and youths. Merkel stated: "Politicians have to be committed to people in equal measure." In 1994, in recognition of her scientific expertise, Dr. Merkel was appointed Overseeor of the Environment and Atomic Reactor Safety Commission. With her policies, the coal industry was motivated to mine black coal rather than brown coal, which emits large amounts of sulfur. Mercury, copper, and arsenic were greatly reduced in the environment; stricter regulations helped ensure safer water and air. She also encouraged businesses to utilize recycling programs, especially for hazardous materials.

Merkel in 1998 lost her prestigious cabinet job when the Kohl government was replaced by a coalition government under Gerhard Schroeder. Kohl, leader of the Christian Democratic Union (CDU), and Wolfgang Schaukel, then chair of the CDU, were involved in a financial scandal. When neither of the accused would cooperate with the investigation, Merkel was elected chair of the CDU. Although her party's reputation had been severely damaged by the scandal, the CDU under Merkel's leadership was able to win enough seats in the Bundestag to become the majority party. Merkel believed she had sufficient support to challenge Chancellor Gerhard Schroeder in 2002, but without a strong coalition to back her and strong political support, she lost.

Clearly she had to improve her image: she was criticized as "too analytical;" she seldom smiled in public; she was accused of being a "lackey" of the U.S.; and somewhat unfairly she was judged on her personality and personal appearance. Apparently, she succeeded in re-making her public persona, for the CDU won the 2005 election by a very narrow margin. In Germany, when no party wins more than 50 percent of the vote, the various political parties vie to form a coalition with a winning majority of the votes. After a series of negotiations, the dowdy Protestant woman from the former East Germany became the first female to head the government of Germany. "And I think that a woman as chancellor can also serve as a good example," said Merkel.

Soon after her election she visited President George W. Bush in the White House to cement relations with the United States. Merkel was honest and direct as always. She spoke at the White House for the first time in the United States:

> This is my first visit as chancellor, heading a new federal government. And I explained that there are two objectives we have set for ourselves. First of all, we would like to strengthen our economic force....Secondly, Germany wants to be a reliable partner to our partners in the world, but also to our partners in Europe. (Clifford Wills. *Angela Merkel.* [New York: Chelsea House, 2008]. 78).

Chancellor Merkel was concerned not only about the future of Germany but about the world situation as well. Her two initial concerns were the economic situation of Germany and the European Union and the war waging in Iraq. She supported an increase in the VAT (value-added tax on goods and services) from 16 percent to 18 percent. She advocated less government and more competition in world trade. She supported George W. Bush and the war in Iraq because she viewed it as "inevitable." She is a strong critic of Iran's nuclear energy program and a defender of Israel's right to exist.

She regularly travels abroad to meet heads of state and to form alliances with their countries. Germany is a member of NATO and the European Union and of the G6 (Group of six leading nations, now expanded to twenty and renamed G20). She was host to the G8 meeting in Germany in 2008, which focused on world poverty and economic cooperation with and assistance to undeveloped nations. She believes that poverty and environmental problems are global issues that need to be solved cooperatively. Merkel stated: "In Europe it is particularly important that we build good relations with everyone who holds political responsibility because Europe can only be built together." She believes Germany partly because of its geographic position can stand as a mediator and balancing factor.

On September 1, 2006, Merkel was voted the "World's Most Powerful Woman" by *Forbes* Magazine. She has traveled the world networking wherever she goes and impressing leaders from George Bush and Tony Blair to Jacques Chirac and Vladimir Putin and more recently Barack Obama.

The President of France, Nicolas Sarkozy, awarded Merkel the Charlemagne Prize in 2008 for her efforts to reform the European

Union. She is also a leader in the Council of Women World Leaders. The purpose of this international organization is to muster the strength of the most distinguished women leaders to examine together issues of serious significance to women around the world. Merkel is eminently qualified to be a member. She, no doubt, will continue to be a strong leader of her own country and the international scene.

★ ★ ★

Cropped photo of President of the Philippines, Gloria Macapagal-Arroyo, meeting with Commanding Officer, 31st Marine Expeditionary Unit, Colonel Walter L. Miller near the site of a devastating landslide that struck Leyte February 17, 2006. (work of an employee of the U. S. Navy Wikimedia Commons)

Gloria Macapagal-Arroyo was born in San Juan on April 5, 1947, to Diosdado Macapagal and his second wife Evangelina. Arroyo spent the first three years of her life with her parents and step-brother and step-sister. Then she went to live with her maternal grandmother for four years in LLigan. Between the ages of eight and eleven, she lived part of the time in Mindanao and the rest in Manila. As a result, Arroyo became fluent in several languages still spoken in the Philippines. In 1961, when she was fourteen, her father was elected president, and the family moved to the presidential palace in Manila. Her father served only one term after which time Arroyo returned to a more normal lifestyle.

Arroyo had had a strict Catholic elementary and secondary education at the Assumption Convent where she was a good student; she even gave the valedictory address at her graduation in 1964. Soon after, she traveled to Washington, D.C. to attend Georgetown University. She graduated magna cum laude with a degree in economics. One of her classmates was the future president of the United States, Bill Clinton. After graduation, she returned to the Philippines to continue her graduate studies. She earned a master's degree in economics at the Ateneo de Manila University in 1978 and a doctorate in economics from the University of the Philippines in 1987.

Arroyo did other things besides studying. In 1968, she met and married Jose Arroyo, a lawyer and businessman. Together they raised three children, Juan Miguel Arroyo, Diosdado Arroyo, and Evangelina Lourdes Arroyo. Today in 2012, Miguel and Diosdado serve alongside Arroyo in the Congress.

Arroyo also taught classes in economics at three of the same schools from which she graduated. So when President Corazon Aquino wanted a new undersecretary of the Department of Trade and Industry, she chose Arroyo for the position. As the daughter of a former president, Arroyo was already well-known and had many political contacts. Arroyo once said: "I believe that public service is a public trust." In 1992, she was elected senator, and in 1998, she became Vice-President serving under President Joseph Estrada. When Estrada was accused of corruption, she joined with opposition forces that called for the President's impeachment. Estrada was forced from office, and Vice-President Arroyo became President. Arroyo spoke these words: "I want justice to be so persuasive that it will be taken for granted, just as injustice is taken for granted today." She is only the second female, after Corazon Aquino, to hold that high office. In 2004, Arroyo was elected to a six year term.

The Philippines ranks high in the quality and quantity of its information and technology workers. Arroyo worked diligently in this area of development as president and today in the Congress. She spoke these words:

> This is why another goal of my administration is to promote and support the development of the information and communication technology sector in the Philippines. At present this means establishing the policy and legal framework for the IT sector, attracting more investments for the building of infrastructure and expanding the human resource development currently available. (Julian Weiss. *Tigers' Roar.* [Armonk, New York: M.E. Sharpe, 2001].x).

The Philippines is a major center for outsourcing by American Internet firms. America Online has most of its help-desk support handled by young Filipinos from a site north of Manila. Huge investments in telecommunication and use of the Internet, cell phones, and PCs have greatly expanded markets. Arroyo has been a major player in this revolution.

A major terrorist problem continues to this day. A Philippine Muslim separatist organization known as Abu Sayyaf Group (ASG) with ties to radical Islam that in the past was connected to Osama bin Laden continuously threaten not only outlying areas but also urban areas, including Manila. Murder, kidnapping, naval piracy, drug dealing, and human smuggling are all part of the terrorist threat.

Arroyo was the first Asian leader to express support for the United States after the 9/11 terrorists' attacks on New York and Washington; she also offered the use of Philippine air space for any reprisal. She participated in the Iraq War and President George Bush's Global War on Terror. In return President George Bush promised economic aid and military equipment. In 2004, Arroyo withdrew its small force in Iraq when a Filipino driver was taken hostage. The U.S. has poured millions of dollars into the region since 9/11 that has been used for education, telecommunications, and infrastructure. The Philippines stand as our strongest link between the U.S. and East Asia. The Philippines is the fourth highest recipient of U.S. military assistance and the highest in Asia.

President Barack Obama has visited the Philippines twice since he took office. He cites efforts on behalf of the Arroyo government to make peace with the Moro Islamic Liberation Front in Mindanao who are seeking to create a separate Muslim homeland.

While the major American military bases were closed in the Philippines years ago, the U.S. still maintains hundreds of soldiers on rotation in the southern Philippines in the fight against terrorism.

Arroyo has committed to reduce poverty. She stressed the need for the government to partner with various sectors in education and in job creation. She sponsored the construction of new schools, restored English as medium of instruction, improved teacher welfare, and launched an internet-based education program.

In spite of attempts to impeach her and acts of open rebellion, Arroyo completed her second term as President in 2010. She immediately announced her intention to run for Congress. She won and currently is serving as a Congresswoman. Economic problems and problems with militant rebels plague the nation. Her first official act was to file a resolution calling for a Constitutional Convention. She wants to reform the Congress by changing it from a bi-cameral legislature to a uni-cameral parliamentary system.

In September 2011, Arroyo underwent a serious third spinal surgery. She and her husband Jose Miguel Arroyo face major charges of bribery, corruption, voter fraud, and unexplained wealth. As of this writing, none of the charges have been proven.

One thing is certain: Arroyo will continue to make a difference in the lives of the Filipino people. "I shall stay married to my country."

EPILOGUE

In the course of pre-history and history, there have been many, brave intelligent women who have exercised leadership in their small communities, tribes, nations, and even empires. My focus has been on the most famous or infamous, according to my judgment, and on the effect they have produced on their nations or in the world. There seems to be no set pattern for how each of these great women achieved their positions of power.

Cleopatra inherited her throne from the Ptolemaic dynasty, but she had to struggle to keep her power with the forces of Rome, and in the end she lost. Theodora had been a prostitute and came to be Empress through her marriage to the Emperor Justinian. Catherine the Great had her husband murdered, so that she could rule Russia. Boudica was married to a king in early England but had to rebel against the Romans to win back her throne. After initial victories, she lost due to the overwhelming power of Rome. In recent times, Indira Gandhi and Benazir Bhutto were daughters of the leaders of the two new nations formed from the British ruled sub-continent of India. Similarly, Suu Kyi's father led his country towards independence. He was later assassinated while Ms. Arroyo's father became president of the Philippines. Suu Kyi's contribution to her native country of Burma was to suffer with patient endurance the oppression of a tyrannical military regime. Gloria Arroyo, on the other hand, became President, and later on, a member of the Philippine Congress. Golda Meir, Margaret Thatcher, and Angela Merkel both rose up from middle-class environments by their own talents and efforts to the most powerful positions in their respective democratic governments, Israel, England, and Germany. It is worth noting that Nancy Pelosi, Golda Meir, and Margaret Thatcher were elected by members of their own party, not the whole country. Each of these women was unique and each found her own road to power, fame, and glory.

It is the hope of the author of this series of biographies that every reader will find something to admire and emulate in this march of heroines, and that each reader will be inspired by their examples to strive to be the best that she or he can be.

Finis

NOTES

As this book goes to press, I wish to include several women who have recently assumed political power.

Laura Chinchilla was elected first female president of Costa Rica on February 9, 2010. She won in a landslide in a campaign advocating free market policies in Central America's most secure country.

Chinchilla is the protégé of the current president, Nobel Peace Prize laureate Oscar Arias. She has promised to continue the same trade policies that brought the country into a trade pact with the United States and China.

Considered a social conservative, she opposes abortion and gay marriage. As a female president, she is following a movement in South America where Nicaragua, Chile, Brazil, and Argentina have all elected female presidents.

★ ★ ★

Yingluck Shinawatra was sworn in as Thailand's first female Prime Minister on August 5, 2011. She is the sister of Thaksin Shinawatra, the controversial ex-Prime Minister who is living in exile. No doubt her family name helped garner public support. Even so, Thailand is hardly known for fostering equality of the sexes, so this is a milestone in Thailand politics.

★ ★ ★

In 2006, Portia Simpson Miller was elected as the first female to serve as Prime Minister of Jamaica. She was re-elected in December 2011.

Miller is promoting a break with the British monarchy and hopes to see Jamaica as a republic. Moreover, she is calling for full civil rights for gays and lesbians, a courageous move considering the country's violent history of homophobia. She is an inspiring example to young women of the Caribbean diaspora to make a difference in political involvement.

★ ★ ★

The highest number of women world leaders ever in history in power simultaneously was thirteen. In 2002, Latvia, Finland, New Zealand, Ireland, Sri Lanka, Philippines, Indonesia, Panama, Bangladesh, Senegal, Sao Tome, Principe, and South Korea all had female leaders. Again in 2006, Ireland, New Zealand, Latvia, Finland, Philippines, Bangladesh, Mozambique, Germany, Liberia, South Korea, Chile, Jamaica, Sao Tome, and Principe all had female leaders. In 2007, there were again thirteen female world leaders in power simultaneously: Ireland, New Zealand, Latvia, Finland, Philippines, Bangladesh, Mozambique, Germany, Liberia, Chile, Jamaica, Switzerland, and South Korea. In May 2010, the first female prime minister in Australia was elected.

Women have made great strides towards equal rights during the nineteenth and twentieth centuries, especially the last half of the twentieth. In 2010, women made up more than 50 percent of the workforce in America. Over 60 percent of the degrees awarded by universities in America and Europe went to women. Throughout the world women have achieved the most progress in democratic societies. There were more women in the Spanish cabinet than men. Forty-percent of the members of the Swedish Parliament were women.

Women politicians the world over continue to work for human rights and human rights are women's rights. They also focus on educational, economic, health, and political issues. Harriet Tubman, a former slave, who escaped to freedom on the Underground Railroad and spent her life helping freed black children struggling along the path to freedom during Reconstruction spoke these words:

> If you are tired, keep going,
> If you are scared, keep going,
> If you are hungry, keep going.
> If you want a taste of freedom, keep going. (Hillary Clinton. *Living History.* [New York: Simon and Schuster, 2003]. 462).

Unfortunately, women in middle-eastern countries and other areas around the world often living in theocracies are denied basic human rights. *Time* Magazine in August 9, 2010, featured on its cover a woman whose nose and ears had been cut off. She was resisting abuse by her husband and in-laws. Her husband in turn administered this horrific mutilation as a form of punishment with the approval of the Taliban leaders. This is not an isolated incident, and I am not writing about ten years ago but 2010. No doubt these occurrences are going on at this moment. The woman is in protective custody and came to the U.S. for plastic surgery.

The Taliban in Afghanistan believe in and wish to establish an extremist fundamentalist Muslim rule that withholds basic human rights from women. Women under the Taliban accused of adultery were stoned to death, even if not proven guilty. Often women who showed an ankle were whipped. As the U.S. moves to giving Afghanistan its autonomous rights and departs the country, there is much world concern over the rights of women. Hillary Clinton addressed women in President Karzi's delegation in Washington in May 2010: 'We will stand with you always.' (Aryn Baker. "Afghan Women and the Return of the Taliban." *Time* Magazine. August 9, 2010 20-28). It remains to be seen as the U.S. negotiates its way out of Afghanistan.

A prominent Pakistani acid victim, Fakhra Younus, committed suicide March 17, 2012 in Rome by jumping out of a sixth floor window. Allegedly, she was attacked with acid poured over her face and body in May 2000 by her–then husband, an ex-parliamentarian and scion of an important political leader, a former governor of Punjab, Pakistan's largest province. Younus claimed her then-husband abused her physically and mentally and she left him.

Much international focus was placed on the attack, and Younus endured over thirty-six surgeries in an effort to give some relief to her horrific injuries. Her skin was literally melted away. The Italian government provided her with medical care and enough money for her and her son to live, while she fought to publicize to the rest of the world the plight of many Pakistani women. (Associated Press by Sebastian Abbot, March 28, 2012, Islamabad)

In 2011, more than 8,500 acid attacks, forced marriages, and other forms of violence against women were reported in Pakistan. According to the Aurat Foundation, a women's rights organization, these figures are no doubt undercut. Yet for Younus and others like her, there is no justice in

Pakistan. Many of these victims are blinded, and scar tissue often becomes infected with gangrene or septicemia

According to a survey conducted by the Thomson Reuters Foundation in 2011, (link.reuters.com/jet92s) after Afghanistan and the Democratic Republic of Congo, Pakistan is the third most dangerous country for women in the world.

Sharmeen Obaid Chinoy, a Pakistani filmmaker, received an Academy Award on February 27, 2012 for her documentary, "Saving Face," which deals with acid attack victims. The movie chronicles the work of British Pakistani plastic surgeon, Mohammad Jawad, who has performed reconstructive surgery on survivors of acid attacks. Chinoy dedicated her award to the women of Pakistan. Moreover, with a global audience, she hopes people will hear her message, and that ultimately Pakistan will change in its attitudes to girls and women. (Reuters by Rebecca Conway and Chris Allbritton February 27, 2012, Islamabad)

Female genital mutilation is being practiced in many places in the world, including the U.S. Some Muslims wish for law violators to be prosecuted under Sharia Law, which would deny women their basic human rights. Men and women the world over must never allow fundamentalist Islamic philosophy to gain a foothold in their respective societies. Who knows what problems our daughters and granddaughters will have to face in the future? And as women we have to speak out for equality and human rights the world over.

ACKNOWLEDGEMENTS

I would first of all like to express my deepest appreciation and gratitude to the Dominican Sisters at Mount St. Mary-on-Hudson, Newburgh, New York, for helping to inculcate in me at an early age a great love of learning. I had the privilege to be educated by these dedicated women for twelve years. The Franciscan Sisters at Ladycliff College, Highland Falls, New York, further stimulated my interest in the classical writers and ancient history. And to my parents, especially my mother, I wish to say "thanks" for keeping me always loaded up with books even in my earliest childhood. My father, of course, was my inspiration in the political arena. Parents and teachers leave their indelible imprints and help define the person we ultimately become. How fortunate am I.

My dear husband Wayne titled the book and understands my great love of history. Don Branham read some of my first draft chapters, advising on publication submission. Vincent Kelly suggested I cut out much material, and I finally came around to agreeing with him. I also owe him a great debt for helping me with clarity in sentence structure. Nancy Smith Becker was kind enough to read an early draft and made many positive suggestions. Karol Omlor advised me on punctuation matters and was of great assistance. To Shirley Rowe, I express my gratitude for helping me with my photograph requirements. I am enormously indebted to Bud Brooks for his very helpful comments and corrections. My daughter-in-law, Barbara Lamb, helped with the design for my book cover and encouraged me to include my notes. Gary Goodwin, my computer guru, was always there to solve my computer issues. Many thanks to George Davis who gave me astute counsel and faithful friendship. And to my devoted niece, Sandra McMahon in New York City, I extend my gratitude for her photography endeavors. I am deeply indebted for the critical reading they gave my copy, and I hope they will observe the improvements without being unduly upset that in some places I tenaciously clung to my own convictions. I remain thankful for their interest and advice. Many friends and family, especially my children, Richard, David, Dianne, Douglas, and Darlene have given me great love, support, and encouragement during the three years it has taken me to write this book for which I always will be grateful.

BIBLIOGRAPHY

Barry, Kathleen, *Susan B. Anthony*. New York: New York University Press, 1988.

Bhutto, Benazir, *Reconciliation*, New York: Harper Collins, 2008.

Burgan, Michael, *Clinton*, Hillary Rodham, Minneapolis, Minnesota: Compass Point Books, 2008.

Burkett, Elinor, *Golda,* New York: Harper Collins Publishers, 2008.

Cesaretti, Paolo, *Theodora Empress of Byzantium*, New York: Vendome Press, 2001.

Clinton, Hillary Rodham, *Living History*, New York: Simon and Schuster, 2003.

Cole, Mary Hill, *The Portable Queen,* Amherst, Massachusetts: University of Massachusetts Press, 1999.

Collingridge, Vanessa, *Boudica*, London: Elbury Publishing, Random House, 2005.

Cronin, Vincent, *Catherine Empress of all the Russians*, New York: William Morrow and Company, Inc., 1978.

Englar, Mary, *Benazir Bhutto*, Minneapolis, Minnesota: Compass Point Books, 2006.

Felsenthal, Carol, *Sweetheart of the Silent Majority, Phyllis Schlafly*, Garden City, New York: Doubleday & Company, Inc., 1981.

Flexner, Eleanor, *Mary Wollstonecraft.* New York: Coward, McCann and Geoghegan, Inc., 1972.

Foss, Michael, *The Search for Cleopatra,* New York: Arcade Publishing, 1997.

Frank, Katherine, *Indira,* New York: Houghton Mifflin Company, 2002.

Fraser, Antonia, *Boadicea's Chariot*, London: Weidenfeld and Nicholson, 1988.

Friedan, Betty, *The Feminine Mystique*, New York: W.W., Norton & Inc., 2001.

Gage, Matilda, *Susan B. Anthony, Elizabeth Cady Stanton, History of Woman Suffrage,* Salem, New Hampshire: Ayer Publishers, 1985.

Gardiner, George, Member of Parliament, *Margaret Thatcher*, London: William Kimber Publisher, 1975.

Gerard, John, *Autobiography of a Hunted Priest,* Translated by Philip Caraman, S.J., New York: Doubleday, 1955.

Goldstone, Nancy, *Four Queens*, New York: Viking Penguin, 2008.

Grahm, Webster, *Boudica,* New York: Batsford, 1978.

Graves, Robert, *I, Claudius*, New York: Harrison Books, 1934.

Gregory, Philippa, *The Boleyn Inheritance,* New York: Simon and Schuster, 2006.

Gribble, Francis, *The Comedy of Catherine the Great,* New York: E.P. Dalton and Company, 1942.

Haigh, Christopher, editor, *The Reign of Elizabeth I,* Athens, Georgia: University of Georgia Press, 1985.

Harding, James, *Alpha Dogs,* New York: Farrar, Straus and Giroux, 2008.

Hasday, Judy L., *Aung San Suu Kyi,* New York: Chelsea House, 2007.

Hennessee, Judith, *Betty Friedan,* New York: Random House, 1999.

Hughes, Libby, *Madam Prime Minister,* Lincoln, Nebraska: iUniverse.com, Inc., 2000.

Leon, Vicki, *UppityWomen of Medieval Times,* Berkeley, California: Conard Press, 1997.

Levin, Carole, *Heart and Stomach of a King,* Philadelphia, Pennsylvania: University of Pennsylvania Press, 1994.

Loach, Loretta, *Women in the Miner's Strike, Digging Deeper Issues in the Miner's Strike,* London: Verso, 1995. ISBNO-86091-820-3

MacCaffrey, W.T., *Elizabeth I: War and Politics, 1588-1603,* Princeton, New Jersey: Princeton University Press, 1981.

Macdonald, Fiona, *Women in Ancient Greece,* New York: Peter Bedrick Books, 1999.

Madariaga, Isabelle de, *Catherine the Great, a Short History,* New Haven: Yale University Press, 1990.

Mayer, Alan J., *Madame Prime Minister,* New York: Newsweek Books, 1979.

McLaren, A.N., *Political Culture in the Reign of Elizabeth I, Queen and Commonwealth, 1558-1485,* United Kingdom: Cambridge Press, 1999. Electronic Resource Call #306.2/0942/09031.

Meir, Golda, *My Life,* New York: Putman Sons, 1975.

Mills, Clifford W., *Angela Merkel,* New York: Chelsea House, 2008.

Oldenbourg, Zoe, *Catherine the Great,* New York: Random House, 1965.

Parliamentary History Yearbook Trust, United Kingdom: *An Age of Transition, British Politics 1840-1914,* 1997. Electronic Resource Call # 320.94109034.

Pelosi, Nancy, *Know Your Power*, New York: Doubleday, 2008.

Pranay, Gupte, *Mother India*, New York: Charles Schibner's Sons, 1992.

Rounding, Virginia, *Catherine the Great*, New York: St. Martin's Press, 2007.

Sandalow, Mark, *Madame Speaker*, New York: Modern Times, 2008.

Saprio, Virgina, *A Vindication of Political Virtue*, (The Political Theory of Mary Wollstonecraft), Chicago: University of Chicago Press, 1992.

Somerville, Barbara, *Gandhi*, Minneapolis, Minnesota: Compass Point Books, 2007.

Starky, David, *Elizabeth*, New York, Collins Publishers, New York: 2001.

Steinem, Gloria, *Moving Beyond Words*, New York: Simon and Schuster, 1994.

Stern, Sydney Ladensohn, *Gloria Steinem: Her Passions, Politics and Mystique*, Secaucus, New Jersey: Carol Publishing Company, 1997.

Stewart, Whitney, *Aung San Suu Kyi*, Minneapolis, Minnesota: Lerner Publications, 1959.

Thatcher, Margaret, *Margaret Thatcher, The Downing Street Years,* New York: Harper Collins, 1993.

Thomas, William, *Aung San Suu Kyi,* Milwaukee, Wisconsin: World Almanac Library, 2005.

Time Magazine

Troyat, Henri, translated by Joan Pinkham *Catherine the Great*, New York: Plume Books, 1994.

Tomalin, Claire, *The Life and Death of Mary Wollstonecraft,* New York, Harcourt Brace Jovanovich, 1974.

Tyldesley, Joyce, *Queens of Egypt*, London: Thomas & Hudson LTD., 2006.

Ward, Geoffrey and Ken Burns, *For Ourselves Alone.* New York: Alfred Knopf Publishers, 1999.

Weiss, Julian, *Tigers' Roar*, Armonk, New York: M.E.Sharpe, 2001.

Weir, Alison, *Eleanor of Aquitaine*, New York: Ballantine Publishing Company, 1999.

Wikipedia commons for images.

Wintle, Justin, *Perfect Hostage*, New York: Skyhorse Publishing, 2007.

Wollstonecraft, Mary, *Maria or the Wrongs of Women.* Introduction by Moira Ferguson, New York: Norton and Company, Inc., 1975.

www.creationism.org.images

www.wikipedia.org for background information.

Yahoo.News

INDEX

Page numbers with *italicized* "*ph*" indicates a photo on page

D

F

O

Q

R